FOUR MONTHS IN A [illegible]ABEEH;

OR,

NARRATIVE OF A WINTER'S CRUISE ON THE NILE.

BY

M. L. M. CAREY.

> "Flies and mosquitoes hold divided sway,
> Half sting by night, the other half by day."

LONDON:
L. BOOTH, 307 REGENT STREET, W.
1863.

Dedicated

TO

'COUSIN PHIL' AND SELINA.

CONTENTS.

PLATES.

FOUR MONTHS IN A DAHABËÉH.

CHAPTER I.

FROM ENGLAND TO EGYPT.

'COUSIN PHIL' is seventy-five years of age; he is crippled and paralysed by a sad accident which it pleased God should befall him some two years back; but he is still a hale and hearty old gentleman, carrying out to its fullest extent the maxim he has held to through life,—never to allow another to do for him what he can contrive to do for himself. The consequence is, that although now unable to move without crutches, or a stick on one side and the arm of his faithful servant Thomas on the other, he is thinking of setting out on his travels! Of course he is; and why should he not? There is a reason for moving; and we shall soon see that 'Cousin Phil' can move quite as easily as any one else.

Many a day in the month of September, 1860, may he have been seen in his study, with guide-books, maps, and accounts around him, planning how he and his 'little Selina' shall keep themselves warm this coming winter. 'Little Selina' is a grown woman now; but with all her father's tender care of her, she is very delicate, and the M.D.'s have said that she must be 'kept warm.' 'Cousin Phil' fetches down his books for himself, and is not a bit discouraged because, stick and all, he has fallen several times in his attempts at reaching a high shelf, and has thus been forced to delay his planning until Selina or Thomas have come in to pick him up!

But 'Cousin Phil' resumes his work as bravely as ever. He will do it all for himself,—aye, and far better too than many a younger head would do it for him. Bermuda is rejected, because "we do not like it"—Madeira, because of its steep hills, up which 'seventy-five' could not possibly walk: and walk he must still. Italy is too cold during the winter. The Cape of Good Hope is too far off. Algiers is strongly recommended: but the fame of the air of Egypt, for the benefit of consumptive patients, is wafted more and more on the cold English breeze, and 'Cousin Phil' in his study has finally decided that, for the coming winter, they shall "warm up" in Cairo, and take a trip on the Nile.

It was further chalked out for me that I should go with them; and I went.

I do not know exactly what my companions expected at that time; but I expected nothing! I was not disappointed. No: although formed rather for glaciers and mountain-passes, than for cloudless, burning skies, and although my health did give way for a time under the winter's 'warming,' I can honestly state for the benefit of future adventurers, that we spent five whole months in Egypt, and that we enjoyed ourselves. It would make but a sorry home, it is true, but Egypt is well worth a visit; and because the friends in my truly favoured home would naturally expect something of me on my return, all the events of this 'warm winter' were carefully committed to paper, as they occurred; and now at the request of the same friends, I lay them before them, that they may be amused or stupified over their pages as the case may be, and judge whether they will endeavour to 'keep themselves warm' in the same manner, next winter or not?

Our rendezvous was at the London Bridge Terminus, where we took leave of all our friends: and thus, on Oct. 9th, 1860, with Thomas the man-servant and Sarah the lady's-maid, our trio started under the favourable auspices of a bright, sunshiny day.

Happily for us, bad sailors, the Southampton steamers were so full, for this and the following month, that we could obtain no accommodation in them; and it was decided that the heavy baggage should alone have the chance of sea-sickness, and that we should go overland to Marseilles.

It is not usual to take European servants up the Nile. The expense is great, and they are, generally speaking, voted "in the way." But 'Cousin Phil' could not do without Thomas, and Sarah proved a treasure which we could ill have spared, were it only for the perpetual ironing which she cleverly accomplished. The Arabs wash well enough, but the iron is beyond them; and therefore the choice for Europeans must frequently be between a lady's-maid, a couple of irons for their own use, or doing without ironing at all.

With no more than the usual stock of linen required at home; a few *common* dresses for the river; the lightest possible shawl or mantle for the daytime; plenty of warm wraps for the night; round hats, neckhandkerchiefs, veils, gauntleted gloves, and large, lined umbrellas, to guard the white skin against the unscrupulous burning of the Egyptian sun; two pair of strong boots for desert and temple excursions; light ones to baffle mosquitoes at all hours of the day; goloshes, for the mud on the banks of the Nile; elder-flower water for the eyes and the complexion; a preparation of zinc — one grain to ten drops of water — one drop of which, applied to the corner of the eye on the point of a fine camel's-hair brush, and repeated night and morning, is an *infallible cure* on the first symptoms of the dreaded Ophthalmia; a large quantity of quassia, to destroy the flies; thermometers and guide-books — Murray, Wilkinson, Warburton, &c.; and, finally, as there are no M.D.'s on the Nile, a good book and box of medicines — homœopathic, of course;—we considered ourselves armed against all emergencies.

Thus equipped, we left London for Folkestone,

crossed over to Boulogne, and travelled through France, stopping at Amiens, Paris, Dijon, Valence, Avignon, and finally at Marseilles, where we arrived by these easy stages on October 18th. We met with a few little adventures *en route*, and 'Cousin Phil' ran some small dangers on steamboat, train and staircase, but escaped in safety out of them all.

An amusing instance of French *politesse* occurred in the train-carriage between Valence and Avignon. The number of passengers was so great, that we were forced to divide our party. My companions pulled down the blinds, to hide the beautiful scenery of the mountains of Dauphiné, as commonplace to them, no doubt, as High Street and Regent Street to me. They then closed their eyes, and slept soundly! 'Cousin Phil' and Selina, in the adjoining carriage, shared much the same fate, and a dead silence reigned until 'Cousin Phil' *sneezed twice.* When 'Cousin Phil' did sneeze, it was always like an electric shock to every one in the neighbourhood. All the ladies awoke with a start, shut up the windows, and seized the hat which lay beside him, with strong exhortations to Selina, that he should put it on his head; giving practical indications of their determined intention to place it there themselves, *bon gré, mal gré.* "Car, Mademoiselle, Monsieur s'enrhume!" While Monsieur, not hearing one word of what was passing, began to suspect the necessity of police interference, to prevent the theft of his comfortable, old travelling companion, which Selina had vainly exhorted him to throw into the old-clothes bag a long time past. He knew too well the value of an old friend and prepared for a fight, but their good-humoured French faces soon betrayed their charitable intention; 'Cousin Phil' was re-assured; the mystery was soon cleared up, the blinds raised, and the lovely scenery admitted to view.

Travelling through France as far as Marseilles is so common an occurrence now-a-days, that I need not trouble my readers, nor waste time or paper in describing it; suffice it to say, "Beware of the hotels near the harbour" at Marseilles, until some improvement has been made in the drainage of that town. To the Hôtel de l'Orient we went, and were, one and all of us, taken ill from the noisome odours which rise from the harbour in this quarter. Indeed, the consequence to me was, that I went on board ship, on the evening of the 19th, more dead than alive; no very pleasant state in which to leave Europe for the first time in one's life, my consolation being that to get out of Marseilles was at any rate a luxury, and inwardly resolving that nothing on earth should ever induce me to set foot there again. We were allowed to embark on board the Vectis, Peninsular and Oriental steamer, at night, in order to avoid the confusion of the morning and the large influx of passengers and baggage. It was nearly dark, and as the tide was low, the only means of descent from the quay into the small boat, which was to row us to the steamer, was by a jump downwards of from five to six feet.

'Cousin Phil'—undaunted 'Cousin Phil'—prepares quietly to take the leap himself, but a stout 'Marseillais,' equally quietly, and by 'French leave,' lifts him in his arms, and in spite of remonstrance, deposits him carefully in the boat; and so was each one of our party disposed of in turn, not excepting the long-legged Thomas.

It was an augury of our Eastern mode of transport, and certainly the only safe one on this occasion. The ladder of embarcation on the Vectis was perpendicular *up;* and the 'companion' ladder was perpendicular *down:* but all was accomplished in safety, and we went straight to our cabins alongside the saloon. One of these Selina and I shared, and there I remained during the whole of the following day, October 20th, whilst at 10 A.M. the Vectis started with all her unknown freight of passengers on board.

It was a fine day, and with the assistance of 'belladonna' and starvation, by 1 P.M. of October 21st I reappeared on deck as lively as possible. It was Sunday. There was no clergyman of the Church of England on board, but from my cabin I had heard the service read in the saloon by a Presbyterian; 'Cousin Phil' and Selina attending with all the other passengers. It was a glorious sight that I now saw for the first time on reaching the deck of the Vectis. The wide expanse of the Mediterranean in its own deep blue, not a ripple on its surface, the distant coast of Sicily the only land in sight, and an exquisitely blue sky overhead. And there sat 'Cousin Phil' in his camp-chair, looking the very picture of contentment, although he could hear nothing of what was going on around him. For some unaccountable reason of his own, totally incomprehensible to me, he was always peculiarly happy on board ship. Selina lay comfortably reclining on her couch beside him,—a couch which served as bed or chair: and here let me remark, that travellers on this route will do well to be provided with their own couch or chair, or they may have to stand during the greater part of the day.

'Cousin Phil' and Selina slept out half their day, and as they alternately awoke I had a chat with either. The former went down to the saloon for meals, and I accompanied him, but Selina had her meals brought to her on deck. I had never faced roast beef and boiled chicken on board ship before, and I felt very shy of them, even in this lovely weather; but I could not desert 'Cousin Phil;' not that he was a bit shy, but then he was deaf, and so I went to sit beside him, and give him the benefit of a little chattering. It was not nearly so bad as I had expected, and although when any richly cooked mess was passed by me, "my heart jumped into my mouth," to use the expression of an

Irish servant we once had, yet I survived it. The descent into the saloon was of great advantage too, in facilitating the process of making acquaintances among our fellow-passengers. I had felt rather lonely in this lovely weather, when both my companions were asleep, at seeing around me groups of pleasant-looking people, yet being unable to impart to any one of them the thoughts that would naturally arise in a mind entirely new to the whole scene. But this did not last long. The necessity of offering a chair on deck, or one of those objectionable dishes in the saloon, and no doubt a desire for sociability on all sides, soon made introductions an easy matter. The weather was so fine that no one could think of being ill; excepting poor Mrs. T——, whom the Fates had fixed upon for the 'victim' which is to be found in every society; and thus before Monday, October 22nd, had passed away, I found myself acquainted with half of our fellow-passengers. There were the Earl and Countess of A—— with their daughters, who were acquainted with one cousin of ours, and carried letters of introduction to another; Mrs. S——, whose husband was commanding in India on the same station with one of my many brothers; Lieut. N——, in the same regiment with this brother of mine, and of whom he told me the following story. That having, soon after his arrival in India, gone 'pig-sticking,' he had jumped horse and all into a well, the mouth of which was hidden by brushwood; where, after fruitless attempts to extricate himself from both horse and water, he must certainly have been drowned, had not his Indian servant, perceiving that he was missing, and guessing the cause, gone straight to the well, and pulled him out by means of his turban. It was a providential escape, and what seems more wonderful still, the horse was also pulled out in safety. There was Mrs. E——, also going to join her husband in India, whose friends were stationed with a second brother of mine in the city of S——, and had met him at Aden a short time since. Such, thought I, is one at least of the advantages of belonging to a military family. We find friends ready made for us wherever we go. Then there were three young brides who all wore Fez-shaped caps, made out of the scraps of their husband's new travelling coats; most useful head-dresses for lying down on board ship, and very becoming too, though they give no shade whatever to the face. There was Col. B—— politeness itself; Capt. L——, who paced the deck making confidential remarks to a friend on the various passengers around; Mr. R——, a *very young* man, who, sitting in the saloon close to our cabin door one evening, reported upon 'Cousin Phil' in most pathetic tones as "a very, *very*, VERY, *old* man:" and, lastly, there was M. Lesseps, the French engineer for the Suez canal, besides a variety of others who entered not into this select circle.

The histories and destinies of each one were

gradually unfolded, and those of the "Cairo party" found to be not the least romantic of them all. Our projected trip up the Nile caused quite a little excitement among our new friends; the most general opinion being, that the charming young ladies and "very old man" would never more be heard of, if they undertook anything so rash: others, again, declaring that it was perfectly safe, and the most delightful expedition that could be imagined.

'Cousin Phil' only smiled, and said, "Time will show!"

Between all this and the sketch-books, which afforded no little amusement in the way of a few shaky caricatures, the time passed pleasantly enough.

On Monday not a speck of land was visible till the vessel approached Malta at 10 P.M.; and though there had not been a sail to relieve the monotony of the sea, it was a magnificent sight, and one which the eye could certainly have dwelt upon for more than a day without wearying. Alas! our eyes did not try it much longer.

The night approach to Malta was exceedingly pretty, with the rows of lights along the shore and in the gaily-painted, junk-like boats that came alongside to fetch away passengers. The Maltese costume was curious, and the "patois," a mixture of Italian and Arabic, very amusing to hear. Brave and enterprising as we were, the darknesss effectually prevented such a party as ours from landing.

Almost every other passenger did so, and we then resignedly retired to bed and to suffocation during the operation of "coaling."

Four long hours did the coaling last. All the port-holes were closed, to keep out the dust, and *hot* is no word for the state of the atmosphere. The time was, however, slightly enlivened by the bargaining carried on between the few remaining passengers and a portly Maltese, who, with the best grace in the world, offered for sale all the trash which he had collected from his store, asking the most exorbitant prices for it, assuring his customers at the same time, in his blandest tones, that "he, at least, would not deceive them." He contrived to dispose of a few articles, and the morning light revealed that they were trash indeed.

No one need be thus taken in, for it is a well-known fact that nothing really valuable is ever brought to the passenger-boats for sale.

At length the old acquaintances returned, and new ones arrived. What a noise had been going on over our devoted heads all this time, as sacks of coal, baggage, and passengers, rapidly succeeded one another on the deck. But down come our lively dinner-companions, and, considerately seating themselves near the partly-open cabin-door, they dispel our headaches and restore our mirth, by making us the subject of their conversation.

Between two and three o'clock A.M. on Tuesday,

the Vectis resumed her way; the port-holes were opened, and the travellers breathed again. Little sleep did any one get that night, either of those who had landed, or those who had remained on board, as the sleeping forms in every available corner of the vessel during the day-light hours of October 23rd, but too plainly showed; of course I did not sleep; but sat "watching the waves with all their white crests dancing." The day was lovely still, with the same exquisitely blue sea and brilliant sunshine; late in the evening, after considerable exertion on the part of some of the gentlemen, the ladies were induced to sing; and, finally, quite a little concert was got up, as we sat on deck in the brilliant moon-light. Alas! for us all, we "made hay whilst the sun shone," but the hay-making was over for the remainder of this voyage. The ship took to rolling in the night, and in the morning, when 'Cousin Phil' reached the deck, it was with too much difficulty to allow of his attempting the descent again for breakfast. I lay on the top of one of the cabin lights getting worse every hour, and unable to move without evil consequences; Selina lay on her couch beside me; until, by a sudden lurch of the vessel, 'Cousin Phil' in his camp-chair fell forward upon the deck, and roused us both in alarm. A number of passengers ran to the rescue; happily, he was not in the least hurt, but henceforth sat lowly upon the deck, with shawls and pillows for support and safety. Selina and I were completely "finished" by the start and the fright, and felt very wretched to the end of the journey. Later in the day, a loud crash was heard, another lurch, and down goes poor Selina, couch and all, overturned after the example of her father; I began to quake for myself, but friendly hands were ready again to assist, and in order to secure her for the future, her couch was lashed firmly to one of the cabin-light bars. Oh! the miseries of the descent at night, and the issuing forth again in the morning; whether the Mediterranean were blue or not, the two succeeding days seemed quite interminable. 'Cousin Phil' lost his companion at dinner time, and had no more chatting to enliven him. The fat, comfortable stewardess assured me that I should starve if I "went on in that way," but I always find it the "best way" on these occasions, though Selina maintained the contrary, and certainly the stewardess's "way" appeared to agree well with *her!*

Every passenger on board was upset, and yet the treacherous sea looked calm, and the spirits of the gentlemen seemed to rise, with the rolling of the vessel. Though full of compassion for the ladies, the first signs of a pale face, among their own number, was a signal for merriment and fun, in which each one was the victim in his turn, and their shouts of laughter at the dinner-table were incomprehensible to our dejected minds. There was one unfortunate man, whose very green and yellow appearance brought him in for an extra share of this kind of fun.

He was resolved to face the enemy, and downstairs at dinner-time he goes with the rest. Fat pork, stewed beef, greens, and salad, are simultaneously thrust before him, and he rushes away in despair. 'Try again' however, he will; he is determined to discover the remedy for sea-sickness, and he descends once more. Shortly after, he returned on deck, as lively as possible and looking perfectly well; and so he continued to the end of the voyage. He said he had drunk a glass of porter, and eaten a slice of rich plum-pudding, and henceforth recommends them to the public, as the surest remedy under similar circumstances.

Our misery came to an end at last, and at about half-past 8 A.M. on Friday, October 26th, the Vectis arrived in the Alexandrian harbour. What a change! The water was green now instead of blue, but the sky-blue was as lovely and brilliant as ever; and it was so warm that we could not stir a step without holding umbrellas over our heads.

The Pasha's flat-roofed palace is now the prettiest object in view. The groups of windmills, seen through a forest of masts, are curious to behold, and quite in the distance appears Pompey's Pillar. It is a white, barren-looking scene altogether; the land a dead flat, the flat roofs of the houses giving them no additional beauty; but the variety of boats around, and the costumes and varied complexions of the Egyptians and Arabs who surround the vessel, are most picturesque and amusing; and I perceived that the Arabs in this harbour pulled the same effective double-stroke with their oars as the Irish boatmen used to do in the Cove of Cork.

The Arab pilot comes on board as the vessel enters the harbour; and, when she is anchored, a small steamer takes away all the Indian passengers, and lands them near the railway station for Cairo. Those who purpose remaining in Alexandria are next attended to, and taken on shore in small row-boats, opposite to the Custom-house.

It was now our turn, and, having no one to meet us in Alexandria, and not understanding one word of the language, we were prepared, according to the accounts of travellers and guide-books, to meet with the greatest possible difficulty. 'Cousin Phil's' grey hairs probably ensured respect; but, be that as it may, we were most carefully and tenderly deposited in one of the boats, under the superintendence of a handsome, coal-black, turbaned Arab, who understood a good deal of English. Our luggage followed in another boat, and we were rowed to shore. A crowd of turbaned heads, and faces of every shade of brown,—those of the women veiled from below the eyes,—camels, waterskins, donkeys, donkey-boys, &c. &c., met our astonished gaze, but no fuss or incivility of any kind. The population were apparently as much amused and interested with *us*, as we were with them; and our wondering glances at the new world we had reached, were returned with the most perfect good humour by the Africans. The Custom-house was easily passed by means of a small silver coin; one box only on the truck being opened, and quickly closed again. Thomas was left with his new black friends to escort the luggage, and we took our seats in the omnibus for the Hôtel Abbat. Here began a loud clamouring in Arabic for extra pay on the part of the porters and other 'hangers-on,' in which, as in many similar instances, 'Cousin Phil' found his deafness useful. Finally the horses started off, and with a jolting which threatened to throw us off our seats at every instant, we arrived, in a quarter of an hour's time, at the hotel.

M. Abbat is a very portly Frenchman ; we spent five days in his hotel, and found him a very attentive landlord. If he would but destroy the flies and mosquitoes it would be better, for they were a perfect plague, and tried the temper of the newcomers sadly. Later experience also led us to prefer the Hôtel d'Europe in the grand 'Place' of Alexandria.

Now came the first breakfast in Egypt! I am not quite sure that we did not expect to see 'stewed crocodile' or alligator, but what we did see was *omelette aux fines herbes*, *côtelettes*, and cold meat, dried figs from Smyrna, bananas, dates, and apples. We were not to be pitied. This was a private breakfast. The 'table d'hôte' was served twice a-day, at noon, and at 7 P.M., and had it not been for the presence of the foreign fruits, the mosquitoes, and the costume and language of one of the waiters, who was an Arab, we might have imagined ourselves still seated at a 'table d'hôte' in Europe. There is but one *salon* in the house, and as that one was occupied, we were obliged to put up with the small public room; which would have done very well, but for that intolerable habit of spitting, which all foreigners *will* still keep up, and in which we found Egypt by no means behind-hand. We used this room, then, for a short time only before the dinner-hour; sitting in the 'verandah,' or in the open air in the little garden earlier in the morning, and in 'Cousin Phil's' room in the evening. Here, while undergoing a process of slow suffocation, we systematically slaughtered the mosquitoes that well-nigh slaughtered us, until, wearied out with heat and bites, we despairingly brought our first Egyptian day to an early close; obtained a momentary solace from a draught of delicious lemonade, and retired to our beds.

In the afternoon we had taken a drive along the great Canal. It is called 'Mahmoodëéh,' in honour of Mohammed Ali, who began it in 1819. He completed it in January 1820—it is said, with the loss of the lives of 20,000 men. The banks are barren and monotonous enough, but along the roadside are the gardens of the Pasha and several good-looking houses belonging to him, to one of the consuls, and to some rich residents, chiefly French. Here and there the windings of the canal afford a landscape, which, with a little stretch of imagination, might be called 'pretty;' but the 'dahabëëhs,' or Nile boats, seen upon its waters, were the chief and most interesting objects in our eyes. Some of them were already occupied, and looked extremely pretty and comfortable. We did not examine these, for we had been told that it was better to engage one in Cairo.

On the opposite banks were many of the dwellings of the poor. It is hard to believe that human beings, living so near civilised lands, can own such homes. They are the most wretched mud hovels that can be conceived, roofed over with bundles of dried cane, conveying no idea but that of pigstyes of the worst description. Indeed, our pigs at home would probably object to inhabit them. The appearance of the poor creatures who live in these hovels is wretched in the extreme.

Returning again along the Cánal, another road led us to 'Pompey's Pillar.' It is a plain column with a capital, upwards of 98 ft. in height, formed of three pieces of granite. The cause of its bearing Pompey's name is unknown, but the inscription, as mentioned by Sir G. Wilkinson, tells us that it was "erected by Publius, the Præfect of Egypt, in honour of Diocletian." It stands at the head of the present Arab cemetery. A dreary-looking spot this is; the soil around as white as its closely-packed grave-stones, which are almost universally surmounted by a short plain pillar, its cold dead look raising in the Christian mind the longing desire for the day when the 'Cross' will be seen there instead, as an emblem of faith and hope, and the sad thought removed, that 'the truth as it is in Jesus' is still hidden from the multitudes inhabiting a land which contains so many interesting reminders and proofs of our Scripture history. Continuing the drive we passed through the old town of Alexandria. Here the scene is strange and amusing indeed to a new-comer. The streets very narrow; the upper stories of the houses projecting with supports from the lower; the little open shops on the ground-floor full of every imaginable article of commerce. The men in their variously-coloured costumes, seated cross-legged, or half lying down on the counters, smoking their long pipes, hookahs, or narghillæ, or drinking *café noir* out of tiny cups, and bargaining for the sale of their goods; whilst other figures, with turbaned heads and venerable beards, lie coiled up in front of their wares fast asleep. Money-changers walk along clinking their money in their hands, to make their office known; and donkeys trot briskly by, rattling a bunch of rings under their necks, to warn foot-passengers out of their way. Our Arab driver looked round ever and anon, in evident satisfaction at the astonishment of the travellers, and ejaculated in patronizing tones the words "Good!" "Very good!" the only English expressions that he knew, which were two more than his masters could utter of his language.

The men in general wear a long, loose garment

of blue, red, yellow, green, black, or white cotton; a Turkish fez on the head, with a white or coloured turban twisted round it in a variety of folds, according to the taste of the wearer, and carefully confining the ends of the beautiful blue silk tassel, which we always felt a great desire to set free. They wear red or yellow morocco shoes with pointed toes, and the greater number go without stockings. The men of the higher classes, and the military, have adopted the Turkish costume of a loose jacket and full trousers, and, as our dragoman informed us, showing his own feet with a look of pride, 'English boots' and stockings. The ancient dress of the Egyptian women, composed entirely of white cotton, is still kept up by the lower orders, and pleased us more than any of the other costumes. It so completely envelopes the wearer that no feature but the eyes and the hands are visible, and must be a most effectual shelter from the burning rays of the Eastern sun. It consists of full white trousers tied in at the ankle; a loose white dress over them; a long, narrow, white muslin veil, called the 'yash-mak,' with some edging or embroidery round it, reaching to the ground, and fastened across the face just below the eyes; a stiff white band resting on the top of the forehead, and descending to the veil, hides the nose; and a large white drapery thrown over the head completely conceals the remaining portion of the forehead. We saw numbers of these white 'ghosts' walking about in the 'Place,' with little European children under their charge, and we wondered that their strange appearance did not startle the poor babies; but they looked quite as happy as if their nurses had worn coloured dresses, unveiled their faces, and shown white hands instead of black ones. The dress of the upper classes of the women is the same in fashion, but the material is Persian silk, of all colours; the most general appeared to be a very delicate pink or yellow; the veil of clear muslin, embroidered elaborately, or trimmed with lace, and the mantle of black silk, which they are careful to dispose in such a manner that their European sisters may see and admire the beauty of their attire, and the splendid jewels which many of them wear round their necks and arms, as well as in their hair. The really poor are miserably clad in a single garment of blue checked cotton, with a scarf of the same material thrown over their heads and shoulders; with this they carefully cover their mouths when any stranger or any man passes by. All this must be seen and *heard* to be appreciated; the attitudes, the countenances, the variety of colour, both in complexion and costume, and, not least, the *sounds*, which surprise a civilised ear on all sides, constituting the attraction of the whole scene. The atmosphere in passing through this portion of the town is none of the most agreeable; and although many individuals are quite clean in their appearance, there is such an amount of dirtiness, that a European will much prefer driving through the old town to walking, and we were not sorry to pass out of it all into fresher air.

The moonlight night was lovely: evening closes in immediately after sunset, and the air becomes sensibly colder; but within the precincts of Abbat's Hôtel nothing was cold: the suffocating heat of noon was there securely bottled in for the night. Mosquito curtains enveloped the beds; but no peace was in store for any one of us on this first or the three following nights; and poor 'Cousin Phil' appeared at breakfast next morning, his face entirely covered with bites, most distressing to himself and to all who beheld him. We thought the mosquitoes, like their betters, might at least have respected his age; but they were too wise; they knew the vigour of 'Cousin Phil's' constitution, and treated him accordingly. Selina and I were equally tormented, but, happily for our vanity, the discerning insects had spared our faces!

The voices of the watchmen shouting all night long, to keep one another awake, are alarming: they startle a poor traveller in the most cruel manner just as he is dozing off, after a violent scuffle with a mosquito; and if he contrives to reach the verge of a second doze, up start a whole chorus of wild dogs in their turn; then comes the same all over again, until, with the morning light, arrives the chattering in all languages of the servants of the hotel in the court below. These have a peculiar faculty for playing and working at the same time, and the unfortunate European lifts up the mosquito curtain in despair, and turns out of his sleepless bed, wondering what he ever came to Egypt for! At breakfast, for the climax, comes the '*plague of flies!*' This is the cool season, and the thermometer points to 76° Fahrenheit in our bedrooms.

Oct. 28*th.*—This morning, being Sunday, was ushered in by more than the usual noises and voices in the hotel. It turned out to be a general washing, and, it might have been supposed, extra talking day as well. This was a second Sunday without a church to go to for public worship, for the clergyman of the place had died a month since, and the one from Jerusalem, who had undertaken the duty after him, was absent at Cairo for the moment, on account of his health. The mail for England was expected hourly, so we prepared our letters for home, and then drove to the Pasha's gardens, where all the world is to be seen on Sunday afternoons at about four o'clock. The carriages remain at the gate, and the parties get out and walk, or sit on seats under the acacia-trees. The garden was barren enough. This was not the season for flowers, and there were but few to be seen, with the exception of the beautiful yellow bignonia, and a very large convolvulus, the blossoms of which were of a more brilliant blue than we had ever seen at home.

We were fortunate in making the acquaintance of an English gentleman who had resided for many years in Alexandria. Mr. B—— was well acquainted with the manners and customs of this country, and was most kind in giving every information and assistance regarding our trip up the Nile. He brought us a dragoman named 'Mohamed el Adlééh,' whom he recommended for our *factotum* during the journey. Mohamed had handsome bronzed features, was a stout, strong-looking man, showed a number of good testimonials from former travellers, and appeared willing to do everything that we could desire, at such terms as Mr. B—— thought reasonable ; and, what was more than all besides, the fear and dread of his displeasure hung over the dragoman's head like a drawn sword. It was finally agreed that, as our boat was to be engaged at Cairo, he should proceed thither at his own expense, to be formally engaged there. When the other preliminaries of the trip were arranged, Mr. B—— kindly promised to come to Cairo himself, and engage a boat for us, that 'Cousin Phil' might not be cheated in more ways than were absolutely necessary; whilst we, on our side, promised to make no agreement until he arrived. Meanwhile, when a guide was wanted in Alexandria, we engaged one of those who sat at the hotel door waiting to be hired. They are either paid a small sum for a trip to a particular spot, or they are engaged for the day. Four-and-sixpence is a sufficient remuneration for the day, although many will make a stand for six shillings. And here it may not be out of place to remark, that for the sake of their countrymen, if not for themselves, travellers in Egypt or other foreign countries should be careful not to give lavishly the first price they are asked, or, as many do, even more than that. Those who receive these sums are never afterwards satisfied with less, but, on the contrary, they learn to grasp at more. Their fellows see no reason why they should not be equally well paid, and the sum thoughtlessly given by one becomes henceforth the standard price for all. The prevailing opinion in the country is, that "Englishmen are made of money." And the more they act as though this were true, the higher the claims of the natives will rise—whereas if 'Cousin Phil' was made of money, and if some very few others may be in the same happy case, we know well that many an invalid is debarred from trying the effect of the air of Egypt, simply by the exorbitant premium now placed upon the trip.

Monday, Oct. 29th.—Our hats were covered with folds of white muslin, to keep out the rays of the sun; and although, with the white flaps hanging behind, we thought we had somewhat the appearance of a procession attending a funeral, the hats were voted to be much improved in appearance as well as in comfort thereby. At 4 P.M. Mrs. L——, an Alexandrian lady of rank, kindly called and took us out for a drive in her carriage; she had a little dog in her lap, and had just finished smoking a cigarette, which she strongly recommends as a cure for toothache. The drive took us along the canal, round by the Rosetta gate: and greatly astonished were we at the glowing description of verdure and flowers, where our unsophisticated eyes could see nothing but desert and dust. Surely, we thought, we are in the true desert now, and there are the poor camels traversing it, carrying skins full of water on their backs for the thirsty traveller! But no: here, a few months hence, will be the green fields of Alexandria; here they were a few months back, and then, no doubt, so enchanted the eyes of the parched-up residents that they see them green still, when not an atom of anything but white dust remains; or, maybe, the burning rays of the Egyptian sun have rendered them colour-blind. Our amusement reached its height when our kind friend ordered the driver to stop opposite three *very dusty steps*, surrounded by a few *very dusty trees*, called a 'Terrace,' and when, after feasting our eyes with a distant view of the Lake Mareotis, we sat talking there, in the dust, because it was "such a pretty spot!" Perhaps before we leave Egypt we shall have arrived at this also; and what shall we think of home and real green when we return to them again? Again we smiled inwardly, and said, "Time will show!"

Tuesday, Oct. 30th.—This morning, with Thomas, Sarah, and a dragoman to escort us, we walked through the bazaars. It was a very amusing and interesting sight; but as these bazaars are not considered good, it will be better to describe those at Cairo, only pausing here to observe, that the foulness of the air was absolutely sickening. It would seem, however, that travelling improves the powers of the body as well as those of the mind, for on our return we not only saw beauty and freshness in what we had despised before, but we breathed the same atmosphere with comparative comfort. Our walk on this occasion terminated with an amusing hunt after homœopathic medicines. In the hurried embarkation at Marseilles, mine had been left behind; and now, after trying five chemists in succession, who were sufficiently behindhand in science to scout the idea of having any connexion with such 'quackery!' we sadly gave it up; when Mustapha, our dragoman for the day, stopped at one more door, and, preparing to usher us in, said, "And this will be *six.*" Much amused, we complied, and lo! globules in abundance were produced. There is nothing like perseverance after all, and we will never give up 'trying again.'

Mustapha had introduced himself to us as brother to 'Mohamed el Adlëéh;' and as matters were not thoroughly arranged with the latter, the brotherly affection oozed out, and Mustapha recognised the duty of not losing a chance for himself. He came up to us, saying, "I, dragoman like him for Nile: if you like him, you take him: if you like me best, you take me: just the same: no difference at all!" And so he made himself most disinterestedly agreeable and useful during the expedition, in hopes of outdoing his beloved relative. It did not succeed, and he was soon engaged by another party.

A heavy shower of rain, which laid the dust and

considerably refreshed the air, drove us in for a time, and then, as we had made several lady acquaintances in Alexandria, we mounted *en voiture* again, and set forth to make "a round of calls."

One or two flights of stone steps lead to the drawing-room doors on each story in the Alexandrian houses. In many they are old, worn, and badly kept, being in a manner public property; but the rooms are comfortable enough when once you get into them; and some rejoice in a good sea-view, and fresher air by far than we breathed at Abbat's Hôtel. Some few private dwelling-houses appeared by contrast like palaces in this uncivilised land; and there sat the owners, surrounded by every European luxury of furniture, books, pictures, and *cleanliness;* endeavouring thus to shut out the white, dusty world beyond, which we are quite sure they must all dislike extremely. The mere treat thus afforded to the eye might have lengthened our "calls" considerably, but we continued the drive towards Aboukir, where the famous battle of the Nile took place, and saw some really green fields of cane, cabbages, and small clover, besides extensive plantations of fig-trees, though with neither leaves nor figs upon them; and here we breathed some deliciously fresh air.

'Cousin Phil' did not feel very well this evening, and we all retired early to bed. Wednesday morning dawned, October 31st—but, alas! what of the night's rest? Poor 'Cousin Phil,' he had not slept a wink, neither had he one flat speck left on the whole of his head, forehead, or face! He was one mass of mosquito bites all over, in a sad state of bodily, and,—we doubt not,—mental irritation also: I had had no less than five mosquitoes feasting upon my hands all night, and was conscious of being in an equally exasperated mood. I hope I did not show it much more than he did. Being still a novice, I had carefully tucked the intruders within my curtains; but 'Cousin Phil' confesses that, in the despair inspired by suffocation, he had thrown up the protecting curtains altogether, and was immediately assailed by about 150 of the enemy! There will not be much left of him to return to England, if this continues.

There is an art in arranging mosquito curtains, as in everything else, and if it is not well understood, these protections are useless. When properly gathered up on the frame round the top of the bed, no mosquitoes can penetrate during the day. A short time before retiring to rest, a vigorous flapping with a fly-flapper or towel should be resorted to, the curtains instantly dropped and carefully tucked in all round. If one small aperture be left, good-bye to sleep! Although the Arab servants are supposed to go through these manœuvres in a masterly style, we always found it necessary to repeat them again for ourselves just before getting into bed. In this last operation, too, unless you are very expert and expeditious, the mosquitoes are on the watch, and will be sure to accompany you. At about sunset these little tormentors of our race congregate upon the window-panes in large numbers. A few moments spent in destroying them at this time will be well repaid. The slightest stroke of a handkerchief puts an end to their fragile existence, and renders that of the traveller so much the more endurable for one day.

The rain poured down this morning in refreshing torrents, and the thermometer fell to 71°: a sensible and welcome change. The shower was soon over, and under Mohamed's escort, at half-past two P.M., we drove to see the Pasha's Palace, and through the great Egyptian Bazaar; when a second shower, which we welcomed with joy, sent us in again, and afforded a view of the most magnificent rainbow we had ever seen.

The Palace is situated near the entrance of the Harbour. Its rooms are very handsomely furnished and hung with damask, and the floors beautifully inlaid with different kinds of wood. They are for the most part state-rooms, in which the Pasha receives his own and foreign officers, and visitors. Our guide's version was, that in one he "held his Parliament," in another his "Church," and in a third he showed the divan upon which he reposes for a time after dinner, leaning back against one pillow, whilst two other very large ones are placed in front, upon each of which, Mohamed said, one leg reclines, "*because he is so fat.*" And this was uttered in a tone of intense admiration! The chandeliers in two of the apartments are magnificent, and come from Paris: indeed, all the decorations are of French workmanship. The Haréem is close by: and the ladies walk in the surrounding garden. The Pashas are allowed four wives by the Korán, but Mohamed told us confidentially that they owned about sixty or seventy.

The name of 'Cleopatra's Needles' has been given to two large obelisks in red granite, bearing, in hieroglyphics, the name of the third Thotmes, B.C. 1493. One of them is still standing; the other lies on the ground at its feet, almost entirely concealed by accumulated dust and rubbish. It was given to the English by Mohamed Ali, and was to have been removed to England, as a record of their successes in Egypt. This was, however, relinquished, the mutilated state of the obelisk making it, as it was said, not worth the enormous expense of transport. We could not but regret that it should lie thus neglected upon its own soil, instead of standing like its fellow, a memorial of the gigantic works of the ancients. There is little else of interest in Alexandria besides the site of the Great Library, St. Mark's Church, the supposed tomb of Alexander the Great, and the mosque of 1001 columns; these last we had not time to explore. From the end of October to the end of March is the full season for journeying on the Nile, and the earlier in this period that travellers can set out the better, in order that they may not lose the fair winds which usually blow during the two first of these months, and are the more appreciated whilst the dahabëëh has to sail up the river and against the current, which in some parts is very strong. If the passage of the Cataracts is contemplated, it is also well to be in good time, for the waters of the Nile at this season decrease rapidly. The rise and overflow of this remarkable river begin in the end of June, and continue till the end of September; it recedes during the months of October and November; and having fertilised the surrounding country by the rich deposit which it leaves behind, returns again to its usual bed.

We had now reached the last day of October, and found the air of Alexandria oppressive in the extreme: half the families in the city were laid up with fever; and as everybody said there was nothing there worth seeing, we determined that, whatever might be before us, the sooner we made a move the better. At a quarter past 8 A.M., of November 1st, we took our departure, without one pang of regret, notwithstanding the kindness of our friends, and the interest which we certainly had felt in all we had seen. On our return, after an absence of four months and a half in more southern climes, we fully appreciated the *European* aspect of Alexandria, and even found it refreshing to return to its now maligned atmosphere.

CHAPTER II.

FROM ALEXANDRIA TO CAIRO.

The dragoman, Mohamed el Adlëéh, accompanied us on our departure from Alexandria, and from the first proved himself to be a most useful and active servant. He began at once acting as commander-in-chief, with great good temper towards us, and with vigorous cuts with his stick upon the shoulders of Arab intruders. Cousin Phil's surname was beyond the powers of Mohamed's utterance. "Very hard for me," he complained; and he therefore adopted that abbreviation which appeared to him most suitable to the head of our party. "Pap-pa," he says, "sit here." To Thomas and Sarah, "You stand there." To Selina and me, "You come with me. We take the tickets; come back; pay for the luggage; then 'Pap-pa,' come in; get into carriage directly;" and so it was all done with lightning speed, and not a little to our amusement. We followed our retainer most obediently, and did all we were bid to do: no time was allowed for thinking, but we hoped it was all right, and wished that a faithful artist could have taken a sketch on the spot of the active figure with brown face, scarlet fez, red and yellow turban, dark blue jacket, and large loose trousers, Damascus silk sash round the waist, and walking-stick in hand. Our kind friends saw us into the train for Cairo: the carriages were of English manufacture, built suitably to the climate, and painted a very light dust colour. We soon found ours the most comfortable place we had been in for a long time. It was Thursday, Nov. 1st, and the interest of its associations as 'All Saints' Day' was heightened by the reflection that many of the early Saints of the Church had once trod the ground over which the noisy locomotive was now conveying us. These recollections increased as we penetrated further south, into the region of the waving corn-fields of Egypt. In some parts the rich, luxuriant soil was freshly turned up by the primitive wooden plough, drawn now by two oxen, now by two buffaloes, whilst one man, in loose white dress and turban, guided it from behind. In other parts the country was still inundated: rice was growing up in the midst of the water, and some fresh grain was being scattered in; large tracts of barley, already ripe, lay in the sunshine, of a brilliant golden hue, and in many fields the harvest was going on. The waters of the Nile had risen this year, we were told, to six feet above the ordinary level. The crops of Indian corn had been consequently spoiled, but the rice was proportionably luxuriant. The beautiful rich green of the 'coffee' shrub, and plantations of the 'cotton' plant in pod were seen as the train passed on at slow Egyptian pace, crossing the river over the suspension-bridge built by Robert Stephenson. These latter were not sufficiently near to be recognised by our inexperienced eyes; indeed, we first noted them down as crops of 'tomatos!' Interpersed amid this rural scene were the mud villages of the natives, rising at very short intervals all along the road. Wretched in the extreme they are, like those which first meet the eye in Alexandria; and there were the poor little girls on the banks of some of the water channels, gathering up the mud with their hands and making clay, wherewith to build or repair their miserable dwellings, their bodies but half covered with the dark blue checked cotton dress of the country, and yet many of them wore bracelets on their arms, and bead necklaces round their necks. Each one of these small villages has its mosque with its minaret, from whence the people are daily called three times to prayer; these, with the distant palm-trees, and frequent strings of laden camels passing by, complete the landscape of this part of the country.

The number of persons traversing the road between Alexandria and Cairo was very striking. They were to be seen along the whole way; some walking, staff in hand, or carrying it behind their shoulders, as if for support to the back; some riding on camels or donkeys, and a privileged few upon horses; while others were lazily working in the fields; all contributing to the life and beauty of the landscape by the variety in the colours and forms of their turbans, fez, and scanty drapery. As the train stopped at the various stations on the river-side, little girls pressed forward offering the water of their beloved river, in pretty, long-necked, porous, earthen bottles, called 'goolleh.' These are common all over Egypt, and in them the water is kept deliciously cool. When well filtered the Nile water is exceedingly clear and very good, but as it flows in the river it presents in general a dull red hue, far from tempting. There is considerable elegance in the figures of the half-dressed children, and in the playful manner with which they endeavour to attract attention, and to gain "Baksheesh," in other words, "A ha'penny, please, Sir." They seem to be born with this word in their mouths, and never cease repeating it, although their efforts are but seldom crowned with success. Cheerfulness and dirtiness may apparently exist and thrive together, at least in southern climes, for if we were struck with their merry faces, we were far more so with their utter want of cleanliness, and a close contact with these lively creatures is a perpetual dread to the pedestrian. Their skin seems to have lost all feeling in this respect, and we saw many of them literally *covered* with flies all over their faces, and grinning away at us all the time in perfect unconcern. There were others, however, who, like their brothers and sisters in the towns, presented in every way a sad picture of misery. Men were carrying water skins on their backs, and in their hands small brass dishes, which they rattled together, offering 'sherbet' or liquorice-water out of them to the people of the country. The skins are goat-skins in their natural form, and are filled from smaller skin bags: by their means the water is carried on the backs of men, camels, or donkeys; while the women fetch it from the river in large pitchers, which they bear on their heads, supporting them lightly with one hand, or frequently balancing them without any support at all. In one instance we saw a man giving drink to his stately camel out of a small iron dish. It would have made a good subject for an artist. Large groups of people were squatted Egyptian fashion, that is, with their knees up to their chins, the fashion of sitting adopted by the Egyptians from time immemorial, and which they do not seem inclined to desert for chairs or other modern innovations. These groups were apparently doing nothing, but they were supposed to be looking after the cattle that were grazing around. A few dark brown-wooled sheep were here and there to be seen; and camels and buffaloes in large numbers. Birds of passage were seen flying high in the air or closely skimming the waters; some lanky storks stood watching at the water's edge; and there were numerous flocks of white pigeons on the wing. On one tree they had settled in such numbers that it appeared to be completely covered with a rich white blossom, which, on our nearer approach, suddenly spread its wings and flew away. The date-palm trees seemed different from those near Alexandria; they were very tall, but the leaves shorter and less elegant; and they had none of the rich clusters of dates with which the latter were adorned.

The air improved as we proceeded towards Cairo, and the most delicious breezes refreshed our parched-up frames. An excellent dinner is advertised at the station half-way to Cairo, called 'Kafr el Eash'—"the best dinner in all Egypt," however much or little that may say for it; but we were sufficiently cautious or economical to have provided ourselves with luncheon at Abbat's Hôtel, rather than pay five shillings a-piece here on the chance of what we might find. The train stops at this station for nearly an hour, which is tedious enough. But we are off again: as we draw very near to Cairo, the Pyramids are the objects of expectation, and at about half-past three o'clock P.M. we really behold them. There is a shout from our carriage of "There they are!" and as if electrified all our party start to their feet; 'Cousin Phil' making his way from the opposite side of the carriage with as much excitement and emotion as the younger travellers. There, indeed, before us rose the Pyramids of Geezeh, in a misty distance, which seemed to add to the solemnity of their appearance. Not all the oft-repeated accounts of soldier brothers rushing by on their way to India,

China, or Australia, and so familiarising the ear to their name, that in Europe, by our comfortable firesides, we begin to think of the Pyramids of Egypt as mere half-way houses to Bombay, Madras, Hong Kong, or Melbourne, could take away one atom of the pleasure and surprise of this moment. Little had either of us ever dreamed, till a few weeks past, of seeing with our own eyes these wondrous resting-places of Egyptian kings, the antiquity of which, beyond all certain date, takes the mind back at once through all the field of history to ages known and unknown. There are no certain records of Egyptian history beyond the sixteenth dynasty, or about 1800 years before the Christian era, and the Pyramids existed then. The Pyramids of Geezeh — a group of three, two of them large, and one by comparison so small that from this point of view it is nearly hidden — were those which charmed us on this occasion. Our fancy revelled in the mine of antiquarian speculation which these venerable mounds presented; our enthusiasm was at its height, and for the moment it seemed as though all that the world contained of real interest were placed before us in that one view. But the train passed heedlessly on, and the busy and truly Oriental city of Cairo soon diverted our meditations into a new channel. We arrived at about five P.M., and were greeted at the terminus with all the confusion and noise described in the guide-books. Happy for us that we had our faithful dragoman to talk down and repulse the crowd of Arabs, who immediately seized upon us and our bags. Even with his assistance 'Cousin Phil' was here several times in imminent peril of being thrown down, and the question frequently rose in our minds, whether we should ever reach the carriage or the hotel in safety at all. This was accomplished in time, and, much amused with the scuffles which other unfortunate travellers were going through with the world-famed 'donkey-boys,' we arrived at half-past five P.M. at the entrance to Shepherd's Hotel, on the 'Uzbeköéh.'

Imagine our delight at the lofty rooms and cool passages of this hotel, and the inviting arm-chairs in a certain parlour, which received us with open arms, and where we immediately reclined our wearied frames, with dreams of future comfort. Imagine the subsequent horror at being obliged to relinquish it all,—the parlour, the only one on the ground-floor, was already engaged! When it is to be had, it is at the price of 1*l.* per day, extra to the 10*s.* paid daily by each person for board and lodging in the hotel. 'Cousin Phil' could not mount upstairs: his bed-room, then, must act as sitting-room; and the poor young ladies, who, of course, have a weakness for sitting-rooms proper, must put up with it. We had spacious apartments above, but the cool passages and very fatiguing stone steps were not just the thing for an invalid; and from what we heard and experienced afterwards, the 'Hôtel des Empereurs' would be far preferable in cases where comfort, equal temperature, and cleanliness, are desirable items.

The quiet *table-d'hôte* dinner was served at half-past six o'clock. There were about twenty persons present, the British Consul and Vice-consul among the number; and all were very chatty and agreeable. 'Cousin Phil,' not being able to join in the general conversation, was contented to sit between the two ladies: thus we had the opportunity of making acquaintance with our next neighbours; and from many of them, as time went on, we gained a great deal of useful information, which was retailed to 'Cousin Phil' in our bed-room parlour.

The next morning (Friday, Nov. 2d) we met at nine o'clock at the *table-d'hôte déjeûner à la fourchette*, with mutual congratulations on not having been eaten up during the night, as in Alexandria. It was a very good breakfast: ham and eggs fried up together into a most exemplary pancake; fried potatoes, cutlets, cold meat, tea and coffee; home-like gooseberry jam, in a large salad-glass, fruits, and *lard*, calling itself butter! I believe it was made of buffalo-milk, but it looked like lard, and that was enough for us. When we said good-bye to our island home, it was good-bye, as a matter of course, to butter also; so that this did not trouble us much, and we never tasted a bit of it till we returned home again in the summer of 1861.

Carriages with two horses are engaged at the hotel at sixteen shillings per day. If not engaged there, travellers are generally asked one pound for them. Ours now stops the way, and we set forth to hunt for a 'dahabëéh,' suitable for our excursion up the Nile. A black figure with white dress and red fez, legs and arms mostly bare, sits as coachman; at his side the dragoman; a black 'sais,' or runner, —with a tight jacket of coloured cotton, large loose sleeves tucked up over the shoulder, caught together behind with a string, and flapping about as he runs, a very short loose skirt, bare legs with a bit of wool tied round the ankle ("to assist his running"), a common fez, and small stick in hand—runs before the carriage, shouting at the top of his voice, "ō—ā! —ō—ā! Riglac, riglac!" (Out of the way! Out of the way! Take care of your legs!) and knocking out of *his* way, in the most unceremonious manner, old and young, camels, donkeys, and donkey-boys; whatever impedes the progress of the carriage, in which the Europeans sit in a high state of amusement and amazement, as well as of interest at the scene before them.

To our northern ideas the noise made on our account, as we whirled through the narrow streets, and the good-humour with which the crowd moved out of our way and put up with all the antics of the 'saïs,' were incomprehensible; while the 'saïs' himself, who could run thus for hours, keeping up with the pace of the horses, and making them go all the faster for his shouting, seemed to us but little short of a maniac. On we fly through the town of

Boulak (the port of Cairo), the dragoman pointing out and naming bazaar, mosque, gate, and fountain, as they succeed each other, so rapidly as to leave in the minds of his hearers a confused vocabulary of unpronounceable names, associated with a still greater confusion of all the novel objects which so simultaneously meet their gaze. The monuments of ages gone by appear crumbling to ruin in the midst of those of later times, and of those of the present day, still in course of erection. Side by side the new and the old exist together in this ancient city. Nothing apparently is ever moved away, but ruins and heaps of rubbish lie as they once fell, or accumulate afresh day by day. Houses, of which one half only still stand, are inhabited, while the rest of the original building strews the ground below in the form of dust and fragments. The pretty "Mushrabëéh," the Moorish wooden lattice-windows, still remain in many of them, though in most cases they are broken and mutilated, and hang from the walls as it were by a thread. This beautiful remnant of antiquity will soon, alas! have disappeared from Cairo, for the Mushrabëéh are no longer allowed to be put up there, on account of the danger of fire. The upper stories of the houses project from the lower and overhang the streets, which are so narrow that it is quite surprising how so much business and traffic can be carried on in the open shops which line them on either side, as well as before them in the street itself. Yet the streets of Boulak are considerably wider than those of 'Old Cairo,' which we have not yet seen.

But we have reached the Nile, and are now examining the many 'dahabëëhs' anchored in this port. It was a work of some difficulty to get to them—first over very irregular ground into a small boat, and thence to the larger vessel. Very pleasant was the refreshing breeze as we rowed along; and this was the first thing which gave me any idea of comfort in connexion with the Nile trip. Once on the water, we should have fresh air again, and Selina and I began to feel our fears disperse. The Arabs hoisted each of us up the side of the 'dahabëëh' in a wonderful way of their own; and between three of them 'Cousin Phil' was safely deposited on the deck. It was so fatiguing for him to repeat this very often, that he afterwards remained in the small boat whilst we carried on the inspection of the rest of the fleet. The 'Cairo' was the only boat that offered the required accommodation of five separate cabins. Our dragoman was amazed; he could not understand, if Selina and I must have each a separate cabin, why that luxury should be granted to the two servants: he thenceforth looked upon Thomas and Sarah as very great personages, though rather inconvenient ones; as to himself, there was no thought of a bed for him at all—he sleeps outside, "wherever I can!" Five cabins, however, we must have; and, finally, we rowed to a boat belonging to a man whom Mohamed called the 'Persian Vice-consul,' but whose real position we never could ascertain. This boat was also too small. While we were on board, the Persian lady looked out from her window on shore, and invited the strangers into her house. 'Cousin Phil' did not much wish to go, but the dragoman insisted, and, knowing that in the East the refusal of an invitation may be taken as an insult, we all mounted a narrow, dark staircase, and were shown into a plain-looking room, entirely devoid of ornament, with the exception of some pretty carving on the wooden ceiling. There were 'divans' against the walls on two sides of the apartment, and common tables against the others. The lady soon made her appearance, very shabbily dressed, in a dark, claret-coloured silk dress, open in front, very low indeed, and showing a clear white muslin habit-shirt, open also. Her hair was plaited in two long, black tresses, hanging behind; and she wore a red fez, almost entirely concealed by a very thick black silk tassel. It was by no means a scene of luxury or grandeur, which may be partly accounted for by the fact, which the husband revealed, through the medium of our dragoman-interpreter, that their eldest son had two months before been drowned in the river. Since that time, the poor mother told us, through her tears, she had not cared to "dress becomingly," or, in fact, "to have anything nice about her." Upon this the poor thing wept copiously, as she did repeatedly during the visit, whenever her husband recurred to the distressing event. She certainly did not care to have her surviving children 'nicely kept,' or dressed: those that now came forward to offer us the customary salutation, were surely the dirtiest little animals that ever kissed a lady's hand; and while submitting to the compliment with becoming courtesy, we inwardly rejoiced in the protection afforded by the European habit of wearing gloves! The visit was prolonged until the 'English gentleman' had taken, or pretended to take, one whiff of the proffered hookah; for 'Cousin Phil' had been reared in the good old times, when the pernicious habit of smoking had not taken rank as an essential accomplishment of youth. The whole party then partook of strong black coffee, in tiny china cups; each cup placed within a beautiful silver filagree stand, resembling an egg-cup. This was the only sign of wealth we could discover in this our first Oriental visit. Thus it ended, and, after mutual interchanges of compliments and a few more hand-kisses from the dirty children, we descended the dark staircase, and by boat and carriage again reached the hotel. We took a slight luncheon at the *table d'hôte,* at one P.M., and in the course of the afternoon set out on another hunt for a 'dahabëéh.' And now, behold us mounted on the arms of two strong, black, bare-armed, and bare-legged Arabs; our arms resting affectionately on their black shoulders as they carried us across the thick mud, and through the water, to a 'dahabëéh,' which there was no other means of reaching. We laughed heartily at the comical appearance of the whole scene, though in the momentary expectation of being dropped into the water by the swarthy bearers, who seemed to participate in our merriment. It certainly would have made a charming picture; our modern European costume surmounted by the knowing little felt-hat and scarlet-tipped black feather, contrasting strangely with the flowing robes of our Arab bearers, and the portly figure of our dragoman in an equally helpless condition closing the procession.

'Cousin Phil' sits the while, patiently scorching in the open carriage, surrounded by an admiring crowd of every shade of brown, not capable of understanding one word of theirs, or of making himself understood by them. Yet there he remains without harm of any kind, and in perfect confidence of safety on his own side; for what should such a brave old gentleman have to fear! The boats proved all too small, with the exception of the 'Cairo,' before mentioned; but nothing could be decided till Mr. B. appeared, whose name was held up by the travellers as their watchword, against cheating of all kinds.

'Hassan Effendi's' boats had been strongly recommended, and we found them well fitted up, though too small for us. 'Hassan' himself escorted the ladies back to the carriage, with what Mohamed called most "*sweet*" eloquence, and a flow of

English words, quite astonishing from Oriental lips. He was very handsomely dressed, wore a profusion of gold chains, and was very proud of the honour of the visit, though evidently rather shocked that his boats could be found too small for any party, however large.

Dinner-time this second day, added to our party a most agreeable acquaintance in Mr. H——, with whose writings on this country the public are well acquainted. He also was going up the Nile for his health.

Saturday, Nov. 3d. We ascended the hill of the citadel, and stood at the entrance of the magnificent Mosque of Mahomet Ali, where our feet were clothed in slippers, made of dirty bits of cloth or canvas, rudely run up into a kind of shoe, before we were allowed to step upon the highly polished marble pavement. In the court before the mosque, which is also entirely paved with polished marble, is a large fountain, at which many poor misguided Mahometans were devoutly washing, before entering the mosque for prayer: their apparent devotion, worthy a truer creed. Many of the Mahometan derweesh, 'clergyment' and 'big clergyment,' as our dragoman insisted on calling them, were squatted on the floor within the mosque, repeating passages from the Korán, or lying down, because, as he said with great reverence, "they have nothing to do but to pray." The interior of the mosque is very fine; the pavement, the greater part of the walls, and the pillars, entirely of marble. The dome and the gallery which runs round it within, are very elaborately gilt and handsomely carved. A splendid circle of glass chandeliers is suspended from the centre, and lighted upon grand occasions. Issuing from the mosque, Mohamed led us with pride to the view of the city, which lay spread out at our feet below the citadel. It seemed to us that it could hardly be surpassed in beauty or in interest. Hundreds of minarets and domes rise from all parts of the town, ruins of years gone by, or fresh erections of the day. Intermingled with them, groves of graceful palm-trees raise their feathery foliage against the clear, blue, cloudless sky, whilst, as far as the eye can reach, the venerable Nile winds its course in the bright sunlight, speckled with innumerable sails; those pretty lateen sails which add so much to every picture in the South. The burning sun lighted up the whole to a wonderful brilliancy, and soon scorched us away from a scene we could otherwise have looked at with pleasure for hours. Then followed the Mosque of Sultan Hassan, the finest in Cairo, date A.D. 1363, that on the tomb of the Sultan being 764 of the Hegira. The blocks of stone of which it is built were brought from the Pyramids. We continued our drive through the bazaars, longing ever and anon for a breath of fresh air, although the constant succession of the novel sights which meet one there at every step will make amends for this, if necessary, for a day or two.

Another acquaintance commenced to-day, a Mr. and Mrs. M——, also going up the Nile, in search of health for the former. Very pleasant friends we found them; but our quiet and sociable party was disturbed by the great influx of strangers, caused by the arrival of the mails from Southampton and Marseilles; and later in the day of that from Suez. The dining-room was changed, the seats at table were changed, so that friends of a few days back were separated. One hundred and thirty people sat down together, and the waiters were so few, and in such constant request, that had not Mohamed and Thomas stood behind the chairs of our lucky 'trio,' we should not have had anything to eat. Most of the Nile travellers had their dragomen in attendance, so that they were not so badly off. We made a tolerable dinner, and then retired to discuss our neighbours, with all that they had said and done, to detail to each other the romantic histories we had attached to each new party, and to hope that Mr. B—— would appear to-morrow.

Sunday, Nov. 4th. We started for church. The morning service was at eleven o'clock. Mohamed produced a very tumble-down looking arm-chair, in which 'Cousin Phil' bravely seated himself, and was raised aloft on the shoulders of two Arabs, or three as the case might be; first they seized one arm of the chair, then one leg, and that not answering very well, a turbaned head was poked suddenly against the back of it, experimentalizing in every possible and impossible way to carry it straight, at the imminent risk of the poor gentleman's being pitched out at every step. Down many a dark, narrow street, we at length reached the room set apart for the service of the Anglican Church; and no small relief it was to the rest of the party, if not to himself, that the occupier of the wonderful chair did arrive without a fall. The travellers for Suez had been sent on early in the morning, so that there was but a small congregation. Mr. R—— officiated in the absence of Mr. Lieder, the resident missionary. His German accent was peculiar, but the service was our Church of England service still; doubly prized in this Mahometan land; and it was with regret that we, and others learned, that no afternoon or evening service was to be offered us here as at home.

For want then of better occupation, we accepted Mr. H——'s kind offer of an order for the Pasha's gardens at Shoobra. These orders are procured from the Consul. At three P.M., our friend joined us, and we set out in a carriage for the drive. A long avenue of acacia-trees and Egyptian figs leads to the gardens of Mahomet Ali's palace; and stretches for a considerable distance along the banks of the Nile. The gardens are much more prettily laid out than those in Alexandria, but there were not many flowers in bloom. The 'Cape jessamine' was very fine, and the small green Tangiers oranges, which the Arab who piloted us round the gardens, brought to us to taste, were very sweet and refreshing. The great 'kiosk,' or fountain, in the centre of the garden, is the chief point of attraction. 'Cousin Phil' could not walk so far, but remained seated near the lesser 'kiosk,' while we with our friend and his fly-flapper, for he wisely never stirred without one, proceeded to the larger, and enjoyed a very pleasant half-hour, sitting on the divans, which are placed under a covered corridor, surrounding a large fountain-basin of Carrara marble. The pillars and the encircling balustrade are of the same material, the panels on the walls are painted by Italian artists, and the pavement is very prettily tessellated. The whole is lighted up of an evening on particular occasions by gas-lamps. How deliciously cool it felt, how orientally luxurious it all looked, and how sorry we were to emerge again into the broiling sun. The thermometer was at 76° in the shade.

Evening drew on, but no Mr. B—— had appeared. Mohamed began to be excited. Two other parties were looking at, and longing for, the 'Cairo;' and the Reïs, or captain of the boat, promised to wait till to-morrow morning only for our decision.

Monday, Nov. 5th. We went to the Telegraph Office to make inquiry through that medium for our friend. Those who were anxious to bring us to an agreement without his protecting care, confidently affirmed that '*His Excellency*' had been taken suddenly ill, and that he could not come at all. But the telegraph in due time answered 'no,' Mr. B—— would be in Cairo to-morrow, or next day at latest. Mohamed meanwhile discovered another dahabëëh, the property of El Halim Pasha, who had died at Constantinople. "It is the best boat on the Nile, which, if we take, I be very glad," says the dragoman: so off we start to see it. Selina and I were mounted again on the arms of the good-tempered grinning blacks; and the inspection of the dahabëëh was so satisfactory, that the "great gentleman" was fetched out of the carriage to see it for himself. He came rowing along in a little boat; the boatmen singing their curious chant-like song to the splashing of their oars. It is a wild, curious sound, but according so well with the scene around that it is not unpleasing. We then visited the 'Cairo' once more; it looked small after the grander and much better finished vessel, but the arrangement of its cabins was in many respects more convenient.

In spite of all exhortation and persuasion we would keep our promise and wait for Mr. B——. The Reïs again agreed for to-morrow. It was quite as serious an affair as choosing a house; we talked it over and over again; and then we drove through the streets, or alleys rather, as they appeared to us, of 'Old Cairo,' the original portion of the great city, which now consists of three divisions,—'Cairo,' 'Old Cairo,' and 'Boulak.' Alas, what pictures of misery and destitution did not these streets reveal! They were heart-rending; the women and children in particular were pitiable to behold. Many we could not bear to look at, and, rightly or not, we formed no favourable opinion of a government which could thus leave its subjects in a condition but little raised above the beasts of the field.

At dinner to-day the various plans of the several parties for the Nile were discussed, and the climate of Nubia up to the Second Cataracts so extolled, that our party, who were before afraid of a *six weeks'* journey, now began to give in to the recommendations of their friends, and for Selina's sake to extend their plans. A few hints were first thrown out, and, finally, something very like a petition for three months, instead of two, was dropped into 'Cousin Phil's' ears, which as he had never entertained any fears on this, any more than on any other subject, easily took effect there. Dreams of cooling breezes; of social meetings in each other's boats; of obsequious dragomen providing every Oriental luxury, as the dahabëëh glides peacefully along, now replace the alarming pictures which had been conjured up, of helpless invalids at the mercy of savages, whose language they could not understand; of unruly boatmen, requiring fire-arms to alarm them into obedience; and, not least perhaps, of the most doleful, unbroken solitude, in scorching sun, with plague of flies!

Tuesday, November 6th. We visited to-day the tombs of the Circassian kings on the south side of the city. The dates are of the fifteenth century, and the tombs are crumbling to ruin. Near to them are those of Mahomet Ali and his family. These are very handsomely painted and gilt, and many of them bear Arabic inscriptions upon them. But the most curious sight was that of a number of men sitting on carpets at the foot of the tombs, or along the sides of the Mosque, repeating portions of the Korán in a chanting tone, in memory of the departed: each one of the deceased being thus honoured in their turn at particular times, and every day during the season of 'Ramadan.' It was a strange kind of chant, and there was very little of solemnity apparent in the faces or attitudes of the chanters who sat or lay there all day; at the present moment, we were told, in memory of 'El Halim' Pasha before mentioned as the owner of the handsome dahabëéh. Another very handsome tomb in this neighbourhood Mohamed pointed out with great veneration, calling it 'Sahaba' (companion), it being one of several erected to the memory of the companions of the Prophet.

In order to lose no time, though the dahabëéh was still unhired, our next visit was to 'Turnbull's shop' in the Frank Street; a very important house in Cairo, whence travellers for the Nile lay in their winter store. There sat Selina and I in state; Mohamed el Adléëh squatted in front, vigorously brandishing before us a fly-flapper to keep off the myriads of flies, who thought Mr. Turnbull's shop a very excellent one, whilst samples of biscuit, rice, arrowroot, pickles, lemonade-syrup, tea, sugar, jam, English and Egyptian, of which the latter proved by far the best, &c., were brought out for our inspection and approval of their several qualities only, for the dragoman was to have the sole responsibility of ordering the proper quantities, to satisfy the appetites of our party of five, for three months' time. This *séance* occupied upwards of an hour, and then we went to another shop higher up the street, for macaroni and potatoes. Mohamed always knew the best stores for each separate article, and evidently thought that good feeding was the chief business of *our* lives; that of *his*, to supply us with it. I think his idea was that it would always be easy to please us, so long as we were supplied with a good dinner, breakfast, and tea. The carriage then fetched 'Cousin Phil' from the hotel, and Boulak was honoured with another rush of the Europeans, through its narrow streets; the wild saïs as usual tumbling everything before him. A number of lanterns and chandeliers suspended gave notice of an approaching illumination. It was the last night of the festival of 'El Hassan el Hossein,' the two sons of Ali. The dragoman says it will be "Peautiful! peautiful indeed!" and "we must certainly go to see it at eight o'clock this evening."

Just before dinner-time appeared the Reïs of the dahabëëh 'Cairo,' to say that a third party were looking at his boat, and that the 'English gentleman' must decide at once, or lose it. The redoubtable Mr. B—— had not yet arrived; but there was no help for it; we were intimidated, and finally resolved that no other boat gave the required accommodation, that one after another was being rapidly engaged for the Nile trip, that the price asked for the 'Cairo' was a reasonable one, 'as times went:' and so the balance was weighed in her favour, and the Reïs admitted into the 'presence-chamber.' He looked imposing, with his dark brown skin, bright black eyes, black whiskers and moustaches; his long loose dress of much the same shade with his complexion, his voluminous turban, and solemn manner, as he sat on a chair, while Mohamed el Adlëëh stood before him and detailed the conditions upon which he in the service of the "English gentleman," would engage the boat 'Cairo.' At each pause the Reïs' hand was placed upon his head, or one finger in the corner of each eye, in token of agreement and good faith. A strong and affectionate attachment was supposed to exist between these two Arabs; they were to each other "my very dear friend." Nevertheless the national craving for "Baksheesh" was not lessened, and even now the Reïs tried hard to raise the hire of his boat. It seemed at times, likely, that the bargain would not be struck after all, but when about half an hour of Arabic and gesticulations had passed away, a long string of "Teieb, Teieb," (Very good! Very good!) from the mouth of the Reïs, announced, that, "for the sake of his friend," and the "charming strangers," he was well content to submit to the "self-sacrifice," of letting his "beautiful dahabëëh" for the small sum of 52*l.* per month, for three months, and to go as far as the Second Cataracts—saving always the approval of 'His Excellency'—whose arrival, be it confessed, Selina and I began now in our turn to await with a certain degree of awe after our daring act. For how did we know, after all, whether we had done wisely or not.

Dinner came again, and we discussed with our friends the grand illumination, and all the invalids determined for once to do the imprudent, and to go. Mr. H—— accompanied us, and, chiming in afterwards with the general opinion, pronounced the expedition even worth a fit of neuralgia. The illumination was well worth seeing. All along the narrow streets and bazaars hung pyramidal chandeliers, some with as many as fifty lights in each of them, the variously-coloured large balls of crystal, seen between the tiers of light, glittering most brilliantly in the surrounding darkness. Besides these, there were smaller lamps of every variety in size, shape, and colour. The dark outlines of the mosques and minarets rose at every turn against the illuminated streets, and the deep blue sky above, with the moon and stars far larger and brighter than in our home latitudes, completed a picture which is rarely seen by Europeans. The sea of turbaned heads through which our carriage wended its way, and the good-humour on the part of the crowd so unceremoniously disturbed, was quite striking. Thomas and Sarah walked, and were invited into one of the houses, where coffee was offered them; and we all returned home, pleased and much surprised at the brilliant effect which could thus be produced by small oil lamps, set in custard glasses. But it was a Mahometan festival after all; in the open shops many sat upon their counters steadily reading portions of the Korán; some few at least, of the obsequious crowd, true to their creed, uttered words of contempt at the Christian as the carriage drove along, and it was sad to think that all this joy and festivity was got up in honour of a false creed and false prophet.

Wednesday, Nov. 7th. We started for a morning drive in search of fresh air, on the road to 'Abbas Seïr.' The driver was a Maltese, who made his horses go at such a furious pace, that when the fresh air quarter was just within our reach, the creatures positively refused to stir any further; not all the threats, coaxing, or cruel beating of coachman, dragoman, or saïs—not even the active exertions of the latter at the wheels of the carriage were of any avail; we were forced to give it up and take another road, and the stubborn Maltese received a good scolding on arriving at the hotel. We had brought a letter of introduction to Mrs. Lieder, and called upon her this afternoon. She is a most good-natured person, always ready to do a kindness to strangers, and does not apparently suffer from the heat in this climate. Her house is the same building in which the Sunday service is celebrated; her drawing-room quite a museum of Egypt. What interested me most in our short survey was the head of one of the sacred bulls, and of a calf, taken out of the Apis Cemetery near Memphis.

On our return, Mohamed's preparations for the Nile excursion began, in the form of a bright new 'silver' tea-pot and coffee-pot, feather-brush, foot-bath, &c. &c.;, and henceforth until the day of embarcation, it was highly amusing to see the canteen pour in and accumulate by degrees, in our bed-room parlour, as well as outside of it, in the passages of the hotel; crate after crate, and box after box, containing everything necessary for furnishing and provisioning a house for three months; added to which were side-saddles for the ladies and the maid, and a wonderful chair, manufactured in more wonderfully rude style, in which 'Cousin Phil' was to be carried about by two strong donkeys. It had four posts and a canopy with curtains of white cotton drawn aside in the front, and two huge heavy poles for shafts fastened to it on either side. The donkeys were to be harnessed between these, one before, the other behind; and as the shafts were placed along the base of the towering chair, clever would the donkeys have been, had they carried it straight; cleverer still 'Cousin Phil' should he not fall out of it, and truly praiseworthy, also, if he do not ere long complain bitterly of the invention. For the moment all is very amusing, and looks like preparations for a pic-nic on a large and rude scale, yet with a considerable degree of Oriental luxury intermingled with it.

Mr. B—— arrived at length, business had detained him, he looked grave at any agreement having been made with Arabs by inexperienced Europeans, but still appeared to think the bargain not a bad one, and our minds were relieved. To-morrow will show the result, and meantime we all partake of a cup of *tea*, a pleasing novelty to our friend's adopted Eastern customs.

To-morrow came, Thursday, November 8th. The whole party embarked on board the 'Cairo;' a most systematic inspection of every nook and corner of the dahabëéh was carried on, while the Reïs and dragoman stood watching with countenances expressive of the deepest anxiety, no doubt afraid of the *rat-holes* coming to light. Mr. B——, looking stern as any Eastern despot, examined so carefully every atom of the vessel before he ventured an opinion, that Selina and I began to be alarmed, and to think we had made a mistake, while 'Cousin Phil,' who could only see a very small part of the play, as he sat perched upon the high divan in the saloon, waited in quiet resignation for the final sentence. Mr. B—— still looks grave, and goes off in a small boat to see 'El Halim' Pasha's dahabëéh and some others close by, attended by several of the Arabs. The

Reïs waits in evident anxiety, sitting with a brother Reïs cross-legged, and motionless on the deck until his return. He came at last; pronounced the 'Cairo' decidedly the largest, perfectly safe, and that, with many little additions of cleaning, painting, locks and keys, book-shelves in the saloon, &c. &c., it would do, although not fitted up in the style in which it might have been.

It was agreed, however, that for sailing up the Nile, space was preferable to style; and so the countenances of the Reïs and the dragoman began to assume a more composed aspect, and after many gesticulations and solemn promises on their parts the party retired; the contract was to be passed the following day, and the boat ready to start on 'Monday next.' Mr. B—— left with our grateful thanks, and we returned to the hotel, to welcome the long-looked-for boxes, which we had sent by sea from Southampton. We had had some trouble in fetching them out of the Custom House. From some unknown cause, the several packages had parted company, and arrived by different trains; so that until all were found, we were not allowed to take possession of any. There was considerable pleasure in the sight of the contents of these boxes; not only for the convenience of the possession, but for the home associations which they brought to our minds. Owing to the change in our plans, but few articles were extracted, and they were soon re-packed to be left at the hotel, in a room appropriated to such purposes until the Nile excursion should be over, and we on our way to more civilised lands.

We went to see another of the Mosques in the course of our afternoon drive; and no words can express the beauty of the soft rich tints of sunset which we saw on our return that evening. There was no great brilliancy; but warm soft hues, such as we never see at home, blended into each other in the richest beauty. Feelings of quiet and mystery stole over us, as the warm glow came suddenly on, and passed almost as quickly away, to be succeeded by the grey shades of night; these, in their turn, to be as suddenly replaced by the exceeding brilliancy of the moon and stars; for there is no twilight in Egypt.

Friday, November 9th. A boy in light blue dress and crimson turban took the place of our dragoman to-day; that important personage being fully occupied in making purchases for the journey, and in arranging matters on board the 'Cairo.' 'Cousin Phil' remained at the hotel, writing volumes to all his grand-nephews and nieces at home, to go by the next mail, whilst Selina and I went forth in all our grandeur, with the rushing saïs and the shabby though intelligent substitute for 'Mohamed el Adlëéh' to the Turkish Bazaar (Khan Kaleel). We *walked* through it, that we might have time to watch at leisure the numerous trades carried on in the little open shops, to admire the silk scarfs of Damascus, and to hear the exorbitant prices asked for them. "If we could but go to Damascus!" our guide informed us that there the silk shawls with long hanging cords and tassels, called 'Hufieh,' and worn as a turban round the 'tarboosh,' are sold for five shillings. Here, he said he could get them for us for fifteen or eighteen shillings; but we were asked 2*l.* in the Bazaar. On our return, after a good deal of bargaining, we purchased some in the Syrian Bazaar of very superior quality for 1*l.* 3*s.* 6*d.* each. A man embroidering a portion of a saddle with gold thread on green leather attracted particular attention. The work was most beautifully done, and the workman never for a moment took his eyes off his work whilst we stood watching him. He first pierced the leather through with a sharp instrument, and then passed the needle up, and down again, into the same holes, catching in the gold thread with some coloured silk, which was thus quite invisible as a stitch, while the surface of gold was left perfectly smooth. There is a great deal of this work done in Cairo, and the saddles thus embroidered are extremely handsome. The attention of the workmen to their work was very striking, for even the little boys would go on steadily weaving the silk borders to the blue cotton scarfs, or shoe-making, or whatever their trade might be, without so much as lifting their eyes to look at us, while we stood watching them and talking about them. It is highly amusing to walk through these Bazaars, where shoemakers, tinkers, tailors, weavers, cord and tassel makers, cooks, barbers, coffee-makers, ply assiduously their respective callings; whilst rich merchants sit on the counters, before their silks and cottons, smoking out of 'hookahs,' or the pretty glass 'narghillae,' in which the water makes a low bubbling sound; venerable old men sit in the same way reading portions of the Korán; scribes are writing, holding the sheet of paper in the palms of their left hand, the little brass inkstand and penholder on the counter at their feet; numbers of others are reclining, the very picture of the *dolce far niente*, sipping coffee from their tiny cups, whilst many a picturesque figure lies full length and fast asleep before his goods. All this is very interesting, very curious, and very pretty, but then comes the other, the dark side of the picture: the *désagrémens* of very close contact with donkeys and donkey-boys, the dirtiest set of men and women that eyes ever looked upon, (scarcely one man among them possessing two eyes of his own); children's faces one mass of flies, with the very least rag of clothing to cover their puny black bodies; beggars of the most wretched and loathsome appearance, who will shake a withered limb before you, or show off a deformed child in the most revolting manner, to excite your charity. One and all of these are pushed away by your attendant without ceremony; but the contact is too close, and when you add to all this, indescribably horrid smells, even the interest of the Bazaar soon ceases. In a short space of time we were glad to make a quick exit to the carriage, and to seek for a breath of fresh air before the dinner-hour.

This evening our kind friend came to write out the contract between 'Cousin Phil' and our dragoman; it was very good-natured of him to undertake the task, which was no light one. A very droll picture it was; his 'Excellency,' in Oriental costume, seated, with pen, ink, and paper before him, in our quaint little parlour, exhibiting all the sternness of manner and expression so essential in dealings with the Arabs; and the dragoman deferentially standing by, and making the same signs of acquiescence and true faith in this matter as the Reïs had done with him before. When the dragoman hires the boat and provides for the party, as Mohamed did for us, the cost of the trip varies from 4*l.* to 6*l.* per day, according to the number of the party and other circumstances: the hire of boats varying from 40*l.* to 75*l.* per month. Some persons prefer hiring the dahabëéh, and providing for themselves, in which case the dragoman is paid merely for his attendance as a guide. The former plan may be rather the more expensive, but it is found to be by far the best way. Boat, board, lodging, washing, &c., and sight-seeing, are thus all provided for, and the travellers may enjoy themselves without even the cares of housekeeping.

A large cargo of news was scribbled off for home, whilst the contract which was to take us so far away was being drawn out, for this is our last opportunity of writing until we reach the famous ruins of Karnak.

Saturday, November 10th. Mohamed continued his purchases, and was also fully occupied with the contract between himself and the owner of the dahabëëh. This contract for the hire of the boat and crew must be drawn out, signed, and sealed, before the governor or the Consul. Mohamed junior was therefore our escort still, and we accomplished the drive to Abbas Seïr. This road is the only one in or near Cairo, worthy the name, the others being, all of them, striking illustrations of the nursery rhyme—"Here we go up, up, up," and "Here we go down, down, down." It is the road which leads from Cairo to Suez, and was made by Abbas Pasha, whose palace stands near it, on the desert waste. We enjoyed this drive extremely; it was the first sight of the true desert that we had had, and the air was so deliciously pure and fresh, that we all agreed, that if a cruel fate were to cast our lot in such a country at all, we should certainly build our houses out here.

Sunday, (November 11th,) came round again, and this time the English service was well attended; all the newly arrived passengers being detained till the morrow. Mr. W——, an Englishman, assisted in the service, and preached an impressive sermon on "Watchman, what of the night?" &c., from Isaiah, xxi. 11, applying the term to the night of the 'life' of every one of us on this earth, as opposed to the 'day' which will dawn hereafter, bright and glorious to the true believer, who shall have watched faithfully during the hours of the present night. The singing was very good; every one took part in it, and the room was quite full. Mahomed takes no share in our Sunday services, so he went down to Alexandria to-day to fetch his 'canteen' and to buy flour and dried fruits for the expedition, these two articles being very superior, and at the same time cheaper there, than at Cairo. The dahabëéh, he said, could not be ready till Thursday; and we were told that we must not be surprised at further delays. Arabs are neither given to hurrying nor to punctuality.

Monday, November 12th. Every excursion boat on the Nile has, besides the national flag of the party in possession, a distinguishing flag of its own, so that friends may be able to recognise one another as they pass. We chose for ours a 'Crocodile,' and after a great deal of trouble succeeded in drawing one of a sufficient size on paper. We then took it to Mr. Pay in the Frank Street, to be made up, together with a large 'Union Jack' for the dahabëéh, a small plain pennant, and a small 'Union Jack' for the row-boat in which we were to land at the various places of interest on our way. We drove through the Bazaars, for the heat of the day was too great for the open space; but towards evening we again tried the road to Abbas Seïr. The air was clearer and purer the further we went, and we were tempted on, rather too far for prudence. Night comes on so quickly and the changes of temperature are so great, and so sudden, that even by a quarter to six o'clock when we reached the hotel, shawls and wraps had become needful. Invalids should be extremely careful in this climate to be within doors before sunset. Mr. B—— came to wish us goodbye, for we were not to see him again till our journey was over. A new set of passengers had arrived, and had been sent on immediately, so that our original small party met again sociably, in the smaller dining-room. We were now quite a family party of travellers for the Nile, and began to talk of a Christmas meeting, and to fight amicably for the honour of the entertainment—none of us however, did meet till Christmas day was long past, and those who boasted plum-puddings had them all to themselves.

Tuesday, November 13th. We drove to Kasr e'Neel, the Pasha's new palace. A large body of black cavalry were passing through the gates, returning from watering the horses. A little further on was a very pretty scene. A camp, tents, men, and horses in large numbers on one side, with a picturesque, rising back-ground covered with groups of people and camels; the Mokattam Hills, and the citadel in the distance. On the other hand, a regiment of Nubians going through the sword exercise with great perseverance. Their uniform, a white shirt, jacket, and loose trousers; red sash and tarboosh, contrasting well with their black hands and faces; the *shout* which ran along the several lines in succession at each sword-cut, producing a very peculiar effect. Further on, among the tall plantations of 'prickly pear,' the band was stationed, and played its everlasting tune, for it seemed to us always the same. The bugles were in one division, at some distance from them the drums, again in a third position the fifes, all sounding together, very much as though the object of the players were to try who could make most noise. Of *piano* and *forte* they can have as yet no idea; and so they go on and on, and the sound rings harshly in our ears at all hours of the day. Near the barracks is the soldiers' market, and great boilers full of soup were passing by on carts, while people were carrying on their heads large circular trays full of eatables, carefully covered over, with conical-shaped covers, made of plaited grass or date-leaves. Mohamed returned from Alexandria to-day: his contract with the Reïs is duly signed and sealed, and we are to go on board the dahabëëh on Thursday evening.

Wednesday, November 14th. The new flags were taken to the boat, and taken back again by the indignant dragoman, to be made some "fifteen yards longer;" he declaring that "that Englishman Pay knows nothing about Nile boats, flags, or crocodiles;" and "Cairo, best boat on the Nile, is not to be laughed at as she sails along!" Whilst they were being lengthened, we drove again to

Shoobra, along a road which threatened to jolt nearly every bone in our bodies out of joint. It had its interest however, in the inspection of the Arab potato plant, with its large handsome leaf; the barmia, a very excellent vegetable, somewhat of the shape of a diminutive capsicum; and large crops of the French aubergine, all very common in this country. On our return, we were surprised at seeing on our table a card P.P.C. The first of the present assembly of travellers for the Nile had started.

Thursday, November 15th. Shopping excursions had become for some days past the regular routine of the morning drive, and the 'Frank Street' the scene as much as Regent Street could have been. A number of little necessaries had been added to our stock, and with the zinc and elder-water, the quassia and insect-powder, we considered ourselves armed against all exigencies. Our packing was accomplished; we took a solitary dinner at three P.M., the donkey-chair was tried in front of the hotel, to the great amusement of the assembled public of all nations, and the danger of the fracture of the whole concern; but when the shafts had been raised a little, it was pronounced available for the purpose; the huge caravan of heavy baggage was despatched on the backs of camels; 'Mohamed el Adlëéh' looked and sighed, as if rather more than the weight of the whole world was accumulated upon his shoulders; and our carriage rushed away from all this confusion

BOULAK, THE PORT OF CAIRO

to take a farewell drive to Kasr e'Neel, and to reach our new home at six o'clock, when the shades of night would be fast closing in.

Worthy, indeed, of the closing scene of a stay in Cairo, is that which now presents itself in the little port of Boulak. The baggage imposingly towers still on the shore, the crowds and the noises around baffle description, whilst all is in darkness, illuminated only by one or two small oil lamps. The 'Cairo' is moored among many cargo boats. Not the slightest idea has she of sailing to-night, and even the strong wills of our two young ladies are unable to move Mohamed to the necessity of at least gaining the opposite shore and the island of Roda, for the sake of quiet and a fresher atmosphere. We are obliged to give in. All is close and horrid, swarming with mosquitoes and flies; deafening with the singing of boatmen in a neighbouring boat, and the preparations on shore for a 'Derweesh festival,' which is being celebrated within and without a mosque, immediately facing the 'Cairo.' But we have good spirits, and all is sure to come right in time. "Let us console ourselves with a cup of tea before we walk on shore again to see the festival." It comes; the tea-pot as bright as new silver could make it; the tea-set, neat white and gold; and now the refreshing beverage. Alas! first one grimace, then a second, then a third; it is undrinkable! Mohamed is summoned. What can it be? The tea is "the best;" the milk is "the best;" and the water is "*the Nile!*"—that one word and *Mecca* containing the whole idea of perfection in the eyes of the Arab and Mussulman.

The Nile, however, was uncommonly red just here, and, notwithstanding the strongest assertions that it had been well filtered, that portion of it which had found its way into our cups was proved to be the Nile indeed, full of a rich red sediment. Mohamed, failing to persuade us to drink it, was moved almost to tears, that his 'guests' (for as such he evidently regarded us, and there was a good deal of the manner of 'host' in him) should go tealess to bed; and finding nothing at hand to remedy the deficiency, in despair he offered to "fetch the brandy!" Instead of this, however, he escorted Selina and me on shore to see the Derweesh ceremony.

The 'quay,' if this landing-place may be so called, was so densely crowded, that it was necessary first, that a way should be made for spectators to pass through. The mosque stands on the quay, and was full of worshippers within, while outside was a circular illumination, of small triangular lamps, suspended from poles and cords, under which a party of 'derweesh' were ranged in a circle, dancing round and round, hugging each other in pairs, and making the wildest exclamations and gesticulations. They were said to be 'calling upon Allah,' but they appeared like raving madmen. When this had continued for some time, they all seated themselves on mats on the ground and continued their exclamations, rocking themselves backwards and forwards incessantly, in the most apparently fatiguing manner, which Mohamed called 'praying.' This rocking, dancing, and screaming, went on till morning, but we were soon satisfied and glad to get out of the horrid atmosphere, and to return to our unarranged home.

We retired to our cabins; mosquito curtains were ready to envelope each one, and now we looked for a wash—a more than constant necessity in Egypt. The baths were scantily filled with something very like *pea-soup.* 'Nile water' again; and the astonished dragoman imagines it *must be clean!* A very long digression upon clean water and dirty water, upon filtering and upon alum for cleansing it, and the very decided determination of the Europeans not to use such a means for cleansing themselves, were requisite before the veil was withdrawn from his superstitious eyes, and he became aware that the water was dirty, and that alum was to be had. No tea, no wash, plenty of mosquitoes, and something very like bugs. Such was the commencement of our boat-life on the Nile. But with promises of better things to-morrow, and a removal to Roda in the morning, we contrived to sleep and rest our wearied heads a little, though I believe we were inclined to think again that we had made a mistake indeed!

The morning of November 16th dawned, with cleaner water, better tea, and a very good breakfast. Mutton cutlets, cold meat, boiled rice and milk, bread, toast, and many apologies that the jam was not yet at hand, a start for Roda on the opposite shore, promises of alum in abundance, of a carpenter for various little arrangements still unmade, and assurances that the wind was directly cóntrary, and likely to remain so for some time! All the other 'dahabëëhs,' wishing to start, were necessarily in the same plight, and it was a fortunate circumstance for Mohamed, who had by no means fulfilled his engagement of being ready to sail on the 15th; fortunate, also, we incline to think, for ourselves, as we had thus the opportunity of discovering all the discomforts that awaited us from an unprepared start, none of which could have been remedied afterwards; and so Selina and I stole a leaf for once from a gentleman's book, *grumbled*, and insisted, at one and the same time, that all must be put to rights, and yet that we must set out instantly. It was very unreasonable, but it was the only way of starting at all. The dragoman made many excursions to shore, and by his fatigued and harassed appearance showed how much he had still on hand. Selina and I sketched the day away, and 'Cousin Phil' sat in quiet resignation on the divan on deck, murdering the flies and insisting upon whatever we told him to insist upon. Luncheon came at one o'clock—fruits, nuts, and cheese. And now *flies* are discovered as thick as currants in a plum-pudding, and much thicker, too, on the ceilings and walls of all the cabins. Mohamed's promises of annihilating "every one of them," appeared rather fabulous;

but by a vigorous flapping with brush and towels, they were soon considerably diminished. We then produced the quassia, and, to the astonishment of the natives, the flies died in and around it in large numbers. A small quantity of quassia must be put into a soup-plate, and boiling water be poured over it, and it should stand for a night. Sugar is then sprinkled all over the edge of the plate, and well moistened with the quassia-water. The flies are attracted to it immediately; they drink it, and very soon expire. The same plateful will last for a long time.

The dinner was very good, so was the tea; and we retired to rest at Roda, with no greater chance of a start than yesterday. Thomas made friends wherever we went, and now he had been on shore to 'his friend,' an English engineer, and brought us back an invitation for the party to go and see the gardens of Ibrahim Pasha next morning.

Saturday, Nov. 17th.—Things wore little appearance of change. It was broiling hot; the thermometer stood at 80° in the shade. The wind was still contrary: the dragoman again on shore; and we began to think of astonishing the Cairo world by our reappearance to-morrow at the Sunday morning services. Meanwhile, with Thomas and Sarah, we landed on the island, where, according to tradition, Moses was laid in the bulrushes. We visited the Pasha's gardens, under the escort of the engineer's very pretty little niece. This engineer is an Englishman, engaged by the Pasha to lay out his garden in European fashion. He receives a salary of 300*l.* or 400*l.* a-year, besides very handsome presents ('Baksheesh'); yet he says he will be glad when his work is accomplished, and he can return to Europe. His niece is of the same mind, she being the only European woman on the island, save one French lady, who cannot speak a word of English, and our little friend cannot understand French.

The time spent upon this property has not been thrown away. It is a very pretty garden, indeed, planted round the hareem, where the ladies are safely enclosed, and when they take their daily walks no other person is admitted. Here were numberless orange-trees, laden with fruit; the bamboo towering against the enclosing wall, the banana, with fruit and flower upon it, a small specimen of the dôm palm, the fleur de Pasque, in beautiful bloom, and a great variety of small flowers, mostly European; a fountain, or 'kiosk,' of course in the centre: and flying over the water, we noticed some very beautiful specimens of the red dragon-fly. We threaded our way through a curious labyrinth of high myrtle hedges: and, after a thorough baking from the hot sun, feeling quite fatigued, from the unaccustomed exercise, we returned to the boat.

At half-past one P.M. the wind had changed quarters, Mr. H—— had paid us a visit, Selina and I had been on board his dahabëéh to inspect the bachelor-like arrangements, and to see how much superior his accumulation of comforts was to ours. One of these consisted in stretching fine, coloured net outside all the windows of his 'dahabëéh,' to exclude the flies and the mosquitoes. It may be hung in the doorway also; and certainly it does exclude the flies, though it also shuts out a certain quantity of fresh air, and on that account we did not wish to adopt it. Everything in his boat was in first-rate order; and he kindly made use of his knowledge of their language to give parting injunctions to our crew on several points, principally in explaining to them that they are not allowed to walk across the upper deck, but must always walk outside the boat on the ledge which is placed purposely all round it. It is very necessary to adhere strictly to this rule, for otherwise the steersman, captain, cook-boy, and one or two sailors, are perpetually passing by to helm or bow on one excuse or another, which is extremely unpleasant, and by no means safe as regards cleanliness. We had constant squabbles about it with our dragoman; but the crew know very well that they have no right to walk along the upper deck, and, if the rule is held to, they submit at once. Mr. H——'s boat set sail with the first breeze; our dragoman arrived, and, 'ready or not ready,' we sailed away after him.

CHAPTER III.

OUR BOAT-HOME.

Tuesday, November 27th. The dahabĕĕh 'Cairo' is 97 feet in length, from bow to stern, and 14 feet 2 inches in width. There is a saloon measuring 12 feet 7 inches; divans on either side, with large drawers under them, provided with locks and keys. Two looking-glasses, four book-shelves, now well filled with volumes, and a table in the middle at which six persons might dine, 'under difficulties.' There are four cabins, two measuring 5 feet 8 inches by 4 feet 7 inches, the two others 6 feet 5 inches by 4 feet 7 inches. They have sliding doors, but when these were closed the dimensions proved rather too small. The choice lay between being closely cooped up with scarcely room enough to turn round, or leaving the door open, so as to admit a portion of the passage as dressing-room. The stern cabin measures 12 feet in length. Its available space for dressing is about 8 feet 6 inches, and here Selina reclines in luxury, though frequently disturbed by the creaking of the rudder. In the further part the boxes are stowed away; and there are drawers or cupboards for stores and clothes under every bed, and a bath which can never be used. Plenty of windows all round, provided with curtains, shutters, and Venetians, and a sky-light to the saloon. Over all this is the 'quarter-deck,' where there are divans on either side, a table, a chair or two, and an awning which is spread in calm weather. The crew live on the lower deck, and sleep upon it or in the hold. At the further end is the large filter for the water, and the cook-boy's primitive kitchen apparatus for the crew. Beyond, in the bow, is 'the kitchen' for the 'party.' The large mast and lateen yard is fixed towards the bow of the boat, the smaller one in the stern. Twelve oars are provided for rowing, and a number of long poles for pushing off from the sand-banks. The dahabëëh, the oars, and the small row-boat, are gaily painted in green, red, and white; and with the flags flying aloft, and the Arab costumes on board, the 'Cairo' makes altogether a very pretty 'turn-out.' She numbers twenty-five souls on board: passengers five, dragoman and waiter, Reïs, steersman, fourteen men as crew, cook and cook-boy.

We had now spent ten days in the gallant ship, on the waters of the Nile; and how shall I tell of the beauty and interest of each new bend of this ever-winding river; the charming novelty of the new style of life; the deliciousness of the breezes; the clearness of the atmosphere; the lovely sunrise at about half-past six, and the gorgeous hues of sunset at half-past five P.M.; crimson and gold, blue, pink and green, intermingled as we had never seen them before, and increasing in beauty, as each day brought us further south; and of the moonlight nights, which we watched till near nine o'clock, and would have watched till morning dawned, had we not been perfect models of prudence and regularity of hours. The thermometer had mounted to 106° in the sun on the deck of the dahabëëh, with a strong breeze blowing, and to 80° in the shade; whilst in the early morning, and in the evening, it had fallen as low as 60°. Under this latter figure we actually began to feel cold, while at mid-day we were burnt nearly to a cinder, though I alone of our party had then been glad to retire to the saloon from the burning rays, to obtain a little time to cool, before the next baking. The dark faces around appeared to us many shades lighter; the white ones had begun to *peel*. So accustomed was the eye becoming to bare-footed servants, that Thomas' shining patent leather shoes and white stockings began to look quite out of character: and as for our faithful Sarah, she entered so heartily into the whole concern, that we had serious fears lest she intended wearing an Arab complexion, speaking the language of the country fluently, and finally becoming, perhaps, 'Mrs. Mohamed el Adlëëh! It would not have sounded badly; but Sarah was far too wise for that.

The journey up the Nile is usually made as quickly as possible in order not to lose the fair winds which blow now; the places of interest to visit, and the researches into the antiquities of the country, are reserved for the downward course, when the dahabëéh is carried along by the force of the current, assisted by the oars of the crew. Already, then, we had passed many points of interest, and left them in the hope of visiting them on our return.

On starting on the 17th, we obtained the best view of the beautiful palace of 'Kasr e' Neel,' as the boat glided along. It is an immense building, and seemed full of life and music, such as we suppose the Pasha loves; but it was very like a *noise*. The stream in front was gay with small steamers, with white funnels and red flags, all anchored in the precincts of the palace, and belonging to the Pasha. The island of Roda is very pretty, and its gardens green and refreshing to the eye. The Nilometer, a stone pillar on which the height of the inundation is measured, is partly visible from the boat. And the citadel stands out in a very picturesque back-ground, with the Mokattam Mountains, or that branch of them called 'Gebel e' Jooshee' stretching far on the eastern shore. On the western, are the Pyramids of Geezeh, and the village of Geezeh itself, on the water's edge. Then follow in succession the Pyramids of Abousir, Sakkara, and Dashóor; all which gigantic wonders soon found their places in our two small sketch-books. 'Old Cairo' meanwhile, on the eastern shore, looked older than ever; and then followed a long line of those curious-looking windmills, standing in all the glory of unadorned ugliness, without a tree or a stone to relieve their outline in any way: but the beautiful corn of Egypt is ground in them, and they are objects of interest, if not of beauty. A large fort built by Ismaël Pasha now crowns the height, and now a solitary man is fishing at the water's edge. Here a group of camels kneel down for their night's rest, and there a few stray sheep are still seeking to slake their thirst in the stream. Some rafts float by, formed of two boats bound together side by side, laden with some hundreds of the common porous earthenware jugs of this country, laden outside, as well as piled up very high from within. Sails of 'cangia' and other smaller craft are continually passing along; and these, with the date-trees and various other objects on the shore, form a succession of the prettiest little pictures imaginable. The flies are intolerable, and fly-flapping a labour, but it is all very beautiful and very enjoyable. Now we have reached Toorah, whence the stone is taken with which the floors of all the houses in Cairo are paved. Evening closes in, the boatmen bring out their musical noise, and set to it with the greatest energy and evident enjoyment, until boat, passengers, and crew, rest for the night near a small village named Masarah. From thence we started again on the morning of Sunday, November 18th. The same line of hills on the eastern shore extends as far as Sioot. We passed four small villages, the houses and mosques entirely built of mud or unburnt brick, and shaded by date-trees, while the Pyramids before named still formed the distant view.

A little incident presently startled our quiet party. A small cargo boat, notwithstanding all the shouting of our Reïs, dragoman, and crew, incautiously sailed too near the dahabëëh, and sent the top of its long yard, straight through our sail, making a large hole in it. The dragoman stands forth in all his majesty, and with extended arms seems to be pronouncing judgment upon the delinquents. Like lightning four of our crew jump into the water, clothes and all (they are not burdened with many), and standing on the deck of the offending vessel, they knock about one unfortunate man, and carry off two of the long boat-poles as trophies, and in revenge. A long harangue and very stern looks follow this display of authority; but on the earnest petition of the criminals, and the consideration that they are "poor people," the poles are restored to them. The four swimmers quietly take off their garments, and hang them up to dry. Others mount the lateen yard in most monkey-like manner, perch themselves all along it, and cobble up the damaged sail in an equally primitive style. We pursued our course and our music, for when we sailed with a fair wind, the 'band' immediately set to work; and we passed Helwân, where the Nilometer was originally made about A.D. 700, it was removed to Roda sixteen years later. The 'False Pyramid,' apparently a large black rock, next appeared in view near Rigga; it is sometimes called the Sphinx, but retains no signs of a face, or features of any kind.

There was a glorious sunset and brilliant moonlight; boats passed along perpetually with their crossed sails, looking like birds with huge wings wide-spread skimming the water; some storks or cranes, and the 'crocodile bird,' gave us food for conversation, and we moored again a little below Rigga, with a watch of three men seated on the shore, with their watch-fires to guard us.

Monday, Nov. 19*th.*—We passed Rigga, Atféeh and Zowyeh; and here was the true desert spread before us. Hillocks of yellow sand, of various shapes and sizes, stretch far away to the horizon, and owing to the clearness of the atmosphere, that horizon is at a very considerable distance: not a particle of verdure is to be seen around, save the narrow strip of 'dhourra' (Indian corn) or sugar-cane along the river's edge, and this is beginning to diminish sensibly in width. There is something very solemn and grand, in the sight of this wide expanse of desert, and the thought of its only inhabitants, the Bedouin Arab and the Camel; and we longed very much to get out of our boat and try a walk upon it, to prevent which, our dragoman assured us that we should "sink to our knees" in it. After-experience taught us that he was only about half-way from the truth in this statement, but we sailed

CREW AT BREAKFAST ON THE BANK

on to a short distance from Benisoéf; and Thomas afforded a little amusement to us all, by the comical figure he presented, when mounted on the back of one of the crew, and carried on shore for a shooting excursion. They looked like some elongated, double-backed animal, to which, with the Arab and European costume on either half, it was difficult, to say the least of it, to assign any era. Poor man! he found himself stopping half-way in the water, his bearer quite up to the joke, that they might be added to the sketch-book *antiquities*. He grew frantic, as soon as he found out why his horse would not go, and spurred so vigorously with his patent-leather shoes that he was very soon deposited on the shore, where he strode about with his black 'suite,' as we sailed on, but alas, shot nothing.

Lovely pink and blue shades blend together in the sunset, the moon grows brighter as she increases, and here we moor again for the night.

Tuesday, Nov. 20th.—The crew squat on the shore before starting again, in the comical fashion of their forefathers: their heels drawn close up in front of them, so that their knees come to about the level of the chin. The large wooden bowl is in the centre of the circle; the left arm is frequently thrown affectionately round its next neighbour, for balance no doubt; and all the right hands dip into the mess of brown bread and lentil soup at the same moment. 'Fingers were made before forks,' and the Egyptians keep up this old custom as well as all the others of their ancestors, but it is most neatly and orderly done. Hands washed carefully beforehand, and fair-play the order of the day. A wooden bucket is set outside the circle, and passed round for drinking, or used at the end of the meal for washing, as the case may be. Not a breath of wind was stirring, and Selina and I took a walk along the shore, while the indefatigable crew 'tracked' (towed) the dahabëëh along. Very pretty it was to see the boat gliding slowly on the still water, and the procession of 'trackers' winding round each point and mound ; while ever and anon they raised their wild sounding song, as they called upon Allah to assist their efforts. A village of pigeon-houses next appeared, and there are many such all along the shore. A whole village is formed for the purpose of attracting these birds, which fly about everywhere in numerous flocks. The houses are built of mud, and are surmounted by little rounded cones, in many of which are placed pieces of the earthen jug of the country, and in these, the pigeons deposit their eggs and hatch their young. In some cases, where they are poor people, the owners live in the houses underneath the pigeons' mansions ; in others, as at Girgeh, a large 'café,' or room for sitting in, for smoking, and coffee-drinking, forms the groundwork of the pigeon's abode above. The young birds become the property of the owner ; these settlements thus constitute a large item in the wealth of the proprietor, and are sometimes the dowry of a bridegroom to his bride, as was one which we now passed, so Mohamed said, newly white-washed in honour of the wedding.

But what comes now from the shore, swimming quickly to the dahabëéh, with matted, woolly hair, its two arms flung alternately high in the air as it advances? It is a 'derweesh.' Our dragoman and crew watch him with respectful, superstitious looks, their purses come forth, and money and bread are bestowed upon the half-maniac-looking creature. His only clothing is wound round his head as a turban, and his newly-acquired riches are deposited in its folds. He swims back to the shore, unwinds the turban, and replaces it round his naked body; and there we leave him to his solitude and to his tomb, in which he will live and die. Our dragoman believes him to be supernaturally upheld, and says "*he never eats anything: perhaps so—a little bit of bread* (about two inches square) *in five years:*" he calls all such "clergyment!" We cannot quite make out what they really are, and there are various opinions respecting them; but they appear like wild men, half maniac, half idiot, living alone in the desert, or among tombs, and literally *in* their own tombs, which they build for themselves, and where they will probably be visited after death by the superstitious veneration of their countrymen, for of this latter feeling, strange though it may appear, there can be no doubt.

The cry of the jackal was the next novelty which

greeted our ears as evening closed in: it is just like that of a child in distress, for which, with all due respect to the nobler species be it said, it is not unfrequently mistaken. We were *told* that they were very fierce, and would attack and eat up a man with the greatest pleasure if they had the opportunity.

We passed on, and stopped this night near the village of 'Bibbeh.' Three watchers were stationed at the boat, and we walked on shore in the moonlight. These Nile walks were not very extensive, for in general there were not more than fifty yards of even ground before we were effectually stopped by the 'dhourra,' or by the clods of earth. Exercise is, however, necessary for health, and so we took it gratefully, backwards and forwards, on the shore or on the deck as it came to us.

It is something for Europeans, even in these locomotive days, to walk among sugar-canes; and the first plantation of them appeared to-day, Wednesday, November 21st, and they were tasted by such of the party as had not met with them before. They have a sickly, sweet taste; but the Arabs munch away at them with pleasure whenever they can get any. The town of Benisoéf, with its sugar-manufactory, looked pretty in the early morning light, the river here having the appearance of a large lake, or of the opening of a harbour, and the colouring of the whole in the early morning was exquisite. The land on the eastern shore here became higher and rocky.

The narrow strip of cultivation, on the deposit left by the inundation, was dug or cut up into little mounds, prepared for the coming crop of water-melons and cucumbers. Ploughing for fresh 'dhourra' was going on everywhere, with oxen or buffaloes. And now a fishing-boat came alongside, and a large purchase of fish was made for very little money. The 'pilot-fish' was reserved for our table, and 'Cousin Phil,' who is rather a connoisseur, found it tolerably good. The crew had a feast upon theirs, which was of a coarser kind, at their next meal, in addition to the usual bowl of bread and soup. The cooked fish was served in a similar bowl; the crew washed again in the river before partaking of it, and a broad grin of delight sat upon their faces till all was demolished.

Music and noises of all kinds now greet the ear. It is the village of Koloseneh, with its dancing-girls, barking dogs, and screaming babies, all which regaled us through the night, accompanied by the creaking of the rudder, which annoyed poor Selina sadly in her spacious cabin.

Thursday, Nov. 22d.—Here was an opportunity of a walk before breakfast, and a sketch of the 'shadoof,' the pole and bucket commonly used for drawing water from the Nile, for the purposes of irrigation. Numbers of them are seen all along the banks of the river, and, where the bank is high above the water, we have seen as many as five of them, at regular distances behind one another, till they reach the fields on the top. The man who works the lowest draws from the river, and empties his bucket into a channel cut for the purpose; the second draws from this channel, and throws the water into another higher up; and so on the third, fourth, or fifth, until the uppermost bucket is emptied into the tiny channels which surround and intersect all the fields. The people work perpetually at the shadoof, day and night, without any ceasing, as at a treadmill. They relieve each other after a certain number of hours. Mohamed was all this time making purchases of provisions in the village. On his return a fresh breeze sprang up, and off we sailed again, passing barren cliff and still narrowing strip of 'dhourra' and sugar-cane, the way perpetually enlivened by the countless sails which met or overtook the 'dahabëéh.'

On the summit of the hill, 'Gebel e Tayr,' is a Coptic convent, dedicated to the Blessed Virgin, and called 'Dayr el Adra,' the Convent of our Lady. No sooner does the dahabëéh appear in sight than five naked creatures swim towards it, shouting, as they advance, "Ana Christián, ya Hawágee" (I am a Christian, O master!), begging for charity. They were received on the deck, and covered, by the modesty of our crew, with some of their own garments. For the honour of Christianity, we gave them a little 'baksheesh,' though it is very doubtful what kind of religion is professed or practised by these poor creatures. We asked them a few questions with regard to their creed. They said that "Jesus Christ is the Son of God," that "Miriam" was His mother, and that they prayed "three times a-day." They, therefore, knew something; and, strange as it was to feel that such wild, savage-looking beings should be the professors of the true faith in Christ in a land of Moslems, we thought we could discern in their eyes and whole countenance a greater appearance of intelligence than in those of our crew, who call upon Allah, in their fashion, sometimes much more than three times a-day, and regard the Christian in the light of an 'infidel.'

The Copts asked for an 'empty bottle' to put oil in; but on receiving one from Thomas with a remnant of wine in it, they put it to their mouths, and immediately begged for one that was 'full,' to take to their clergyman. The money given them was put into their *mouths*, and one carried the empty bottle in his hand, as they all swam back to the shore.

At half-past three P.M. we reached the city of Minieh, and there the dahabëéh was moored, to remain for twenty-four hours, for the "grand wash," which did not, however, begin till the next morning. Here was the first place sufficiently level for 'Cousin Phil' to walk upon since we had left Cairo. We all turned out with the dragoman, and succeeded in reaching the bazaar of Minieh, where Selina and I left 'Cousin Phil' seated, under the protection of Thomas, and walked with Mohamed further on into the 'Cooking Market,' which is one of the characteristics of all these *villages*, as we then ignorantly termed them, and were forthwith sharply reproved by Mohamed, who informed us that Minieh was no village but a "large city." All things in this world go by comparison, and on our return from Wadee Halfeh, we were inclined to agree with Mohamed. To return to the Cooking Market: very important the cooks look, in their little raised kitchens, and many a steaming hot mess is eagerly bought and carried off from the counters; and it is no more than just to remark, that in the midst of all the dirtiness around them the cooks do contrive to produce very good-looking dishes, and to keep their cook-shops and cooking utensils at least apparently clean. As to this department on our dahabëëh, the cleanliness of the saucepans, the pastry-board, and rolling-pin, would have shamed many a so-called first-rate English cook. Yet our cook was a sun-burnt Arab; he worked on the lower deck in the bow of the boat, and was obliged to do everything in the open air. When a gale of wind was blowing it was difficult to keep the fire in; and only when there was a dead calm, was he allowed to put up the awning over his kitchen.

The bazaar of Minieh is narrow and dirty, but as full of life and business, and clean articles *within the shops*, as all the others we have seen. There was plenty of the dried-locust fruit, which is much eaten here without any cooking. It is a large, long pod, like the acacia-pod, of a dark chocolate colour when dried, and tastes rather like dried figs. It seemed to us far more reasonable to suppose that this fruit formed part of the food of John the Baptist than any kind of grasshopper, however delicious these may have been. Then the pretty red lentils, which abound everywhere in this country, and look like a very small split-pea, explained to us the "red pottage" for which Esau sold his birthright so many hundred years ago; the same mess of "bread and pottage of lentils" which our crew devour twice in every day. We noticed also brown loaf-sugar in the same shaped loaves as our white ones. There is a sugar-manufactory here. It was, unfortunately, not at work, but we were shown some samples of its produce. The brown loaf looked very coarse; the white very good, but it seemed of a coarser grain and softer than the West Indian sugar which we are accustomed to at home. It is almost universally purified with bones. The Moslems have a strong prejudice against the use of blood; and in a manufactory established at Raramoon by an Englishman, the sugar is refined by means of eggs. The finest sample produced was most beautiful; as clear as crystal and made into a twisted stick, like barley-sugar, as a sweetmeat for the ladies of the 'hareems;' "not to eat," as our dragoman very impressively informed us, "but to suck." His sense of propriety being much shocked, we fear, by the unceremonious manner in which a portion of the offered delicacy was now crunched between European teeth. It may be had here for twelve piastres a-pound, whilst in Alexandria and Cairo it fetches twenty and twenty-four.

Let our friends look in upon us in our saloon of an evening, and they will see that, in the midst of our romance, we are of the commonplace Western world still. Yet the ancient Egyptians played at draughts in ancient Egypt itself, and why should not romantic 'Cousin Phil' play at backgammon on the Nile? He sees no reason against it, neither do we. Backgammon, then, concludes each day's entertainment, and the backgammon board comes in as a standing dish every evening after tea. It is rather hard upon me, for 'Cousin Phil,' being up to all the tactics of war, almost always wins the game; yet he is for ever under the impression that some evil genius hovers around him, tumbling a perpetual  out of his dice-box. I never could persuade him that he was throwing 'doublets,' but he always counted my doublets at least four times over;—and so we played on to the end of the winter—.

Friday, Nov. 23rd.—Washing day! The tall boat-poles were stuck in the dry mud-soil, close to the dahabëéh, a sheet spread round them for shelter like a screen, while, at a distance, a line was fastened along other poles where the linen was to be hung out to dry; and the Arabs squatted on the ground and set to with very tolerable good-will.

We were curious to see how Arab men would wash, and are bound to confess that they can do it as well as European women. There was first a large bowl of cold water, in which all the linen was rinsed by one man; then another bowl of very clean, hot water, in which it was well soaped and washed by a second; the fire, on which the kettle was set to boil the water in, was made in a hole in the ground close by, and it was the business of a third person to feed it. The clothes were well washed, and then hung up on the lines to dry. The drying was quick work when the thermometer rose to 94°, and then the whole was brought in to Sarah, who had two good days' work to iron it all. A 'blacky' waited upon her with the irons, but she had frequently a great deal of trouble in getting them heated, and after three o'clock could not have them at all on account of the dinner.

Washing and provision-hunting occupied the whole day, and as evening came on the wind rose so high that it was not possible to proceed. How strangely it sounded, after the calm and quiet of the preceding days, to hear the gusts and squalls, and to feel the boat rolling about in a way which would almost have done honour to the sea. In the morning Selina and I had sallied forth with Mohamed, our sketch-books, umbrellas, camp-chairs, and two of the crew, who were always in attendance with their big sticks, to chase away the admiring crowd. We walked once more through the bazaar; then the

Dragoman went to seek for turkeys, &c., the more humble attendants remaining, and assisting in looking for a subject worthy of a sketch. Their taste was curious, and we were difficult to please, for the heat was very great—about 85°. At length we fixed upon a trio of cobblers, mending up all the old shoes, just within one of the gates of the city. This gate was only a plain wooden door across the street, and the market was on the other side of it. Very proud the cobblers were of the choice of the ladies, and many a more important personage thrust himself in the way, evidently thinking that he was far more worthy of a place in the sketch-book than the cobblers. But the crowds passing through the gate began to press round thicker and thicker, in spite of the great sticks of the crew; and the contact with Minieh's inhabitants was becoming so close that we were just going to give up in despair, when an 'officer' stepped forward and ordered the gate to be closed. The order was instantly obeyed, and the unfortunate populace continued pushing in vain from without. This we thought rather an alarming crisis; and considering all the difficulties under which the sketch was labouring, we made ready to decamp, but the expostulations of the spectators were so urgent that, we sat on, wondering at our own boldness, and wishing that 'Cousin Phil' and our friends at home could have a peep at us and the cobblers. On a sudden a dark figure started up, wielding a huge stick, and speaking in threatening accents. The crowd dispersed on all sides, and a clear space was made and kept for the adventurous artists. It was Mohamed el Adlëéh himself, whose blood was boiling at seeing how near the people had pressed upon his charge; and in answer to our inquiries about the propriety of the gate having been closed for us, he insisted on our remaining, saying, "Of course; take your time: that's our business; we must do it. I think I broke the arm of one man just now!" It was he himself, who, from another quarter of the town, had found out where we were, and ordered the closing of the gate. We had had enough of it, however, and now rose to depart, the gate opened, and the crowd rushed through and followed us. What a nuisance they must have thought us! But they seem to expect to be pushed about whenever a European, more especially an English subject, appears, and in most instances their own countrymen are the ministers of this petty tyranny; an office which, it must be added, they assume with the greatest relish.

The cemetery of Minieh is on the opposite side of the river, whither the dead bodies are ferried over. This was the practice of the ancient Egyptians, and gave rise to the fable of Charon and the Styx.

We left Minieh on Saturday, Nov. 24th, at 7 A.M., and passed by the grottoes and catacombs of 'Beni Hassan.' Very curious and picturesque they appear in the bare steep cliff, and full of interest when we are told that in them many of the ancient Christians have sought shelter from persecution; and in one of them it is supposed that St. Anthony lived, and preached from thence to the multitudes who came to hear him once every year. A small tomb stands alone on the cliff — very small and unimportant-looking; but it is the tomb of 'Sheikh Seyd,' and yearly visits are paid to it by the natives, and illuminations made in it. . . .

The Reïs was not well to-day, and up comes Mohamed with a request for some globules. We could scarcely restrain a smile at the thought of administering three globules of 'nux vomica' to such a sturdy-looking black. His symptoms, however, having been gravely and admirably detailed, we assumed very solemn faces, forbade coffee and smoke for the time being, and administered the globules. It was very like physicking a buffalo. But most submissively the orders were received, and the cup and pipe laid aside. The symptoms abated, and the Reïs grew better; but, alas! the starvation could last no longer, and a request came, "The Reïs—he want to eat!" With much amusement the permission for something 'very plain' was reluctantly given. Soon after, the Reïs was worse; he wanted some more physic, and the angry Dragoman exclaims, "The Reïs is a fool! I make him some soup, and he been eat butter and roasted bread!"

Next day the poor man begged a dose of castor

oil, and it was truly ludicrous to see him fed with it by the Dragoman with tender coaxing and lumps of sugar. He appeared resigned to his fate, and thought, as all these people do when they have the slightest ailment, that "he was going to die most surely." He did look ill for some days—we cannot say pale, but something that showed he would have looked pale if he could.

. . . Now we are stuck on a mud-bank. The crew start to their feet, seize the boat-poles, and sticking them into the mud, push away with all their strength, bending themselves double as they walk along the side of the boat one after the other, and then withdrawing them, return quickly to repeat the operation. The curious shape into which they throw themselves gives them more the appearance of quadrupeds than bipeds, and they call loudly upon 'Allah' the whole time. It is of no avail, and three of them proceed to take off their clothes (no very long process), jump into the water, and put their shoulders to the boat; and while their fellows continue pushing as before from the deck, they lift the huge weight until we float again. It had a strange appearance to see the row of naked copper-coloured busts at the bow, like so many figure-heads, immoveable, though working with all their might. This is a frequent occurrence in a trip on the Nile: the river changes its bed so perpetually, and fresh banks of the deposit are so frequently thrown up, that the navigation is more or less a case of 'feeling one's way along.' In some places the river is quite deep; at others, Mohamed says, no more than one foot and a half, but just sufficient to float the dahabééh. The width of the stream is equally variable, and at times we sail not on the river at all, but in a canal formed by the sand-banks, through which we meet the true river again.

We passed the first specimens of the dôm palm to-day, which henceforth increased in number as we ascended the stream. They are very handsome: the trunk, annulated and smooth, branching out in two stems, and the leaf the shape of a large, indented, almost circular fan; the fruit hangs in heavy clusters from the branches, and resembles a potato in form, but of a dark olive-brown shining colour when unripe, as it was now; the flesh of the fruit is about three-quarters of an inch deep, and within is a large stone remarkable for its extreme hardness, which is valued by carpenters for the sockets of their drills; the flavour of the fruit, we were told, is something like gingerbread; it forms a considerable portion of the food of the natives in these parts, and they keep large quantities for sale: it is sometimes called the 'Bread-tree.'

The beautiful cliffs of Aboolfeydeh detained us for the night, and caused very anxious looks on the careful Dragoman's face. We thought him very cowardly at first, and set him down as an instance of Oriental weakness and effeminacy; but we soon changed our minds, as the vessel began to roll and pitch in good earnest, so that it was almost necessary to hold the glasses on the table at dinner-time. Mohamed said it was quite necessary, and accordingly stationed Thomas at one end of the table to look after the decanters, whilst we were each one enjoined to provide for the safety of our respective glasses. The wind blew famously, and it was soon easy to perceive the cause of the disturbance: the gusts come down through openings in the hills, catching the high lateen yard and sail, which tower to about the same level; and it sometimes happens that vessels attempting to sail here in a high wind are overturned. It was very curious to see the sailors run up the mast, and perch themselves all along the yard to furl the sail. In the moonlight the appearance of height was increased; and with the reflections on the sail, the dark figures dotted like so many monkeys all along the yard, and the picturesque cliffs on one side, the crops of 'dhourra' and the watchmen and watch-fires on the other, it was a scene well worth recording. Indeed every traveller here should be an artist capable of carrying all away home with him in his portfolio.

Sunday, Nov. 25th.—Flocks of wild geese, so numerous as to look like clouds, passed by, flying high up in the air; they rise in a body, and then divide into long strings of single birds, forming waving lines in all directions, or frequently stretching along without the slightest bend, for a considerable length. They are extremely numerous here, and are much sought after by sportsmen; but, though fine-looking birds, they are not good eating. One gentleman, we were told, shot 1400 of them during a short trip on the Nile; Mohamed's version of this story being that the said gentleman had made a vow, on leaving Cairo, that he would shoot 20,000 before his return; that he had already accomplished 18,000, and was retracing his steps in order to complete the remaining 2,000. Mohamed fully believed that he was correct in these numbers, and could not at all comprehend why we should be sceptical on this point: moreover, he evidently set this scepticism down as one of the proofs of our Christian unbelief. Our sportsman on board had tried to bring down some of these birds several times, but they were always at too great a distance; and as he generally aimed straight at a *native*, it was perhaps not very remarkable that the birds did not fall. Happily the natives also found means of escape. There were also flocks of a bird resembling the ibis, and some others whose names we could not make out.

Far away from the congregations assembled at home on this holy day, we could yet join with them in prayer and praise, and our little party assembled in the saloon at 11 A.M. and enjoyed the Church's service together. In the evening we took a walk on shore, at the village of 'Ekrab,' and thought of those who were then walking to church at home for the Evening Prayer. We almost envied them their privilege, and yet surely it was a privilege also to walk along the banks of this wonderful 'river of Egypt,' to think over all its past history and the prophecies connected with it, and to watch the gorgeous sunset hues, blending with the soft shady tints of night, coming on so rapidly, to be followed again by the splendid moon and stars, which here, at the time of the full moon, literally turn night into day. The bright luminaries had shone as brightly, the blue river flowed as freely in those early days, before the eyes of kings, prophets, and patriarchs, the servants or enemies of the King of kings, whose past lives we now realised as we never did before. The pleasures of home will doubtless have a double value when we return to them again, but meanwhile let those granted to us at the present time be acknowledged and turned to account.

The 'Cairo' reached Sioot, the capital of Upper Egypt, at 8 P.M., but continued sailing all night, and stopped on Monday, November 26th, at a small village to purchase milk for breakfast. There was none to be had, the cows and buffaloes were gone over to the opposite side for pasture, to remain there for two or three months; after which time, the whole of the pasture being exhausted, they must live on dry food for the remainder of the year. We therefore sailed after them for our breakfast provision. Milk is procured in this manner fresh every morning, from buffalo, cow, or goat, as the case may be; and we had had the good fortune to find it hitherto very good, as indeed was all our food, with the exception that the meat was slightly tough, whilst the knives wherewith to cut it were more than slightly blunt! Tough and very small mutton was our usual meat, but beef came occasionally. The buffalo beef we found by far the best, indeed that was pronounced good; but so many chickens, pigeons, and turkeys, were slaughtered every day for our table, that the quality of the meat was not of much consequence to the ladies—'Cousin Phil' had it all to himself. The bread was baked fresh every second day; the cook took the greatest trouble about it, and it was at last very light and good; but poor Selina could not eat it, neither could 'Cousin Phil' endure the pistacio nuts, which Mohamed would thrust into the 'Mish mish,' the puddings, and even into the 'haricot.' We, however, finally expelled them, toasted the bread, put up with the meat, and so, on the whole, managed uncommonly well.

In illustration of the changes in the bed of the Nile each year, the village which supplied us with milk this morning, and which was originally built at some distance, was now half washed away. The remains of many of its houses stood crumbling on the edge of the water, yet still inhabited by the owners till the last moment of safety, and several of their date-trees lay uprooted on the bank. Many towns now on the river's edge were formerly a mile away from it, while some others extended far across where the river now flows deeply. The natives are consequently obliged to be continually building themselves new abodes; a merciful dispensation of Providence we thought, considering the dirtiness within their confined walls.

Two king-fisher birds showed themselves here, and it was pretty to watch them plunging into the water to catch their prey: their plumage a very beautiful mixture of black, grey, and white. The tameness of all the birds was very charming, and our deck was frequently covered with numbers of little brown sparrows or water-wagtails, while turtle-doves perched all along the awning cords quite close to us, without showing the least fear. To-day the wild geese were more numerous than ever. There seemed to be millions of them in the clouds soaring above. And now seven stately pelicans swam by very slowly and majestically. These were the first we had seen, and we watched them with great interest, others appeared a little further on, and Mohamed was greatly disappointed that there was no shot on board sufficiently large to kill one of them. He says, "Oh, yes; I shoot very well indeed; and I would stuff it for you to take home." It is rather problematical whether he really could have done so, but he was a clever man in his way, and we were very sorry that we could not give him, at least, the chance of succeeding. Another bird, called by the natives the 'camel of the river,' we discovered on a nearer view to be a crane.

Tuesday, Nov. 27th.—Further we sail from the haunts of men; or, rather we 'track,' for there was no wind blowing, and the thermometer in the shade had reached 80°, and in the sun 106°. All was as still as could be, not even a sail in sight for some hours, and the only sounds that broke the stillness were the shout of the 'trackers' as they moved along; the creaking of the double 'Shadoofs,' worked by two naked, dark, copper-coloured beings on the shore; and the sharp cry of the 'crocodile bird,' a pretty white and black bird, about the size of a cuckoo. The crew were 'tracking' along on a bank in the middle of the river, which they had reached through the water, when somehow the 'tracking rope' broke, and there floats the 'Cairo,'—"best boat on the Nile,"—a strong current against her, and twelve of her boasted crew far away on a bank, isolated from us all! We could not forbear a laugh, but it required all the exertions of the few remaining hands on board to guide the boat against the stream to a place whence two of them could take the small boat to fetch the lost crew. Mohamed, we think, did not feel very comfortable, and looked a little as if he were thinking, "Suppose they should take it into their heads not to come back again?" They came, however, and resumed their 'tracking' as steadily as if nothing had happened.

All sank into the former delicious silence, and I continued reading aloud to Selina about Jerusalem and Bethlehem in 'The Crescent and the Cross.' It was too still to last, and now we were 'in for it!' Far from civilised man indeed, we looked up at some harsh sounds which met our ear. The 'trackers' were attacked by some wild-looking men. All the great sticks were thrown to them quickly from the dahabëëh: one man was wounded. The enemy produced muskets and prepared to load them. The Dragoman made a tremendous bound, and leapt on shore with his great stick: and here were we, with the steersman and two others, sole possessors of the 'Cairo,' and approaching with all speed to the scene of combat.

"Now then, good people," said the beating of everybody's heart, "why did you not listen to your friends at home, and remain quietly nearer to them? Here's an end to your romantic expedition; and the ladies, and the brave old gentleman, are going to be buried in the Nile, or carried away captives to the White River." Selina and I were very brave of course; "not in the least frightened," yet we could not think why the steersman did not turn the dahabëëh the other way and try to make her '*run*,' instead of guiding her straight to the scene of action. The crew fought well, and in a moment of time the brave Mohamed had struck one of the enemy a blow across the chest, which sent him tumbling over the bank, "half killed," Mohamed said. All the enemy's muskets came into possession of our crew, one of whom fired into the air to prove that they were loaded. Mohamed stalks about as fearless as if surrounded by friends alone, speechifies, and vows to bring all the enemy before the Governor at Girgeh, whence they would be "despatched to Cairo and put in prison." The cause of the commotion was simply this. The crew were quietly tracking along, when one of them, seeing a man below the bank, civilly warned him to take care of the rope, or it would hurt him. For answer the savage rushed at him, struck him with his gun, and threatened to fire. The rope was let fall in an instant, and the fight began, while the numbers of the enemy increased from their boat which was moored close by. Our side was still the most numerous, but it was a "glorious victory," and four muskets were carried off to the dahabëéh, in spite of all the entreaties which the vanquished enemy were now most humbly making to have them restored. They tried hard, and offered to give forty piastres to each of the crew as a bribe; but Mohamed returns with his crew to the boat, and we leave them behind. But, no, it was not quite over yet. The sailor who had been first struck still thirsted for vengeance. He was an enormously large, and very strong man: the coarsest specimen of human nature we had ever seen; highly valued by Mohamed, and called by him "the very strong man," but very difficult to appease when affronted. He had lagged behind the rest, and was listening with pleasure to the words of the enemy chief, whom, finally, when the small boat was sent for the truant, he suffered to swim along with it to the Dahabëéh. There he was at the stern. Our brave blood boiled and froze again, and prepared for a hand-to-hand combat on board. This, however, was apparently far from the thoughts of either party, and the Dragoman assured us, that these men would as soon think of trying to take the guns by force, as they would of flying. The chief only wanted to parley, to repeat the offer of his bribe, and to beg that the 'party' on board would be appeased by having the three chief offenders brought before them and "*flogged till nearly dead;*" and that then the muskets should be restored. A novel scene indeed for English ladies to witness, and we are sorry to state that it would evidently have given the greatest satisfaction to the "very strong man" to have seen the proposed sentence executed. Mohamed, however, knew better, and informed the chief, with pompous dignity, that he was not the magistrate, and that it was "the will of the party" that the guns should be "delivered up to the Governor of Girgeh." He was, finally, courteously sent back in our own boat and deposited on shore, whence he continued his entreaties, with uplifted arms and solemn promises, until the dahabëéh was out of sight. I do not know who or what these people took 'Cousin Phil' for; they were evidently afraid of him; and Mohamed, determined to make the most of everything, gave him different high-sounding titles on every different occasion, such as the 'Rajah,' the 'Great Howagee,' the 'Large English Gentleman,' from the 'English Parliament,' &c., so that by the end of our journey there was a pretty long string to his name. Mohamed el Adlëëh was now a hero in our eyes, and when peace was restored, we felt a certain satisfaction at having had 'our adventure' on the Nile, though very thankful that it had terminated so harmlessly to ourselves. Mohamed came up to assure "his party" that "all this is finished;" to inform 'Cousin Phil' that if these men, or any others, attack them again, here, or elsewhere on the river, the 'Paper' which he will procure from the Governor at Girgeh will cause that "these men will all be hung;" which caused 'Cousin Phil' to smile. Then Mohamed turned to us and said, in tender, entreating tones, "If you please not to think any more about this; just talk a little, then go on reading and working as before; because, you know, I see you Mrs. L—— *get very red*, and Mrs. C—— *very white* just now." We had then, alas! betrayed the inward emotion which we had thought to hide so well. As to the title of 'Mrs.,' our Dragoman, though he guessed our ages at fifteen and sixteen, always persisted in giving it to us—alternately with that of "yes, sir," which, to Sarah's horror, he would constantly address indiscriminately to lady or gentleman. She succeeded at last in making him say 'yes, ma'am,' but it always came out in such a ridiculous tone, that we often wished the 'sir' back again, lest a slight convulsion of the lips should meet the Arab's piercing eye and affront him. To assure us still more of our safety, he boldly asserted that he, with his stick, "could knock down any six men, even if they had guns;" and when we suggested that the guns might be useful if we kept them altogether, he looked astonished, and said, "The crew; he don't care for guns, only just sticks!" and, moreover, "Mohamed will kill himself" (be killed) "before any harm can come to any of the party!" "That's my business!" emphatically added our enthusiastic defender. And we did feel very safe in our brave guard, although when we stopped at the village of Menshëéh for the night, and saw that the chief and two others of the enemy had already made their way there by land, we found that we did not yet thoroughly understand the character of these people, and began to quake a little; a little more too, perhaps, when it was agreed in a council of war that the captured guns should for safety's sake be removed from the deck and brought into the saloon for the night, and when they were finally deposited within the stern cabin. I walked along the shore with Mohamed, in the midst of the foe, to show that we were not in the least discomfited by their appearance; and to do ourselves justice, even we ladies were not half so much afraid of them as they were of us; no! although they were dark, wild-looking savages, and only half clothed. They had come here on the chance of our staying for the night, to raise their bribe and to offer the offenders again to punishment. No mercy, however, was shown, and the enemy remained squatted quietly alongside with the watchmen from the village, four strong men, proof against any attack, whilst we bravely retired to rest and slept soundly, although I believe our shoes were placed close at hand in case of a sudden alarm. Mohamed and the crew watched of course.

The enemy consisted of a number of slave-traders from the 'White River,' who were returning from an expedition to Cairo, whither they had been carrying slaves for sale, contrary to the law. They had been stopped by some Governor on their way, and were now returning home. The three that followed us hither said that they were the owners of the guns which had been taken by the first offenders whilst they were asleep in their boat. The offenders meanwhile were far too much frightened by the name of the 'Governor of Girgeh' to appear. The owner of the boat, the chief or 'Sheikh' of the party, had "nothing to do with it," and apparently no responsibility was attached to him by any one on either side; but Mohamed suspected our Reïs of having let out that we were going to Menshëéh for the night, of having held out hopes that the bribe might be accepted, and so of being the true cause of "all this trouble." He was very wroth with him in consequence, and said he would bring him also before the Governor. Matters were not straight on board for a little time, but we could not understand one word that was said, and therefore quietly left them alone to fight it out their own fashion. Only sometimes, when the voices were unbearably loud, we sent word that 'we could not hear our own reading,' and they always ceased immediately. Finally the Dragoman's determination carried the day, and all parties were frightened, bribed, or wearied into peace. The wind would not rise, and on Wednesday, November 28th, we were 'tracking' still; but we finally succeeded in reaching Girgeh. The Governor was away; the wily enemy were beforehand with us again; they had been to the Governor's agent to try to bribe him to their side. 'Truth will out,' however, even on the Nile; Mohamed met the agent on his way to the market, told his story, and brought the agent to see the travellers.

A dumb show was now enacted. The agent could not speak English; 'Cousin Phil' could speak neither Arabic nor Italian, which all these dignitaries understand slightly, but he made him sit beside him, and handed him over to "the ladies" for conversation. Selina and I could both of us read and understand Italian pretty well, and used to hold small conversations together in that language by way of practice, but the peculiar undress, bare feet, and dirty appearance of the said agent no doubt chased it all away, and Selina's perverse lips chose to frame nothing but Portuguese, whilst mine uttered German. Why could not this man talk French, we could all, we thought, have spoken that "like natives!" But where was the use of moralising; we were deficient in the thing required, and so, after a sufficient time of edifying stammering, the agent and 'Abool Gowád,' a fine-looking, handsome friend of our Dragoman, having partaken of coffee, the latter having offered the ladies a Turkish bath, which they politely declined for fear of the consequences, the visit was concluded, the guns lay quietly in the stern cabin, and we walked into the city to see the bazaar.

Mohamed's 'friends' were innumerable; at Minieh he was embraced and hugged at every ten yards, and it was the same wherever we went. Four or six kisses on either cheek alternately, a pressing of hands and most soft sounding dialogue of mutual good wishes, was the 'routine' on all these occasions; and then they hung on each other's necks, reminding us forcibly of the pictures which represent the meetings of Jacob with his brother Esau, or his son Joseph; and which we now judge to be very faithfully drawn. This walk terminated with the performances of an Egyptian conjuror. Near the market-place a close circle was formed around him, the little children within sitting on the ground, the taller ones standing behind them, and behind these again a large concourse of grown-up people. The circle on our approach was broken, with the usual shouting and beating in spite of all our remonstrances, in order that the travellers might see the performance; which we witnessed for a time, because it took place in Egypt, but would certainly have turned away from, anywhere else; and we were soon satisfied. The conjuror had a little child to assist him, who first with a great stick beat him vigorously across the chest, as he knelt on the ground, till you would have supposed he must at least have been hurt, but he was not.

A wonderful box next appeared, playing similar tricks to those that are practised in Europe, with the addition of a snake coming out when a handkerchief only had been put in; and the child took up the snake in its hands and held it as a necklace round its neck. The conjuror then produced some huge irons in the form of a kind of open ring, which he inserted on either side of the child's mouth, clasping in the cheek as far as the ear. It was a horrid sight, and the child screamed and cried to such perfection, if it really were a sham, as we were assured it was, that we could stay no longer and walked away, followed by half of the circle of spectators, who evidently considered us at least as fine a sight as their conjuror.

A most glorious moon rose to-night. She was 'at the full,' and more beautiful than I can describe, as she rose large and golden on the still waters. At six A.M., Thursday, November 29th, she was still shining brilliantly, and at half-past six had disappeared before the gorgeous colours of the rising sun in the east, while these spreading gradually round, soon merged with the soft blue and pink of the west into the brighter day.

CHAPTER IV.

FROM GIRGEH TO ASSOUAN.

The 'Cairo' remained at Girgeh to get bread for the crew. This is no light work for the men. First they must buy the corn, then cleanse it by winnowing through a sieve in the open air, with a little stick or a branch of palm; then they must take it to one of the ancient mill-stones to be ground by the women; lastly, they must make the dough and bake it in the ovens in the town. The whole process takes twenty-four hours. The bread is wheaten bread, made of the whole meal with leaven. It is made into small, flat, round loaves, containing about the quantity of an English penny loaf, and is very well made. The next process is to dry it, for which purpose it is spread out on the deck, cut up into small pieces, and left exposed to the sun, until thoroughly dry and hard, so that it may keep for some time uninjured. The pieces are put into a large box on the deck, and the cook-boy fetches the required portion twice every day to be soaked in the boiling lentil soup for breakfast and dinner. One *ardeb* and a half were made here for our crew, three more will be made at Esneh, which it is calculated will be sufficient until we return again to Girgeh from the second Cataracts. (One ardeb is rather more than five bushels.)

Whilst the crew were engaged in their bread-making, Selina and I were seated on a low divan in an Egyptian house, to which Mohamed had escorted us. We had asked to see the house of Sheikh Abool Gowád. On the way thither we were introduced to a young Nubian slave, who had been adopted by her owner, as a companion for his daughter "to go to school with her," &c. The child was the very essence of ugliness, but her master appeared to be very fond of her, and pulled about her fat black cheeks in a fondling fashion of his own, which did not serve to increase her beauty. Her nose was as flat as nose can be; she was very shy, but was made to kiss the ladies' hands, and she looked frightened, at the suggestion that they might take her away to England with them. The Sheikh's house is built of mud and crude brick. We passed first through a large room used as a store for "all kinds of things," of which, however, there were none then visible: next into the 'cooking-room,' in the corner of which stood a little round mud oven. A hole for the fire was on one side of it on the ground; the opening above by which to admit "the goose" faced in another direction; and on the top were two small excavations for "the sauce." There was no other article of furniture, but one or two pans in a corner, and this room was anti-chamber to the sitting-room, where the divan was spread on the floor, in a portion railed off from the rest, with a slightly ornamented wooden railing. A new-looking, printed, and thickly quilted calico counterpane was spread over a mattress, or a bed of dried cane perhaps, upon the floor, and covered a small raised seat, which ran along the wall at the back of it. This formed the divan, on which we were requested to seat ourselves, Turkish fashion, while the host and the Dragoman sat opposite to us on the ground, the former smoking his cigarettes all the time. This smoking is by no means so unpleasant as the cigar or pipe smoking practised in Europe. The little cigarette of fine tobacco, rolled up at the time of using it, in a bit of paper about three inches long and two inches broad, sends forth a very faint cloud, and though we did not like even that, we hoped it would keep away the fleas, which we could not help expecting in swarms about us on our return: and so, with all our natural antipathy to smoke in any shape, we almost welcomed it here. There was no window beside the old wooden lattice; no furniture beyond the divan, the rail, three rude cupboards in the mud wall, two of which we were told contained "the Bibles," and a stand resembling a 'what-not,' on which our host said that he sat to read the Korán to the villagers, whom he assembled in his house twice a-week. He had been four times to Mecca; and his old mother, who now came to join the party and to sit on the divan beside us, had been there six times. They said it cost 80*l.* to make one journey thither. If that be true they must have expended all their wealth in these journeys; for certainly there was no appearance of even much less than 80*l.* here. Many of these people, however, have money, although to European ideas their appearance is that of poverty. When *Mecca* was the subject, some of our Dragoman's tales were marvellous, and he looked with the greatest veneration on those persons who had made many journeys thither. Selina wore dark gloves with gauntlets, and now her "black hands" compared to her "white face" caused a great deal of whispering and speculation among the hosts, and she was finally requested by Mohamed to pull off her gloves to show that hands and face were suitably alike. The gloves drawn off, her rings were displayed, and poor Selina was in for a special examination. The gloves they had never seen before, but they dearly love jewellery, therefore dress, rings, bracelets, gold beads on the net, and red feather in the hat, were severally inspected and admired. She bore it all with a marvellous good grace; but when the old mother escorted us upstairs, to see the woman-kind of the establishment, and came affectionately close to both her guests, we must confess to having involuntarily shrunk back for safety. She was dressed in blue cotton, and was as dirty and ugly as the rest of her race. The Dragoman was not allowed upstairs, lest he should see our host's married daughter who lived there. Little likely was she, we thought, to captivate anybody; but there is no accounting for taste in this world, and these people see charms in each other to which we are stupidly blind, so there might have been a chance of Mohamed's wishing to carry off the beauty. And what did we see upstairs—a poultry-yard; in the rooms and outside the rooms, chickens, turkeys, pigeons, and a goat; cooking utensils and bed-coverings, all indiscriminately huddled together in one enclosure, and the daughter and a grandchild as dirty-looking as any of the Egyptian community! We had, however, seen an Egyptian house, and thought we should not be in a hurry to go into another of the same class. Three-quarters of an hour we sat, before the indispensable coffee was brought in; and when the little cups did at last appear, they contained, not coffee, but a horrid decoction of brown sugar and hot water, covered over with pounded cinnamon. Ah! good ladies! beware how you visit an Egyptian Sheikh again with your Dragoman. We sipped on, for good manners' sake, till we were nearly ill, and then the 'factotum' Mohamed held out his hand to take the cups from us, and poured the contents of each in turn down his own throat, as part of "his business," we suppose. And so indeed it was, on this occasion, for coffee is the usual offering to guests in this country, and the cause of the substitution had been a previous statement of Mohamed's to our host, that "*we* do not like coffee."

The market at Girgeh is cheaper than in any other town on the Nile; large purchases are consequently made here. Eggs are sold fourteen for one piastre (five or seven piastres answer to one shilling); chickens, two piastres apiece; butter, when it is to be had at all, at five piastres per pound. In other places chickens fetch from three to five piastres apiece; and eight eggs only are given for one piastre. The chickens were not very much larger than European pigeons, and the pigeons not much beyond larks. The eggs of course proportionably small, but generally good.

Friday, Nov. 30th.—We reached Farshoot, formerly a station for troops. The scenery grows prettier as we advance, and the hills of Denderah and Gheneh appear in sight. At a short distance from Farshoot a strange scene takes place. 'Sheikh Selim' sits there, in a hole in the ground; a few dried canes around him for shelter, not an article of clothing upon him, a quantity of horrid matted hair on his head, and several "servants" attending him. There he has sat for forty years and upward, and every boat that passes by brings him offerings of one kind or another. Dragoman and crew all turned out, and Selina and I were turned out also to see the "*holy man.*" After a glance or two we gladly turned away, and keeping at a respectful distance tried to sketch the extraordinary scene. The crew crowded round him; and with a mixture of reverence, sympathy, and superstition, presented their several gifts: chicken, rice, bread, &c., and the Dragoman, foremost in all such things, brought a large canister of snuff. Sheikh Selim sat with his hands across his eyes, as though afraid of the honourable circle; and apparently regarded nothing, until the boiled chicken was poked close under his nose; then he slowly and cautiously stretched out his hands to take it, tore it, and ate it like a beast of the field. The wretched object must surely have been born an idiot, supported and cared for in this strange manner by the superstition of the Moslems. He was apparently entirely devoid of the power of speech, which raises man so distinctly above the brute creation. This scene, together with the Derweesh we had already seen, brought strongly to our minds the poor creatures mentioned in our Lord's time, who "possessed of the devil, lived among the tombs;" and on this particular occasion we could not but think of the king Nebuchadnezzar, when, as we are told, "his body was wet with the dews of heaven, till his hairs were grown like eagle's feathers, and his nails like bird's claws; his dwelling was with the beasts of the field, and he was made to eat grass like oxen." Such is the literal description of Sheikh Selim; and revolting as it was to see the human form in such a condition, there was something very striking and touching in seeing it thus cared for and venerated by its more favoured fellow-beings, if such a term may be correctly applied to anything so entirely devoid of the light of intelligence as was this miserable object. Had the worshippers enjoyed a little more of it themselves, and not been so blinded by their superstitious creed, they would surely have kept such objects at home, and cared for them there instead. Mohamed shook his head at such an idea, and said "the derweesh know everything without learning it, and cannot live at home!" The strange visit occupied about a quarter of an hour, and then the whole party returned to the dahabēēh, the Europeans marvelling, the Egyptians looking as placidly happy as a Christian might after some act of special piety or devotion.

But the breeze was blowing fresh, and 'Cousin Phil,' like a true sailor, was anxious to catch every breath of it; the sail was again unfurled, we bid adieu to 'Sheikh Selim,' and fresh novelties soon took the place which he had occupied in our minds.

First, came a raft of floating 'ballásee,' the large earthenware water-jar of Egypt. Perhaps a thousand of these jars compose the raft. The mouths are first stopped with clay, then, bottom upwards, they are tied together in long rows with the stem of the date-palm leaves. The several rows are connected together in the same manner, and then layers of them are placed and secured one over another in an oblong form. Thus they float on the water, forming their own boat; on the top of which sit two men, rowing it along with four rude branches of the acacia-tree, each man working with two oars at the same time. They were going down to Cairo and Alexandria for sale.

Again not a breath of wind. More fitful and uncertain than elsewhere this element seems to be on the Nile; and we rested again for the night at a small village called 'Woolad Amr.' Here was a plantation of the dôm and the date-palm together, and a very pleasing picture was formed by the intermingling of the two; the more spreading dôm, filling up between, and covering many of the tall naked trunks of the date. Rich clusters of half-ripe fruit hung from the branches of the former. The crew scrambled up and brought down several of them, for us to carry home as curiosities. The trees are private property; but the Arabs appear to think that 'possession is even more than nine points of the law,' and evidently did not anticipate the slightest remonstrance on the part of the original owners. We thought we should not have allowed our apples or pears to be taken away so quietly—but I was very glad to have my branch of dôm to bring home with me, and so I kept it. The castor-oil plant (palma Christi) grows here in great abundance, and here also, in general, crocodiles abound. We were told that there were two at that moment on the opposite bank. We strained our eyes in vain to see them, and suspected the force of imagination on the part of the Arabs. The shout of 'Tèmsáh, Tèmsáh,' (crocodile) was beginning to be a daily excitement; but though we saw plenty of them afterwards, those now in view proved, on a nearer approach, to be only a stone, a lump of mud, or a bit of a tree. Selina and I had been "dying to see a crocodile," and so had 'Cousin Phil' too, we are sure; so we tried to persuade him to remain here till the afternoon of the next day, that we might row to the bank which they frequent and examine them closely. But no; a fresh breeze had again sprung up, far more attractive in his eyes than a crocodile, and in his anxiety to be off, imagination carries him so far, that he looks up into our eager faces with amaze, quietly asserting and maintaining too that we had seen plenty of crocodiles already. In vain we tried to recall the place of their abode; 'Cousin Phil's' world was peopled with them just then, and so off we sailed on Saturday, December 1st, and left the common-place creatures behind us.

The river from hence to Denderah and Gheneh is extremely pretty, owing to the rosy tinge of light which seems always to rest upon the hills. We reached Gheneh at one P.M. Here the donkey-chair was first brought on the scene; after a long preparation, the little steeds were harnessed to it, and 'Cousin Phil' seated in it and raised aloft. All the rest of our party were mounted on gaily accoutred little donkeys, with plenty of rings round their necks, so that we should "have music wherever we go," and, accompanied by a numerous native escort of all ages and sizes, we trotted away through the bazaars to see the manufactory of the 'goolleh.'

The proper clay is found in this neighbourhood, and the manufacture is perpetually carried on. The workshop is of the most primitive kind, built entirely of mud, sufficiently high for a man to stand in, but no higher, and just large enough for two workmen and a small stock of jars. The workmen, a father and two sons, were very clever at their trade; and the process seemed to be much the same as the first proceedings in the more refined potteries in Europe, saving the refinement. They said that one man could make fifty 'goolleh' in a day. They are sold at a very low price, but in such numbers that the present owner of the establishment realises a large fortune by his jars. Back we trotted again, exceedingly amused with the excursion, and with this first appearance of our cavalcade. How we did broil! And the donkeys trotted on as though it were the coolest day imaginable. They appeared to enjoy the fun as much as their riders; and the chair only came down four times, and was pronounced admirable.

The crew meanwhile had taken the opportunity of our trip to engage the services of the barber of Gheneh. On our return, while waiting for our Dragoman, who had gone on his usual excursion for provisions, we had leisure to watch the process. Both barber and patient squatted on the ground in front of the dahabëéh. Soap was not spared; a most extensive lathering went on: and then the barber, razor in hand, threw himself into a succession of the most picturesque attitudes, as he rolled the black head about between his two hands like a ball. Every atom of hair was shaved off, and the bald pate, after another extensive lathering, was dried and polished up in style with a towel, the artist holding it ever and anon at a little distance and surveying his work with the satisfaction of a painter over his newly-finished drawing. But Mohamed returned, we sailed away again, and the remaining heads awaited their next opportunity. Again a magnificent moon arose, and a great deal of sheet-lightning was seen in the sky. The idea of lightning either could not, or would not, enter Mohamed's head. He first declared that it was a watch-fire; and, having slept over it, informed us, the following morning, that it was 'rain in the desert.'

Sunday, Dec. 2nd.—There was a dead calm, and as the mud bank appeared quite dry, and we were sufficiently near to disembark, Selina and I got out for an airing, leaving the dahabëéh to follow us, and rejoicing in the unusual length of our promenade, when, suddenly, we found ourselves in the midst of a swamp, which it was impossible for us to cross on our own feet. We could neither go backward nor forward, and there was no alternative but to allow the only one of the crew who had accompanied us to take us up successively in his arms and carry us across. The great Mohamed was carried in the same manner; and we marvelled at the strength of the young Arab, who set us down, one after the other, without showing the least sign of fatigue, not even staying a moment to take breath. The dahabëéh came slowly 'tracking' along: we could not get back to her, and she did not get up to us till noon. We had not bargained for this. It was one of the hottest days we had experienced, and Selina was now so thoroughly 'warmed up,' that, giving the reins to her imagination as she sat on the camp-chair, which happily had been brought out for her, she smelt *the smell of fire* on her black silk dress, and feared to see the flames rise around her! As for me, I walked up and down, trying to catch one breath of cooling air, and can truly say that, although we did not ignite, we never felt anything so nearly approaching to it as we did then.

Happy Mohamed! He sat the while by the river-side on a bundle of dried cane, took off his shoes and stockings, and put his two feet into the water. Seeing my discomfort, he said, in a patronising tone, "Come, and sit by me, Mrs. C——; there's plenty of room." We thought our dragoman had forgotten his manners; but never had we wished so much to do what would not quite have suited the dignity of English ladies.

The dahabëéh came up at last, and we returned gladly into the saloon, to join together in the morning service of the Church. Selina's voice was so weak, and the servants were so shy, that I was obliged to act in the capacity of clerk to the congregation, wielding the fly-flap incessantly at the same time over 'Cousin Phil's' devoted head, for around it the flies clustered with the greatest tenacity, making repeated efforts to stop his reading, by walking into his eyes, nose, and mouth. No chance for them, however. I was by this time in pretty good practice, so that the service went on with sufficient comfort—under the circumstances.

'Tracking' continued all day, and then the oars were brought into play, in order that we might reach the village of 'El Aradëëh' by nightfall, where two fine-looking watchmen were posted on the bank to overlook the precious freight. Their fires blazed brightly, throwing their lurid flames so as to light up the dark figures, white turbans and scarfs, so strikingly in the darkness, that, to the immense delight of both watchmen and crew, we could not resist an attempt at their portraits.

Monday, Dec. 3rd.—Still not a breath stirred the air, and the crew must have found it hard work to 'track' us along. On account of the shallowness of the water the dahabëëh at times could not get near enough for the rope to reach the shore; and then, off went the clothes of the trackers in an instant, and the procession 'tracked' through the water with as much good-humour and fun, as though it were "all play, and no work at all."

As we passed by his abode, "the Sheikh of Gamouleh and forty surrounding villages" came on board, to pay us a visit, and to request earnestly that the illustrious party would honour his 'palace' with their presence, and accept of dates and sugar at his hands. We promised to do so on our return, not without dread visions of the Sheikh's house at Girgeh: but Mohamed assured us this was a very different affair, quite "a great man's house," and "peautifully clean." So we sent him away with a promise, and a present of a small portion of quassia for poisoning the flies, which, little as it was, afforded him the greatest satisfaction. It was the only thing we could find wherewith to repay his Oriental civilities. It may not be necessary for travellers on the Nile to carry a present in their hand, but it certainly would be much more agreeable to do so, and we frequently regretted that we had nothing to give. It would have cost but little trouble or money to have taken out with us a few penknives, scissors, beads, or needles and thread, all which would have been looked upon as treasures by these grandees. Some lemon-trees and a small vine adorned the bank this morning—a very pleasing variety to the constant, though beautiful, date and dhourra. They were planted in a private garden, and were the only specimens we had yet seen along the river. When night came on, the stars were reflected so brilliantly in the waters as to give the effect of two firmaments, one above, the other below in the stream, and only second in brightness to the original. This occurs constantly on the Nile, and forms one of its greatest attractions. The thermometer to-day stood at 56° at sunrise, and rose to 80° in the shade at noon, and 107° in the sun.

Tuesday, Dec. 4th, brought but little more wind. Not till two P.M. did the 'Cairo' come in sight of the famous ruins of Thebes, and finally stopped at Luxor on the eastern bank of the river.

There we were, at last, in sight of the most wonderful ruins in the world—of buildings raised by man nearly 1500 years before the birth of Christ. Luxor, on its first distant appearance, looks like a fortification jutting out into the sea, with its flag-posts on the top, from which the English and French flags are flying. Soon, however, the ruins of its temples begin to appear: the Obelisk rises high against the blue heavens, and we feel transported into the world of ages gone by: yet the first thought from the 'quarter-deck' is for letters from home, and an immediate rush is made to the Consul's house to fetch them.

And how was the sight of the venerable ruins welcomed on the lower deck? The Arabs are silent, but Thomas and Sarah stand forth with all due excitement and interest. "There it is!" "Yes, that's it!" "Oh, that's Thebes!" "Ah, yes, Thebes: we do the washing here!" Thomas and Sarah were as practical as the rest of us. And what harm to either party? We did write letters home, and we did have another 'grand wash' in view of the famous ruins. But we neither forgot the ancients nor their gigantic works; rather, the thought of them ennobled our more common-place proceedings, and that same evening we visited the temple of Amunoph III., the Obelisk, and the colossal figures, which lie almost wholly embedded in the sand.

Wednesday, Dec. 5th.—The donkey-chair was brought out, and shouldered this time by four of the crew, who placed their large scarfs or warm cloaks as pillows under the huge poles; and 'Cousin Phil' came with us to see the ruins of Luxor. With Thomas, Sarah, and a guide who could not understand a word of English, I mounted to the top of the temple, up the narrow stone staircase within. Such steps—such strides—and sometimes, too, such stooping—and the ascent was begun by climbing on the roof of a modern inhabitant's house. At one stone in particular I thought I must have turned back. The summit seemed inaccessible; but the guide signified that it was quite easy, and I stepped up accordingly. The view from the top, and the recollections connected with it, so well repaid the exertion, that I repeated the expedition the two following mornings, to see the sun-rise, to enjoy the cool air, and to endeavour to note down in my sketch-book all the objects of interest around me. There they lay before and around me, the ruins, the figures, the Obelisk (the fellow to which has been taken away to Paris); the modern mud villages, mosques, and pigeon-houses, amongst which the ancient monuments now stand; the gracefully-winding Nile, Karnak in the distance on one side, Koórneh on the opposite bank; all around, the exquisitely coloured hills of the Lybian and Arabian chains, with the sandy desert at their base, and the clear morning hues lighting up the whole. It was, indeed, a sight worth coming a long way to enjoy—worth even the broiling which must be incurred in so doing. The thermometer stood to-day at 85° in the shade, and 119° in the sun.

In the evening we enjoyed a row in the small boat; the boatmen singing with might and main, in honour of the present company and of all the Moslem saints in succession: the works of their ancestors seeming to inspire them with fresh energy. When darkness came on we took to fishing. Mohamed had made a line on purpose for us, with a long rod of cane; he had also lighted up the 'Cairo,' with a grand illumination of eleven coloured lanterns, one on the top of the great yard which now stood upright, looking verily perched among the stars. He was as proud of his boat as a peacock of his tail; and declared that of course no boat was to beat the Cairo in anything. And now we fall asleep in our boat-home at Luxor, to the splashing of the fish under our cabin windows—the fish that had not allowed themselves to be caught, and we dream whether it is all a dream or plain unvarnished truth!

Thursday, Dec. 6th.—We decided not to remain long at Thebes, but merely to take a general view of its ruins, purposing to examine them more particularly on our return. To-day was devoted to an excursion to Koórneh. The chair and the donkeys were sent across, and we followed in the small boat. The cavalcade set out, all mounted on donkeys, with the exception of the guide engaged for the expedition, who looked stately and dignified mounted on his white Arab, wearing a very large white turban, and 'malâiat,' a voluminous blue cotton scarf with red border, the ends of which were thrown carelessly over both shoulders, and hung down behind. This was a day of great interest, and we thoroughly enjoyed the sight of the 'Memnonium,' or palace of Memnon, one of the earliest kings of Egypt; its fine pillars and capitals, and the hieroglyphic subjects sculptured on its walls; the huge broken statue in red granite of Remeses the Great, on which some hieroglyphics are cut, nearly two inches deep, the cuts being as clean now as though they had but just been made. There lay the giant overturned, with his face to the ground. Then there were the two colossal statues in the midst of the extensive plain; sitting still, and though much mutilated, and one of them almost faceless, seeming grandly to review the surrounding desolation, as though they would be fain still to frame the thought, and to exclaim, 'Monarchs of all we survey.' It is one of these statues which is said to have emitted a musical sound when struck by the rays of the rising sun: and to this day when travellers approach, the Arab who climbs to the top, in order to make the giant proportions of the statue more evident, strikes one of the uppermost stones, which emits a metallic, though not otherwise musical sound. Our luncheon was spread in view of the beautiful columns of the Memnonium and the Catacombs in the hills, and a small bazaar of "antiques" was gradually formed by the Arabs, who pressed round offering their goods for sale. A strange collection, and strange-looking merchants, with their dark faces and grinning white teeth. The dragoman and the guide discerning between what was truly ancient and what was only modern imitation, bargained and purchased for us, and as we knew nothing about the matter, we took all on trust from them, and set down each article as a treasure.

Friday, Dec. 7th.—A large budget was despatched hence, through the Consul, to Cairo. The letters are carried by 'runners,' who accomplish the distance, 454 miles, following the course of the river, in six days. We were not allowed to delay longer; Mohamed declared that "all this was as nothing compared to Karnak," and considered it a point of etiquette that "Karnak, best of all," should be kept for the last, lest, after the sight of its glories, we should not sufficiently appreciate the inferior temples higher up the river. "A bird in the hand is worth two in the bush," always was, and always will be, and it is prudent to take at least a cursory view of Karnak on the way up the river for fear of accidents: 'Cousin Phil,' however, true to his principles, was very submissive to the 'commanding officer.' We obeyed; and as we did see Karnak on our return, I believe also that we did enjoy more thoroughly the less elaborate remains above, for not having first seen this crowning glory of them all. We sailed away then, and around us again were desert, hill, and narrow bordering band of green. Once more we enjoyed the refreshing breeze, and the delicious sensation of sailing on the Nile. We were far away from all we had been accustomed to see and to think about, and an entirely new train of thoughts was thrust into our minds by the strange contrast. All was charming, and dreamily romantic; yet many a longing thought would frequently, it must be confessed, take back to cooler climes; for we had still much heat to endure before we reached our journey's end.

Cranes, vultures, and eagles, next engrossed our observation; we were sailing farther and farther from the busy world of life, and no human being appeared on the shore save a few wandering Arabs and naked children, until we reached the town of Erment on Saturday, December 8th. Here one of the Pashas has established three sugar-manufactories, and built so many pigeon-houses that they have the appearance of a town of small whitewashed towers; too white, and too regularly built in square blocks, to be an improvement to the landscape, but forming a curious and characteristic feature. The modern appearance of the buildings near the water's edge is striking, and there were glass windows in many of the houses. The ancient Erment dates its foundation as far back as that of Thebes, if not earlier.

In the evening we reached Esneh, and here the 'Cairo' stopped, that the crew might make, and take in the remaining quantity of bread required for the journey, until we returned to Girgeh. Little of the city of Esneh can be seen from the part of the bank near which we moored; the most important building in sight being a 'café,' built of mud, from whence, in the still evening, proceeded sounds of music and shouts of applause. Our crew had all gone there with their instruments of music to enjoy themselves, with permission to make "as much noise as they pleased;" the volume of their vocal powers having lately risen to such a pitch on the deck of the dahabééh as to require temporary control. On the shore at Esneh, therefore, they burst forth with fresh vigour, as they watched the 'Almé' (the dancing girls), who resort to the café, to dance and sing for the amusement of the public. The sounds continued far on in the night and ceased finally at two A.M.

Sunday, Dec. 9th.—After our morning service we went to see the temple of Esneh. The portico alone is excavated. This was accomplished by Mohamed Ali, but the rest remains covered still; and we were told, that the present Pasha will not allow it to be touched, for fear, as Mohamed said, of its 'beauties being carried away.' The portico is very fine indeed. It contains a close cluster of massive pillars, displaying great variety of architecture in their capitals, and covered with hieroglyphics, some of which we would gladly have taken off with paper and sponge, but as we had not provided ourselves with paper suitable for the purpose before starting on our journey, we were not able to do so. On the ceiling is a zodiac, which we strained our eyes in vain to decipher, I believe we ought to have been able to do so, but we could not, and had no one capable of explaining it to us. We saw only confused groups of mysterious-looking figures surrounded by stars, and boats apparently conveying animals across the water. The devices forming the capitals of the pillars are of the natural productions of the country, the date, the lotus, the papyrus, and other rushes. The streets of the present town are almost on a level with the roof of the portico, and the wretched hovels of the natives are built so close upon the beautiful ruins that they hide them completely. The descent into the portico is as bad as can be, and very little light is allowed entrance into it. The bazaars were more spacious than those we had yet seen on the river; the market and the whole town very picturesque. In the evening we went with Mohamed to what he called "a private house," that we might see the 'almé' dance. The "private house" was little more than a mud-hovel. The space in which the girls danced could hardly on the raised seat against the wall, were seated on their own chairs, which had been brought with them from the boat. A bed with mosquito curtains was at one extremity of the apartment; a divan at the other. The instrumental and vocal performers crowded at the little open door-way; and a small oil lamp, hanging from the ceiling, was the only light provided, to illuminate the darkness. Had we not brought our own lantern with us, little indeed should we have seen of the performance. The 'almé' dance with their bodies rather than their feet, making a series of contortions, shakings and joltings, which suggest the idea that the figures of these girls consist of two distinct parts, which have very little to do with one another.

They shuffle their naked feet along the ground in a most inelegant manner, keeping time to the music which is played for them. One of the girls played with small brass cymbals, a pair of which she held in each hand; her companion raised one hand to her head, at times as though in grief, at others spying through her fingers with most impudent looks, while the other arm was fixed 'akimbo' on her side. There were regular figures to the dance; the performers seemed to follow the music according to their own inclination, and at the conclusion of the exercise they looked as hot and tired as might be expected after such unnatural exertions. One of them who was pretty, and who was evidently looked upon as a kind of pocket Venus by her countrymen, gave us a song, which lasted for full ten minutes, in a curiously shrill and wild voice. She played her own accompaniment, on one of the funnel-shaped earthenware drums; after the song the dance was repeated in the same manner as before, and would have continued till morning, had the spectators not been fully satisfied long ere this period.

The dress of the 'almé' is always gay and handsome. They wore on this occasion striped India silk, and necklaces of gold coins, crocodiles, and other forms, all in gold. Their fez-caps were sewn all over with small gold money; a handsome crown-piece of solid gold fastened the rich black silk tassel; and a number of long braids of silk, equally covered with coins, forty of them at the least, dangled behind amongst the tiny plaits of their black hair, which between the silk braids and the tassel of the fez were very little seen. The fiddler, and the fiddle that accompanied the dancers, were the most curious part of the whole scene. The instrument was made of a cocoa-nut, cut crosswise in half; across it a bladder was tightly stretched; the handle was a rough stick, and two bundles of horse-hair, white and black, were stretched along the whole, by way of strings. Two very large pegs at the top served to tune the strings, and a projecting iron stem beyond the cocoa-nut shell to rest the instrument on the ground. The fiddler was a remarkably fine, dark-coloured man, father to one of the girls; and wonderfully well did he perform on his primitive-looking instrument. The fingers of one hand moved at the top, on the two bundles of strings, with the greatest agility; while the other hand and arm worked away with the fiddle-stick, which was formed of another bunch of horse-hair, loosely stretched and tightened by his hand in holding it. The variety of very peculiar sounds caused by the contact was almost incredible, a good deal of expression being arrived at by suddenly jerking the instrument first to one side, then to the other, in a way which would no doubt, have astonished slightly the talent of Paganini. We set down the old man as a decided musical genius, and regret extremely not having brought back to Europe a faithful picture of the musician and his instrument. A younger musician holding a somewhat smaller instrument, made of the other half of the cocoa-nut, kept buzzing on, one continued monotone, as a 'second part' during the whole performance. We were sufficiently pleased with these curiosities to be enabled to express truthful admiration and satisfaction, notwithstanding the sensations of disgust and pity which the dancing itself could not fail to raise in a European lady's mind. We were very glad to have seen it, but were equally sure that we should never wish to witness it again; though the fiddler and his fiddle we would most gladly have captured and taken away along with us. Honest Sarah's sense of propriety received even a greater shock than ours, and her looks of undisguised horror were an amusing part of the play: indeed I am not sure that they had not their effect in increasing the impudent looks of the 'almé,' which were towards the conclusion mostly aimed at her. But Sarah could not get over a great number of the daily sights she saw in this strange land, as her averted eyes and frequent sudden disappearances into the depths of the cabin abundantly testified. But we will not quarrel with her for this; it is a fault on the right side. And we like her all the better for her true English modesty.

Monday, Dec. 10th.—At a quarter before nine A.M., the Pasha of Esneh rode up to the dahabëëh on horseback, and came on board to visit "the Large Lord." He remained till ten o'clock, most cruelly depriving us of our breakfast, while he sat smoking his two pipesful, and drinking a cup of coffee and glass of lemonade. When the latter was offered to him, he looked at it in consternation, refusing to touch it; until the dragoman, after a considerable flow of eloquence, had succeeded in persuading him, that it was not 'spirits,' which he, as a good Mussulman, was bound not to touch. The horror depicted on the dragoman's face at such a suggestion from his own countryman, was equally striking and amusing. This Pasha was a very intelligent man, and we had more conversation with him, Mohamed acting as interpreter, than we could have had with any of our former visitors. He asked many questions about India, Australia, and China, which taxed our historical recollections considerably. In each one of these subjects, our party, it might reasonably have been supposed, would be "well up;" but it is astonishing how little people really know when they come to be catechised. Our eyes were found frequently meeting each other's with silent interrogatories, but we quickly remembered, first, that there was no one there to contradict what we might happen to say, and, secondly, that it was many chances to one that whatever we did say would be wrongly translated by our interpreter; therefore putting aside all doubts on the chronological points of our English history, we passed the examination—at least fluently. The Pasha said that 'Cousin Phil's' head betokened "much knowledge and good sense," and that in the "old times" when 'Cousin Phil' "was young," people knew "a great deal more than they know now." He was much shocked at the precocity of the young ladies, who assured him, that the present generation in Europe were much wiser than their forefathers. But both he and Mohamed looked at us incredulously, and their horror was turned into admiration, when we assured them that children of six and seven years old were now thought rather stupid if they could not read, write, and count by that advanced age. The Pasha said he had read about London "in books," and he only objected to it, that "being such a fine city, there was no land in it for sowing corn."

This dignitary rules from Esneh to 'Wadee Halfeh,' and has held his appointment for eighteen years, not a little proud of this being the longest term that any Pasha in those parts has remained in office, they being liable to be removed at the pleasure of the chief Pasha or 'Emir.' He showed us his watch, which was an English one, enclosed in three outer cases, two of silver, and the third of tortoise-shell from Constantinople. He spoke a great deal of Edfoo and its temples, and of the rapacity of the French, whose ways of dealings with the "Emir" he compared to "the detours of a cat running after a rat." It was a pity we could not converse with this man in his own language. He was very entertaining, and, moreover, was the first clean, well-dressed visitor we had had; he was likewise the highest in rank, which no doubt accounted for the difference. He appeared very shy of looking on the faces of the ladies; and I fear he considered it a proof of great boldness in us, that we could look at him without blushing, although he contemplated our beauty fully as much by his repeatedly cast side glances, as if he had looked us straight in the face, like a Christian.

At length he left us, remounted his horse, which his servant had paraded up and down the bank during the visit, and rode away, leaving our famished appetites to enjoy a late breakfast. We had to wait till the afternoon for the supply of bread for the crew. It came at last, the 'Reïs,' as Mohamed expressed it, having been "all day in the oven—I sent him in by force. If he not been in the oven, we not be ready for forty-eight hours." So the poor

Reïs was no doubt well baked. The fact was, that he, with a servant of the magistrate, provided by Mohamed, had been keeping watch near the oven, lest other bread should be put in, before our stock was all baked. Bag after bag began to be emptied on the further end of the deck, like so many sacks of coal, there to remain till it was cut up, and dried in the sun. A sheep had been slaughtered, two new ones purchased at about a 'dollar' apiece, turkeys, chickens, and geese, had been added to the poultry-yard, which consisted of two not very large wooden cages, placed in the stern of the vessel. Thus well provisioned we resumed our way, the thermometer standing at 83° in the shade, and 110° in the sun.

A table of antiquities was now spread on the deck, and, much to 'Cousin Phil's' amusement, as well as our own, the *factotum* dragoman proceeded to divide the spoils of Luxor evenly between Selina and me. In his purchases he was most anxious always to have duplicates of everything, and would sometimes even reject an article because it could only be possessed by one of us. He evidently feared lest any feelings of jealousy should arise, and was as grave at his present business, as though his head were to pay for the slightest deviation from equity, until, when one last treasure stood alone, he knew not what to do. Each of us wished to give it to the other, but this was more incomprehensible to Mohamed than anything else. He would resort to lots. And now the Arab nature came out. He had been honest long enough; with the idea of 'lots' came also the idea of 'cheating,' and a side signal was given, which Selina could not obey. Fate, however, assisted him: I drew the shorter slip, the 'scarabeus' was handed over to Selina, and then the conscience-stricken looks of the penitent dragoman were worthy a greater crime. He became so much impressed with the love that existed between us, that one day, when Selina was not well enough to undertake some expedition which he had proposed, he looked at her quite reproachfully, saying with emphasis, "You know very well Mrs. C—— will not move one step without you." He was certainly quite a character in his way this dragoman of ours, and much enlivened our trip by his peculiarities. The wind had gone down again towards evening, and we sailed but slowly along. The stars were beautifully reflected in the water; a little steamer, collecting the taxes for the Government from the villages along the river-side, passed by, puffing and paddling away, making as much fuss about its journey as any six European steamers of more than double her size, and the thick cloud of black smoke from her funnel stretched across the clear sky, as far as the eye could reach, as though it would remain there a fixture for ever.

Tuesday, Dec. 11th, dawned, and an unusual stillness pervaded the dahabëëh. The night-watchers from among the crew had slept during their appointed watch. Mohamed, who was watching below, because we were near no village, and could therefore have no watch from the shore, discovered the crime, watched himself with the Reïs, and reserved the culprits for punishment the next morning, lest the passengers should be disturbed by "a row" in the night. They were allowed breakfast as usual, and then the men lay down on the deck, and *the cook-boy stepped across their heads.* A strange idea! But the degradation was great, and not a word was spoken for a considerable time. One man would not touch a morsel of food till the end of the day. Mohamed said the Reïs made the cook-boy do it by force. It was as great a punishment to him, poor boy, as to the criminals, who begged hard to be beaten with a hundred "*sticks*" (stripes) rather than submit to such humiliation. But Mohamed was greatly impressed with the heinousness of their offence, and the necessity of discipline and night-watches, and he was inexorable. No sound of music or singing was heard during the day. The 'tracking' continued in silence, and everything in the dahabëëh was in painful harmony with the stillness of surrounding nature. More and more desert she became; less and less of life did she show. The water-drawers at the 'shadoof' were now of a much deeper copper colour; very few birds were to be seen; here and there a few white camels trudged by, this being the district in which the best camels are reared. Large detached stones studding the sandy plain; the remains of an ancient quay appearing in the water on either bank or a solitary tomb on the top of the highest hill; the white smoke of burning charcoal in the distance; a large-leafed plant, called by the Arabs 'milk of the hill' from its milky juice, which is a deadly poison, used by them sometimes to injure their eyesight, or to make one eye entirely blind, in order to avoid the dreaded 'conscription,' and the seed-pod of which contains such a beautiful silky down that it is sometimes called the 'silk-tree;' a few stray shrubs of henneh, from which two or three women were gathering the leaves, for the sake of its beautiful red dye, with which they colour their nails, the palms of their hands, and sometimes even their faces; a lovely sunset of yellow, pink, and blue shades; a rest for the night on an island mud-bank; a walk upon it by starlight, with the discovery of the print of crocodiles' feet, were the objects of interest which filled in and closed the stillness of this still day; and, as we retired to our berths in the evening, we could hear the night-watchers at their post as usual.

Three days of dead calm succeeded, and only gradually did the men regain their wonted cheerfulness. The sail was hardly spread at all, and our progress was necessarily slow; but the awning was up, which could not be when what we were pleased to call a '*spanking breeze*' was blowing, and this was no small enjoyment. The thermometer was at 83° and 85° in the shade, 110° and 116° in the sun, at midday, while at sunrise it had fallen to 46° and 50°. The trackers tracked steadily along. Scarcely one bird was now to be seen. The band of green had vanished into a mere line; here and there it had disappeared altogether. Yet each day brought its own little amusement and variety, and, strange as it may seem, its hours were numbered before we were aware of them.

On Wednesday, Dec. 12th, we passed Edfoo, leaving its beautiful temple for our return. And now the little steamer of two nights ago was seen prowling about, and the report reached the inquiring dragoman, that the tax-money collected for it had been stolen a few days back by three men from one of the neighbouring villages. They attacked the boat in which the money had been placed awaiting the arrival of the steamer, and killed the two men who were in charge of it, while the brave captain and crew jumped into the water and ran away to tell the tale. The murderers had now fled into the wilderness; thirteen men of their families had been captured and were kept in prison as hostages; a regiment of soldiers was on the look-out for them; and the sheikhs of their respective villages were bound to find and deliver them up to justice in a month's time. Such were the facts gleaned from the shoutings of the respective crews to each other. Mohamed looked anxious, and said we should anchor to-night in the middle of the river, instead of mooring near the shore. Many travellers insist on doing this at all times. but the dragomen and crew are invariably against it, and it was such a manifest inconvenience to them all that we gave up the point. Selina and I had cast the imputation of cowardice upon the crew of the unfortunate boat, whereupon Mohamed boldly asserted, speaking of the robbers, "Thousand men no good against these people: these people only fit, just for to kill." This was pleasing intelligence; but evening drew on, and we ran in to the shore as usual. Our rope was not long enough to cast anchor here, so for want of a rope we were to run the chance of being murdered too. The Reïs assured Mohamed that he knew the place and that these were "very good people;" but the dragoman looked uneasy, until Selina and I made some remark about the danger of our position. The scale was turned in an instant; "Afraid! we never afraid! What for we be afraid?" And as no one could give a satisfactory answer to this query, it was voted universally that we were 'not afraid.' We did not tell 'Cousin Phil' that we really were so, but bravely consoled ourselves with the fact, that the "good people" dwelling in this desert spot, under this clump of palm-trees, were but twenty-five or so in number; and that our brave company, with the captured guns, would certainly not jump into the water and run away, but would easily master double that number if we were attacked. Foe or no foe however, the wind would not rise, and here we must stay; and we slept soundly to boot.

Thursday, Dec. 13th.—The 'trackers' moved on again in the still, desert scene, and at night we reached the hills of Silsileh, the 'Mountain of the Chain,' where, it is said, that a chain was fastened across the river, by the order of an ancient king, to prevent vessels from passing higher up and taking stone from the quarries, whence the materials for almost all the Egyptian temples were taken.

Friday, Dec. 14th.—Tracking still; and now we had a pleasant walk "on the sands," for the deposit was covered with sparkling grains of gold and steel, blown across from the desert, which reached to the very edge of the river's bed. Here again we saw the print of a crocodile, and later in the day a real crocodile appeared, stretched on a bank in the middle of the river. To make sure of its identity we fired off a gun, and the huge creature plunged into the water, to the no small joy of Mohamed, who evidently considered his *protégées* remarkably sceptical on the subject of these monsters. We could not judge of the size of this one from the distance at which it lay, but the splash and the length of time which was occupied by the monster in completing its plunge, showed that it was a large one. There were also traces of snakes on the sand, but they are not likely to show themselves to travellers. Should they do so Mohamed turns pale, and most unhesitatingly affirms, "Then we be afraid, certainly!" and consequently "take to our heels!"

sures within a mud wall about six inches high. In these some natives had been watching, waiting the appearance of a crocodile, that they might shoot at him. They lie down within these enclosures to hide themselves from view, and rest their guns on a small opening in the top of the enclosure till the crocodile appears, when they shoot at him with unerring aim. This part of the river abounds with crocodiles, but they usually come out of the water only at the hottest time of day, to bask in the sun on the bank.

But soon the 'trackers' were obliged to take to the opposite bank, for there was no further walking space; moreover, we were pretty well baked by our charming walk "on the sands," whatever the crocodiles might think about it; we therefore concluded our excursion and returned to the dahabëéh, re-embarking when she had been pulled up to us, for we had walked much faster than she had proceeded, having had time to sit down and take a long rest while she was still trudging slowly along.

Friday, Dec. 14*th.*—A dahabëéh was seen returning from the Cataracts. The small boat pushed off from her side, and we awaited, with pleasurable anticipations, a visit, and an account of the dreaded passage. Only the courier of the party appeared, and the dahabëéh rowed on, ashamed, we feel sure, to own that she had not ascended the Cataracts at all—had had enough of it, and was now making the best of her way home. Her courier came to beg privately from our dragoman for dates and 'mish-mish.' He had exhausted his own store, and, alas! where was the Christmas plum-pudding which had been promised at Shepherd's Hotel in Cairo to all the dahabëëhs assembled at Wadee Halfeh? When Mohamed el Adlëëh had recovered from his amazement that his illustrious party had received no visit from the passing vessel—a fact which he evidently regarded as a personal insult to himself—he expressed his astonishment at our quiet resignation on the subject, and would scarcely vouchsafe one word to the 'courier.' But Thomas and Sarah came to the rescue, and, too glad, no doubt, of a little English chat, they catechised him about the Cataracts, &c. When Mohamed had thus indirectly discovered the proceedings of the unfortunate vessel, the undisguised contempt with which he viewed the whole affair was highly entertaining. He was, of course, entire master of his own stores; nothing would induce him to part with any of them, and we sailed on, in all the glory, as Mohamed expressed it, of our "mish-mish for six months."

Mish-mish is an excellent dish of small apricots, dried and stewed, and served up in general with boiled rice.

We had become so accustomed to the bald-headed Arabs, that we were almost startled to-day at the appearance of a man on the shore, of whom Mohamed quickly exclaimed, "That kind never wear caps." He needed none; his head was covered with very thick cork-screw curls of jet-black hair, reaching to the nape of his neck, and forming a 'thatch,' fully capable of baffling the rays of the Eastern sun. He was the only specimen of exactly "this kind" that we saw; but he came from the Khartoum country, of which we saw many other inhabitants higher up the river. The wind failed when we were about five miles from Kom Ombo, and we moored again for the night. There was a remarkable echo here across the desert. Every word of a sentence, however long, was distinctly repeated, some seconds after it had been spoken, with every intonation of the speaker's voice most faithfully restored on the air. So distinct was it, and so remarkable in the variety of the sounds, that, as we sat in the saloon, we were for some time persuaded that there was another crew in one of the cargo boats near us, either answering or mocking our own. Being accustomed to echoes only amongst lofty hills, it seemed quite unaccountable that so striking a one should come across the desert plain, upon which there was nothing but very diminutive elevations covered with loose sand.

On the opposite bank the cotton-plant was growing abundantly, and there were some specimens of the poisonous plant before mentioned, of whose powers Mohamed stood in such dread that he could not be persuaded to let us gather a bit, even for the sake of science.

The wind sprang up suddenly, and we proceeded

passing by Kom Ombo; but again it failed, and we anchored at some distance from a bank, on which grew some palm-trees, but to which there was no means of nearer approach. Before falling asleep, strange, hideous sounds reached our ears. We listened and wondered, and Selina and I almost went to awake each other, to know what could be the matter. Between charity and philosophy, however, we remained quiet, listening on attentively to what each one finally construed to be the roaring of lions, or, perhaps, tigers, concluding that we were exposed to fresh dangers in this savage land. The morning dispelled the illusion, and we smiled on finding that the growls and howls were but the boasted musical voices of our own crew, pulling the anchor up and letting it down again, according to the caprice of the wind, as it rose or fell, mingled with the creaking, monotonous sound of the 'saghi' (or water-wheel), turned by oxen, which from this point replaces the 'shadoof,' and works on, for the watering of the crops, making this pretty music, night and day, all through the winter months.

This morning, the sunrise had been most beautiful. All who are not invalids on the Nile, will gladly turn out of their mosquito cage to see it, as well as to enjoy the only cool breeze they will have till the twelve hours of the day are past: this I did, of course, and shall now describe one whole day of our dahabëéh life, beginning with the sunrise. I leave the vessel, stand on the shore, and look around me.

The crew issue one by one from the boat, and standing about, with their faces turned to the east, perform their morning devotions; each one wholly wrapped up in his own, and apparently totally undisturbed by anything around him. The dragoman spreads his carpet on the deck, and is always first in his Moslem prayers. He washes carefully, and then, woe betide any woman-kind who shall happen to pass by, and allow even her dress to touch him in the slightest degree. His prayers are thus "all spoilt," and he must "begin over again." He prostrates himself, letting his forehead touch the ground two or three times; then rises and stands quite upright, his arms tight to his side, and in this posture, almost faster than his lips can move, he repeats some portions of the Korán, or calls upon Allah in all the ninety different names which he says belong to the Deity, counting them upon his rosary as he proceeds. At other times he kneels sitting back on his heels, and while repeating the same words, turns his head, first to the right, then to the left; rubs the crown of it with his hand; holds both hands straight up before him, as though he were reading out of an open book; pulls his beard and moustaches, and makes sundry exclamations in a most peculiar groaning tone; all these gesticulations being signs of promises and vows. The men scattered on the shore go through the same forms, some in a less, some even in a greater degree; and all look so devout in their imperfect faith, one cannot but long that they should be brought to know the true Gospel of Christ, and to bring all this apparent humility and devotion to the foot of the cross, to be there purified and made acceptable to Him who hung thereon for them as well as for us.

In a conversation with Mohamed on the subject of his religion, we gathered that he looked upon Jesus Christ as one of the 3000 prophets whom God had sent into the world from the beginning, and some of whom were in it still. He denied the Divine nature of Christ simply, he said, because "It is impossible. How can man be God?" There was a dogged obstinacy of manner about him, which would seem to repel all idea of the possibility of persuading him of any error in his creed, and a sadly curious self-confidence when he concluded the subject with these words, "Very well, Mrs. C——. When come the end of the world, then you be there, and I be there, and then we'll see, and then I tell you how it is true." They do not pray to their saints, he said, although they are perpetually singing out their names in their songs, whether in times of danger or otherwise. The basis of the Moslem faith is the first grand truth, that there is but one God, and that He orders all things, even the most trifling circumstances in life to which order, man must implicitly submit. Mohamed seemed to know no other article of faith; and the imperfect knowledge of the Moslem converted this one into the mere idea of a destiny, to which it was his duty wholly to resign himself. All was destiny, carried to such an extent that Mohamed frequently would not venture an opinion on the merest trifles, even he would not say at what hour we were likely to reach our destination. More than once he begged of us not to ask him "such questions," because, "if I say we get there by five o'clock, the wind sure to rise, and we not get half way there to-night." Swearing and drinking are wholly forbidden by their law; the former vice had one day met with condign punishment in the person of the unfortunate cook-boy, who cried like a real child after the shame of his beating. We looked up from our work and book in astonishment at hearing the familiar sounds proceeding from so unfamiliar a form, for I do think that our cook-boy, though a very good boy in general, was the most *unlike* specimen of the human race that could have been produced, and the idea that he could cry had never entered our heads. It was somewhat difficult to remember also that he was a married man having a wife and child somewhere in Nubia. They said he was eighteen years of age, but he did not look more than fifteen.

To return to our day. No sooner are the prayers over than the tracking begins. 'Cousin Phil' and I appear on deck, for 'Cousin Phil' still maintains his early hours, and rises at six of the clock. The present hour he devotes to his books, I to my concertina, while the dragoman and others, remaining on the boat, listen in raptures to the strain. "Peautiful, indeed!, peautiful!" sighs Mohamed, with uplifted eyes; and at the close of each verse there comes a kind of a groan of delight, with which the Arabs always express their admiration of a musical performance, and which, by its ever novel peculiarity, threatens to turn the song into a laugh each time that it occurs. Sometimes, when the dahabëëh was stationary, Mohamed would say, "Oh, please to turn that way, and sing *that sing;* these people *never* see anything like this." And there was the bank behind me covered with the whole black population of the village, squatted down, listening, with eyes and mouths wide open, to the unusual sounds of the instrument and European voice.

At eight o'clock the merry 'trackers' come tumbling in again, and squat in a circle, on the deck or sometimes on the shore, round the large wooden bowl containing the brown bread and hot lentile soup, the bucket beside them as usual, for drinking, or for washing when breakfast is over. Short work they make of it, and very fair play, as has been before described; and highly pleased they are at forming the subject of a picture. Yet this does not retard their meal for one instant; about five minutes despatch the whole so that the artist had need be quick and expert, if he wishes to catch any likeness in those dark complexions. And now they are off again, 'tracking' along the shore. The sleepy waiting-boy, "my man Ali," as Mohamed called him on his first introduction, has contrived by nine o'clock to get the breakfast ready in the saloon, where we take all our meals. Ali was a tall, slight youth, with a light brown, sallow complexion, and very peculiarly languishing black eyes. He wore the Turkish dress, his 'best' jacket being very handsomely embroidered with gold. He seldom wore this one, and was, without exception, the dirtiest human creature that could have waited upon us. Scolding or coaxing were equally useless, and, although he was once or twice compelled to wash both himself and his clothes, this was so great an exertion on his part that it lasted for a long time, when it was found necessary to enforce the order again. When Ali *was* clean, he made a very pretty figure in his full white trousers, braided jacket, and short black curls, peeping round his head from under the fez which had the largest and longest silk tassel imaginable, falling gracefully upon his shoulders, and adding to the generally languid appearance of the youth.

After breakfast we pace the deck for a 'constitutional,' and then, sitting on the divans, or lying down if we prefer it, we amuse ourselves with reading, working, and sketching. The dragoman comes up at times to name some bird, plant, or hill, making, now and then, it must be confessed, some wonderful mistakes in the classification of the two former, proving beyond doubt, that his knowledge of natural history is very limited. A slight breeze springs up, and in come the 'trackers,' again in their blue, brown, or white dresses, brown or red 'fez,' faded into every shade of yellow, or no colour at all, and sometimes a best turban or two; but when we arrive at a town, they turn out splendidly new and clean. Now they tumble in, like so many children; the sail is spread, with a good deal of singing to help it up, and then they form a circle on the deck again. The musical instruments are brought out of one end of the bread-box, and a full chorus of the most extraordinary music that has ever greeted our inexperienced ears strikes up. The band consists of small kettle-drums (called 'tom-toms'), tambourines, small brass cymbals, and funnel-shaped drums, made of crockery, which are tucked under the arm, and struck with the fingers of both hands. The instruments are distributed round the circle, which closes in, and then they "go at it"—it can be called by no other name—the remaining performers clapping their hands in time with the music, all singing with teeth clenched, or mouths wide spread, just as it happens to suit the sentiment, one for one tune, and one for another, sending forth a combination of sounds more strange and wild than we could have conceived had we not heard them, and of which even four months' teaching could hardly suffice to enable the traveller to give a faithful imitation on his return home. I tried to imitate them frequently, but was obliged to give up in despair. Yet this wild music accords so well with the surrounding scene that, from a distance, when the ear becomes familiarised to it, it might even, by a slip of the tongue, be called 'pretty,' and there was one song which both Selina and I finally 'liked.' The crew had songs for us, and for all the saints in the Mahometan calendar. On they play and sing, in the very height of enjoyment; the dragoman sits by, looking as if he had already entered the seventh heaven, and, in the midst of his ecstasies, casts frequent glances at the party on the 'quarter-deck,' to inquire whether they are not likewise affected, for this is first-rate Arab singing: "Oh, yes; very good indeed." And we respond, that, at least, it is "hearty" to the highest degree. Some days the band is not brought out; but the dragoman leads a game instead, in the same squatted circle; and a merrier party of schoolboys was never seen than this grown-up crew at play. The peals of laughter that ring from the lower deck cannot fail to draw the attention of the 'quarter-deck,' and we are much amused to find that the game very much resembles 'Turn the trencher,' or 'Forfeits,' only that the forfeits here are all paid in one way, namely, by a good slap on the back from the hands of the whole circle, piled one over the other and raised *en masse*, to fall simultaneously on the unfortunate victim, whose head is bowed low in the centre of the ring. Suddenly the game or the concert will lose one member, or two, or three, as the steersman shouts to shift the sail, or to furl it again ; then up jump eight or nine, climbing the mast, perching like so many monkeys at even distances along the lateen yard, drawing the large sail up with hands and feet, and then tying it round with a small rope, which will let it all down again at one pull when required.

Should the morning have passed without it, the afternoon will generally produce some place of interest to see, and to read and talk about, or to sketch as we pass rapidly by ; and, when all these fail, we have one resource still left—we ingratiate ourselves in the favour of the Arab cook, and may be seen seated in the bow of the boat with Mahomed, learning how to make some of the very nice dishes which Hassan sends up for our dinner at six o'clock. A glorious sunset, new every evening, and an equally glorious moon or starlight night, tea at a quarter to nine, and then the standing dish, backgammon and [illegible], close the romance of our day on the Nile.

CHAPTER V.

FROM ASSOUAN TO KOROSKO.

As we approach the scenery of the cataracts, very fine palm-trees again greet the eye, the hills begin to assume a darker hue, and the sandstone gives place to the granite rock. A few Roman ruins crown the tops of the hills on the eastern bank as we proceed. On the western, the sand of the desert lies thickly strewn upon the rock. Here was the island of Kubanieh, and the home of our Reïs. He landed, and was surrounded by a very respectable body of black relatives, for they are Nubians; and before parting he left a basket full of presents for his mother. Each man of the crew, whose home lay on our way, was allowed to pay it a visit, and to rejoin the dahabëëh at the next village at which we stayed for the night. These people never meet their friends empty-handed, and Mohamed had provided a large box to contain his presents for his friends. They were frequently handsome, such as a fez, some coffee-cups, or a silk-handkerchief, and he received many in return, in the form of dates, sugar-canes, and sheep.

At half-past four P.M., *Saturday, Dec. 15th*, we reached Assouan, the ancient Syene; and here 'Cousin Phil' and the whole party turned out for a walk. In the evening I sat on the bank fishing, Mohamed squatted at my side, musing and meditating on the lovely romantic scenery, and on the remains of past glory and grandeur.

But I must not forget the beautiful approach to Assouan. *Here* begins the actual rocky scenery of the Cataracts, and the river appears enclosed as in a basin, or like the opening of a harbour, with lofty hills on either side. The island of Elephantina is in front, and small islands, with the most brilliant patches of vegetation, stud the water. Palm-trees, sont, young barley, and lupines of brilliant emerald green growing on every little scrap of earth (the deposit of the river), between the picturesque masses of granite or porphyry, of which the islets are composed.

In some cases a great number of large, ancient stones are heaped up, as though placed there in preparation for a building; in others they stand erect, singly, and covered with hieroglyphics. Here they assume all kinds of fantastic shapes, human figures, skulls, or old castles; there, they are cut into huge plain blocks bearing the marks of the wedges used to detach them from the larger mass, and lying about as though waiting to be laid in the spot for which they were originally designed. Some of these masses are of enormous size, and we noticed one which had every appearance of having been destined for an Obelisk. In such a scene, it is not to be wondered, that although the next step would take us to the longed-for Cataracts, we were well content to linger awhile because the wind would not blow. In our first walk we met a number of little Nubian girls, with their hair plaited in very small straight plaits, and covered thickly with the castor-oil which abounds here. The beauty of many of their faces led us to coax them to come nearer for inspection. They were very shy, and soon the horrid perfume of the castor-oil, with which they were saturated, caused them to be again most ungratefully dismissed to a more respectful distance. They were quite black, but very pretty and intelligent-looking; their figures very elegant, and their movements most graceful. The Nubian boys were very ugly; yet curiously enough they grow up into fine, and some of them handsome-looking men, whilst the girls lose all their beauty with advancing years, becoming almost like the women of Lower Egypt, who, as far as we were able to observe them, were, old and young, absolutely frightful.

We walked over the site of the old town. The town of Syene is fallen indeed; and the traveller walks over a soil composed of the crumbled *débris* of its palaces, houses, and temples; or if he chooses to dig he may disinter the old inhabitants themselves in their mummied forms. There was one coffin, at the time, which had been half dug out by some traveller a few days before, and left there, having probably been found valueless.

Sunday, Dec. 16th.—Chair and all we crossed

to the opposite side of the river, and after one whole hour spent in preparation, our caravan was set in motion. The talents of Mohamed el Adlëéh certainly did not lie in the harnessing line. His clumsy attempts at linking the donkeys and the chair to one another were ludicrous to behold. 'Cousin Phil' tried hard to show him that all he was doing was entirely wrong; but Mohamed thought, what could an 'English lord' know about Nubian donkeys and Mahometan chairs; he therefore shook his head, shrugged up his shoulders, shifted his head-gear first on one side, then on the other, to assist the workings of his brains, and ejaculated patronisingly on every fresh remark of 'Cousin Phil's,' "Trust to me; trust to me!" The clumsy dodges succeeded at last, and, Mohamed fully convinced of his own cleverness, we started to see the Obelisk, which lies in one of the quarries of Syene. It was never finished, but it lies there still, ninety-five feet in length; one single block of granite, of a very beautiful grain and colour, close under the mass from which it was cut, and which bears the marks of the wedges used in detaching it. All the blocks of granite around bear similar marks, the cuts being as fresh as though they had been but recently made. As on the opposite shore, nothing but ruin and devastation is to be seen. A portion of the gateway of a temple, said to be of the time of Nero, stands near; and there are other trifling remains of interest to be visited. These were too far off for our party, and we passed on through the Moslem cemetery, which is of great extent. Some of the tombs, built with domes and small parapets on the tops of the surrounding walls, formed very picturesque groups; and by the side of some of the smaller ones, jars of water stood for the refreshment of travellers. Mohamed said this was always the custom with "rich people." Little wonder that these poor people should deem that the English are "made of money" if this jar of clear water and the single plant of aloe growing near it was a sign of wealth among them. I was much struck with the simple ingenuity of my little donkey-boy on this occasion. He could speak nothing but Arabic with the exception of one word, suitable to the place of his abode. This was "mort," (no doubt the Italian 'morte'), and when I drew his attention to some of the tombs, which differed so much from the others, that we doubted whether they were tombs or not, and addressed him in our newly acquired Arabic, "Ehe die?" (What is that?) he answered me with a delighted flow of his native tongue. This, failing entirely to reach my senses, he laid his head on his hand, closed his eyes and said, "Sitte, Sitte, mort." (Lady, lady, dead.) I understood him at once, and conceived a much higher idea of my little guide's intellectual powers, than that with which his first appearance and the pig-like grunts with which he urged the donkey on, had hitherto inspired me.

The epitaphs on the tombs are of the earlier

inhabitants of Assouan, and bear date from the third century of the Hegira (A.D. 622). We should have liked to have taken off some of the inscriptions on the tracing paper, which we procured here, but Mohamed either truly considered this a desecration, or he was in a hurry to proceed, for he would not hear of it, and said that it would be at the cost of his life to allow us to do "such a thing." We might sketch the monuments, but touch them—no! not for the world! Of course we were obliged to submit, though we believed the danger to be wholly imaginary. Desolate and dreary, though picturesque, was this Moslem cemetery; a collection of mud or sand-covered graves scattered in all directions, and interspersed with the more pretending domed and parapeted elevations, to all appearance unknown, uncared for, broken, and crumbling. Yet we were told that each grave was 'private property' and watched with jealous care, so that the smallest depredations would be visited with extreme rigour by the "high families" to whom they belonged.

We returned through the city, bazaar, and market-place. The streets were wider than in the other towns we had seen; but what struck us most was the lack of windows to most of the houses. This was, partly, no doubt in order to exclude the burning rays of the sun; and what windows they did rejoice in looked, not on the street, but into the little square court which lay at the back of most of the houses. Mohamed said it was for fear the women should look out and be seen by the passers-by. Here he also informed us, that when he wished to marry, he would go to *Sioot* to choose his wife. "Much the best girls in all Egypt there!"

The young ladies at Assouan who walked about well veiled, were very anxious to see their European sisters; and at Mohamed's request we graciously stopped our nimble steeds, and unveiled our faces before a group of them, who cautiously uncovered their own in return, when Mohamed had ridden away to a respectful distance from the beauties. Dirty and ugly the group were, but they seemed much gratified by their inspection of us; and we flatter ourselves that, by comparison at least, they pronounced us clean, if not pretty. They were dressed in some sort of black material which trailed in the dust, looking as if it had never been washed since it was first put on, and they wore beads and small leathern bags, with portions of the Koran sewn up in them as charms, round their necks, and bracelets of ivory and ebony on their arms. Many articles were offered us here for sale; gold and silver bracelets of filagree work, and other ornaments, which were all rejected because Mohamed promised that we should meet a caravan from the 'Khartoum' on our return; which we never did meet, with the exception of a returning one when all its goods had been disposed of.

Monday, Dec. 17th.—There was another washing-day at Assouan, and we enjoyed ourselves in the small boat, rowing among the picturesque rocks and endeavouring to take a sketch of a dilapidated 'saghi' with its long string of buckets dipping into the river. The current was so strong here that it was impossible to keep the boat still, and frequently when we lifted our eyes from the paper, the subject of the sketch had disappeared.

In the evening we went to see two young lions on board a cargo boat belonging to some rich merchant. They had been caught in the Khartoum, and were going to be taken to Cairo for sale. We might have bought them, for 10*l.* or 12*l.* a-piece, had we wished to bring them home as pets. They were from three to six months old, and about the size of an ordinary English mastiff; but even at that early age, their subdued roar made by no means an agreeable impression; and it was not without some degree of fear that we saw one of them taken out of its crate-cage, that we might view it in all its beauty. The owner, a tall, handsome, coal-black Nubian, who, though very rich, wore no other garment than the loose blue dress common to all the Egyptians, with a fez of very prettily embroidered cashmere, played with the young king of the forest, and fondled it as you might fondle a dog; but this appeared to us by no means a comfortable proceeding. A small and very pretty monkey was afterwards brought to the dahabëëh for sale, and Mohamed, being of a speculative turn of mind, bought it for three dollars, saying he would sell it in Alexandria for five or six guineas.

Tuesday, Dec. 18th.—We were ready to start, but the wind did not rise sufficiently for the passage of the Cataracts; so Sarah enjoyed a quiet day of ironing, and we set off in the row-boat again. Gently we glided between the groups of picturesque rocks, admiring in silence the wild beauties of the scene, when something moving upon the waters called forth a simultaneous exclamation of astonishment from our party. If mermaids have a real existence, and boast a rich, copper-coloured skin, surely here was one of these mysterious beings, and Syene is the place of their abode! A small, human form lay stretched on the surface of the water, moving quickly along by means of its hands and feet. A little lower down was another figure, quite black, apparently sitting on the water, and moving in the same direction. This was a Nubian inhabitant of Assouan, ferrying himself across the river on his ferry-boat, the boat being simply a log of wood cut from a date-tree. He has bound to it, with a cord made from the fibres of the same tree, a bundle of Indian corn-leaves, which he is taking across as fodder for his goat or his sheep on the opposite shore. He wears no clothes, and sits on his log-boat, his legs stretched out horizontally along either side of it, so that it is completely hidden under the water. In his hand he holds a small paddle-oar, with which he pushes the water back, first on one side, then on the other, till he has reached the opposite bank. And yonder is our mermaid—his little girl, of about ten years of age. She also has her log-boat, which is buried under the water, as she lies along it, flat upon her chest, her hands and feet working away above the surface. She, like her father, is taking some fodder across the river. Her laughing face is turned towards us, the very picture of innocence and happiness, her rich copper-coloured complexion is her only clothing; her short, black, curling hair waves bewitchingly round her forehead; and the bundle of bright green leaves, seen above the water in front of her, completes the whole smiling picture. It was an exquisite touch of nature, and its beauty and simplicity were irresistible. Forgetful of the first shock natural to civilised minds on seeing a young lady in such a position, we lingered on, and voted this by far the prettiest sight we had yet seen. At the request of our dragoman, the little mermaid was made to show her swimming powers by working her way towards us. The current seemed almost too strong for her; but she was not to be baffled. She came near, and we held out our hands, and dropped a few 'paras' (the small copper coin of the country) into her outstretched palm, adding, if possible, to the brightness of her pleased and merry countenance. This is the common mode of crossing the river near Assouan, and many log-boats are seen lying on the rocks to dry. Some are larger, and made of two or three logs bound together; these will carry five or six persons across at a time, although how to seat them all upon so small a surface would puzzle most European brains. This piece of primitive nature amused and interested us for the remainder of the day, and we retired to rest, liking the picturesque spot so well that we almost hoped the wind would not rise just yet.

On Wednesday, however, *December* 19*th*, the cloudy sky and cold air at sunrise betokened a breeze, and Mohamed was anxious to start. Our cat had been allowed to escape at Thebes, which had troubled him much; but now that he had manufactured three rat-traps, which we were quite sure could never catch one rat, he could imagine no further attraction at Assouan. The Reïs, or pilot of the Cataracts, with whom a contract had been made, and duly signed and sealed before the Governor at Assouan, was summoned. His brother came instead of him; and Mohamed, ever ready with an excuse when it suited his purpose, said that the Reïs was a gentleman, and never got up so early, but that he would join the dahabëéh near the Cataracts, where his home was. The brother was a Reïs also, but not the chief. With him and a pilot, who is engaged here to take charge of the boat till her return (the Caireen or Alexandrian Reïs being considered inefficient for the difficult navigation of these parts), at about half-past ten A.M. the 'Cairo' started on her way. A strange, wild way it was, growing more and more so at every step, as she wound in and out, between this rock and that, in apparent peril of being at each moment dashed against one or other of them. We soon discovered Mahomed's 'gentleman Reïs' in a small row-boat, from whence he was directing the movements of the great ship. The wind had by this time risen too high, and we were obliged to stop on one of the wild masses of rock. Selina and I got out, enjoyed a walk and a climb, and finally sat down to sketch, associating in our minds the dark black rocks of Assouan with those much nearer home. We sat on, busied with our thoughts and our pencils, the hinder legs of our chairs sinking imperceptibly in the soft mud soil, until the fore-legs toppled up in the air, and down we came. No great harm done, if we may judge from the laughter which ensued. The alluvial deposit made a soft bed, and we were picked up by our black attendants, not a muscle of whose faces betokened any feeling but that of dire dismay, and who henceforth squatted themselves considerably nearer, in momentary expectation of another such catastrophe. They clearly did not think the 'sitte' (ladies) fit to be trusted alone.

The rest of the crew were dotted over the black rocks, enlivening the landscape by the bright colours of their costume, half of their number, including our dragoman, being rolled up in crevices, and fast asleep. At mid-day they were all roused by the pilot, and we were summoned to return to the vessel, as the wind had lulled sufficiently to enable us to proceed.

There were forty helpers at hand, and it required some vigorous exertions to get us off the rock on which we had rested. It was accomplished at last, and we soon reached the first 'door' of the Cataracts. These Cataracts are called 'E Shellál,' and are simply rapids caused by the rush of water through the masses of rock. The falls appear very slight, the highest not exceeding five or six feet. Each passage is called 'bab' (a door), and Mohamed counted five of them, looking, as each one was passed in safety, as though one-fifth of the weight of the world had been lifted from off his broad shoulders. To watch his countenance of alternate fear and joy was a study in itself. And no less amusing were the looks that he cast frequently at each of us, to see if we also were not afraid. More than once the question was repeated, "How do you like it, Mrs. S——?" "How do you like it, Mrs. C——?" with a look which meant to say, "You ought to be frightened out of your senses." But Mrs. S—— and Mrs. C—— agreed that it was very pretty and highly entertaining; and as to 'Cousin Phil,' who sat on the divan, quietly wondering what they were making such a fuss about, Mohamed gave him up in despair, the *sang-froid* which he displayed on the occasion completely puzzling the excitable Arab.

To persons wholly unaccustomed to rocks and sea, the passage up these Cataracts may possibly appear somewhat frightful, and many prefer leaving the boat, and walking along the shore, whilst it is being dragged up; but to us there was nothing alarming in these tiny, picturesque rocks and falls, although the curiously primitive navigation, by means of which we were hauled up, or pushed along, failed to inspire much confidence as to the result. Either there really was no danger at all, or the exciting novelty of the wild scene left us no leisure for fear, or, as Mohamed would certainly have said, had he dared, we were too ignorant of the danger to be afraid of it. But, danger or no danger, there is great difficulty in pulling a large dahabëéh up the falls, and Mohamed el Adlëéh deserves much credit for managing everything as he did. We had passed the rapids in the course of a few hours, instead of being two or three days about it, as some of the other dahabëéhs were, and without any annoyances, so that we thoroughly enjoyed the whole scene. It frequently happens that the natives crowd on board, on one excuse or another, and clamour for 'bak-sheesh' from the travellers, at which time many articles may be stolen from the cabins; but Mo-hamed, being responsible for everything on board, took care to expel all useless hands immediately from our vessel, and we lost nothing. The drago-man was as sharp-eyed as the thieves could have been; he kept strict watch over everything, and, much to the discomfiture of Thomas and Sarah, insisted on their being stationed below. The windows of all the cabins, except one, which was allowed to admit a little light and view, had been trebly secured with glass, shutter, and Venetian blinds; but Mohamed knew the agility of the natives, and assured us they could easily open them all, and take possession of anything within reach of their long arms. Everything then was stowed away in the drawers under the divans, and watch kept below, while Mohamed and Ali patrolled the deck, sending off many a scrambler from the sides of the dahabëéh. We proceed in safety. The agility of the "old man," the chief Reïs, must be seen to be realised. He looks as old as the Cataracts themselves, and as wild. Yet see how he gesticulates and shouts; now from the small boat, now from the top of a rock, which he has reached by swimming, we suppose, though neither Arab nor European can follow his lightning speed; now from the quarter-deck and helm, where he is standing again before we have had time to observe that he has left the rock. He has been Reïs of the Cataracts for the last forty years, knows every stone, current, and eddy in them, and thinks, naturally enough, that no one else does. He is a great man—"a gentleman." But this gentleman appears in a pair of short, white drawers, and a loose, open shirt, like the rest of the crew. Most of his retainers wear much less, and that is constantly taken off, that they may jump into the water, and push the boat along, or off, on their shoulders and backs. All around we see brown or black human beings jumping and swimming hither and thither, holding between their teeth the ropes that are to pull the dahabëéh along; now tying them to one rock, then to another; now swimming round to lift them, first over this one, then over that; while the Reïs shouts his directions, the crew shout them on, the brother Reïs contradicts them, the pilot of Assouan chimes in with his interpretation; and the 'blackies' in the water shout and halloo, because they cannot make out what everybody else is shouting and hallooing for. Now we watch the old Reïs, who is in a perfect fit of excitement on the top of one of the rocks. A sudden sound makes us turn from him for an instant, and, lo! there he is on the dahabëéh, at the helm again, his arms flung wildly in the air, dancing so high with rage that he bounds at least three feet at each jump. He shouts as no one else can shout; and Mohamed el Adlëéh looks indescribable things. We begin to think that, after all, there may be some danger; yet there is too much of the ridiculous in the whole scene: and as we look and listen, and see the shore so close that we could jump upon it in a moment, we laugh heartily to think that all this 'Bedlam' and trouble should be got up to pull a party of strangers up these little Cataracts, when they could far more easily and quietly have gone along the road on shore. But the scene is worth a good deal, and we recommend every one to go through it, and have this 'Bedlam' got up for them also. The dahabëéh must be dragged up in any case if the travellers go to the second Cataracts, and they will hardly see such a scene in any other country. The natives in these parts are called by the Egyptians 'barabis;' they speak a different dialect, and neither our dragoman nor the crew could understand half they said, which was one great cause of the loud tones used on this occasion and of the confusion which followed. When the old Reis was dancing, as before described, it was that his orders not being heard in the general uproar, they could not be obeyed, and he was declaring that the boat would be damaged, and that they should all pay for it. Even the crew were moved to laughter by his gestures. But at length he made himself understood, and the 'Cairo' passed safely up the third rapid. The passages narrow, the current increases in force, natives start up in large numbers from their dwellings behind the hills to help, and children come to shout along with the rest as we proceed. The three first rapids are passed, as already described, by means of small ropes fastened to the different rocks, and the exertions of the men in the water. The two last are the real falls, and the dahabëéh is taken up the fourth by the efforts of about sixty people, collected on the deck of the vessel, and pulling upon one large rope, fastened to a rock on the shore. When we had passed the fourth 'door,' there arose another scene, equalling that at the third. We were approaching the fifth rapid, and the old Reïs prepared to rest from the labours of the day; for some unknown reason our Reïs had told him we should remain here for the night, and do the next rapid to-morrow. Mohamed is furious; a sufficient number of hands have not been provided to pull the huge vessel up. But on we must and shall go! So, after a tremendous storm of words, the old Reïs shouts and halloos again. As though by magic, in all directions figures start up from behind every rock and hill, and at length a rope is fastened, and a procession of two hundred persons, including a number of children, who hasten to have a finger in the pie, is formed, extending from the dahabéëh to the summit of the rock. A large rope is fastened up there, and all pull upon it from the shore. The sheikh stands at the head, waving a white scarf aloft in triumph, and shouting encouragement, no doubt, along with the rest of his party; but so well do the old Reïs and all others remaining on the dahabëéh exercise their unwearied vocal organs, that, between them and the rushing of the Cataracts, the voices of the two hundred are literally drowned.

The moment we reach the top, Mohamed fires off a gun, and then comes up to us with a beaming countenance, congratulates and shakes hands with the 'Rajah' and the ladies. The Reïs and the pilot follow with their 'salaam.' And now the excitement is over, the noise gradually ceases as the 'extra hands' disappear behind the rocks, and all those on deck subside and squat down to munch a few dates and some brown bread, their frugal fare after all this hard labour. It was four hours since we had started from Assouan, we were in smooth water again, and an almost strange quiet and calm succeeded to the noise and savage excitement just experienced.

In half an hour's sail from the last rapid, the beautiful island of Philæ stood before us with its ruined temples and its palm-trees. There it lay as on a still lake, encircled by precipitous rocks and piles of rocks, every stone of which was reflected in the clear, still water beneath. It is indeed a lovely spot, this 'Sacred Isle,' as it has been called by some, and 'Beautiful Isle' by others; long might the eye feast unwearied upon the attractive scene, and gladly "come again to-morrow." We remained here till the morning of the 22nd, giving ourselves two full days to explore the ruins and to rest; for the excitement of the Cataracts had been rather fatiguing.

Philæ is like a gem on the water. It looks about one mile in length, and is covered with ruins of exquisitely carved colonnades, pillars, porticoes, and other portions of a temple dedicated to the Triad formerly worshipped here, viz., Osiris, Isis, and their son Horus. It is one of the many spots which lay claim to having been the burial-place of Osiris, whose death and resurrection are recorded in sculptures, on some of the walls of the Temple.

THE ISLAND OF PHILAE

Among the most interesting of the many other subjects, are the birth of Horus and a curious bird encircled by the lotus flower, having a serpent on one side, and on the other two priests in the act of worshipping another serpent suspended on a cross, which bears a great resemblance to the usual representations of the Brazen Serpent in the wilderness. We had considerable trouble in finding them out, owing to the blackening of the wall, by the 'mashals' (torches) of curious or thoughtless travellers. The temple of Philæ was commenced by Ptolemy Philadelphus B.C. 284, and accomplished during the reigns of succeeding monarchs. Many of the ruins are extremely perfect, and the colouring of blue and green still remains on the capitals of one very beautiful group of pillars, belonging to one of the porticoes of the temple, five on either side the entrance. The pillars are partly, and the walls and roofs entirely, covered with sculpture and hieroglyphics; and we were much interested in endeavouring with the aid of our various guide-books to decipher them.

The ascent of the bank, from the deck of the dahabëëh on one side, or from the row-boat on the other, approaches very nearly to the perpendicular: the natives, for there were natives even among the ruins, were collecting and throwing down the dust of the 'Sacred Isle,' to take it in boats to the opposite shore, to strew it over their fields; this dust being considered particularly good soil for the growth of corn and beans, the only articles of food besides dates, in which these poor creatures indulge. Up this hill of dust and rubbish, brave 'Cousin Phil' was carried by two of the sure-footed crew, though so steep was the ascent that it was necessary that these two should be supported, each by another Arab, to keep the first from falling down, with his precious charge. How they succeeded in getting him up, and about, and down again, is hard to say; we thought it was at the risk of breaking every bone in his body, if not in their own also. Once on the island they made with their hands and arms what Mohamed called an "English sedan chair;" and between this and his stick 'Cousin Phil' got about so well and was so much interested in the ruins, that he determined to repeat the expedition on the morrow.

Friday, Dec. 21st.—We took another look at the temple, and then we sat on a terrace before a more modern-looking chapel, shaded by a remarkably fine and tall group of date-trees, while the Arabs of our crew who accompanied us, plaited slippers most ingeniously from the leaves of the palm. We astonished their weak minds, by quickly copying another plait in the same material, from a little Nubian boy, who was called upon to show his talent in basket-making; it being quite beyond their comprehension that we could copy them without ever having been taught. The boy then brought a shield which he had plaited from the same leaves in imitation of the shield of crocodile skin used by the natives of the

Khartoum, and taking a reed in one hand for a spear, he acted a sham fight with another boy for our amusement. Very pretty, indeed, it was to see the graceful attitudes into which they threw themselves; and how lightly they jumped and sprang from side to side, and round their adversary, to elude his darts. Thus we whiled away the lovely morning hours, and in the afternoon we came again to sketch the beautiful portico.

On the opposite shore, called 'Pharaoh's Bed,' there are a few small ruins, backed by high, wild-looking rocks of red granite, up which I scrambled quickly to obtain a view of the landscape. By far the best view of the island with its ruins and its trees is obtained from thence; the deep blue belt of water surrounding it; the clear reflections on its surface, the hills and the palm-trees of the coast beyond, together with the ruins and trees below, while all is quickened into life, as it were, by the roaring, rushing sound of the Cataracts heard in the distance.

A party of Nubians were sitting outside their small huts among the ruins at the foot of the hills. They were extremely dark, and even the women wore hardly a pretence to any covering beyond that of their long hair, plaited and plastered with castor oil, necklaces of beads, bracelets of ivory, and a leathern fringe tied round their loins, which is worn here by men and women alike. A woman was manufacturing the castor oil into a black paste for her hair, rolling it together with her hands. An old man was sick and begged for a little "oil and vinegar" in a broken soda-water bottle.

In the evening we went out again to see the island by moonlight. We landed and saw on the bank two dark figures, ready to receive us, with flaming 'mashals' in their hands. These torches are composed of a circular piece of wood placed at the end of a long pole above which is a sort of open case made of three or four hoops of iron, which is filled with burning wood. The Arabs shook them about so violently as they replenished them with fresh pieces, that showers of sparks and burning splinters were perpetually scattered around. The glaring flames, the white teeth set in the black faces, the noisy voices, the still ruins, rising more grandly in the surrounding darkness, and the lovely moon shining tranquilly above the whole, offered a strange and striking contrast. Our black attendants darted about hither and thither with their flaming brands; now they shoved us upon this stone, now upon that, in order that we might obtain a better view; the dragoman ordered the 'mashals' first behind one set of pillars then behind another; then up the tower staircases to the tops of the ruins, with those of the party who could mount so high, consenting to swallow an unlimited quantity of sand and dust, and to be half roasted in descending the narrow passages by the over-zealous Arabs, who would persist in thrusting the torches into their faces in order to light them down.

Had it not been a heathen temple which lay in ruins before us, we were inclined to think that the whole proceeding savoured a little of sacrilege: at the least, it was a rude intrusion upon the nocturnal stillness of these venerable precincts, and the silent moon seemed to look reproachfully down upon us.

The dragoman and crew, in the midst of their noise and excitement, frequently stood still, conversed together inquiringly upon the ruins, and apparently admired and appreciated them fully as much as we did. We decreed that Philæ had been very well shown off, and returned to the boat. "Taal hennee! Taal hennee!" ('Come hither! Come hither!') say the Arabs, and we jump from the dusty bank into a pair of black or brown arms stretched out to receive us into the boat, to which proceeding we are now becoming so accustomed, we think when we reach England again, we shall frequently look round for one of our faithful crew, to keep us from wetting our feet or soiling a new pair of shoes.

Mohamed was ill to-day from exposure to the sun, and we had to administer belladonna. Ali showed strong symptoms of ophthalmia, and we were called upon again. Selina dropped a drop of the preparation of zinc into his eyes, with a camel's hair brush, as he of his own accord laid himself down on the floor, rested his head against a chair, and held his poor eyes open. The pain of the application is great, and the brave manner in which the sleepy boy bore it, and asked for more until his eyes were quite cured, surprised us, and formed a striking contrast to the woe-begone looks of the sick dragoman. It provoked a smile to see his despair on the slightest indisposition; but by the morning our reputation as M.D.'s was established, and Mohamed's first words on entering the saloon were "Quite well, thank you, sir"—"Don't you lose that physic, please!"

Sunday, Dec. 23rd.—We arrived at Kalabshee, having yesterday bid a reluctant farewell to Philæ. Here we were close upon the tropic, naturally anticipating an extra roasting, but the day was comparatively cold. The thermometer pointed at sunrise to 47° outside the cabins, and 53° within the the saloon. At the hottest time of the day it was 75° in the shade; and 96° in the sun. A strong wind was blowing, and yet we were glad at noon to take refuge for a short time in the saloon. We sailed on and reached 'Gerf Hossayn' in the evening. A tiny village rose here and there in the desert waste, a very narrow strip of cultivated land bordered the river; and the only sound to be heard was the perpetual, melancholy creaking of the 'saghi' wheels. The air at 'Gerf Hossayn' being recommended for its purity and softness, we determined to spend two days there, and we found it quite deserving the praise bestowed upon it.

Monday, Dec. 24th, and Christmas Eve. This day was spent partly within, partly without the temple of 'Thah,' the Lord of Truth. It is of the time of Remeses the Great, B.C. 1311, is hewn in the solid rock, and must be seen by the light of the 'mashals.' Hundreds of bats rushed out from their hiding-places as the merry Arabs rushed in with their flaming brands. The figures on the pillars of this temple, as well as on those of the portico, are badly executed. Compared to others of the same period, they are thick and dumpy in their proportions; but we could not help admiring the perseverance which had accomplished a work of so much labour. There are single figures on all the pillars of the hall, and other groups of three, in high relief, on panels along one side, and on the wall of the adytum, in front of which stands the altar. Several chambers lie beyond, all in like manner covered with hieroglyphics, but so blackened by the smoke of the 'mashals' as to be now scarcely discernible. We spent some time in trying to make them out, till longing for fresher and purer air, we seated ourselves within the single line of shade afforded by a pillar of the portico, and sketched the grim figures upon its opposite neighbours. An animated conversation was meanwhile carried on by our 'suite.' The dragoman, with the 'clergyman' of the village, several of our crew, and some Nubians, who had joined the group, sat down among the fragments of the temple ruins. The names of the Reïs, the Pasha, the Rajah, the party, and all the towns on the Nile rejoicing in the name of a resident governor, were bandied about with sufficient frequency and gesticulation, to enable us to arrive at the drift of the whole.

Our Reïs had for some time past caused considerable annoyance on board; now requiring one of the crew to do duty so repeatedly out of his proper turn, that the victim at last resented it; now accusing Abdallah, who had the care of the commissariat department for the crew, of having ordered far more bread than was needed; now insisting upon punishing an offender with stripes, which Mohamed out of deference to us never would allow; and now wishing to dismiss some of the crew altogether. Upon this last announcement there was a strike, and the crew declared that if one of their number were dismissed they would all go, or they were "quite ready to put the Reïs into the river."

Thus the peace of our happy family had been perpetually disturbed, and the poor dragoman's system upset. He was always at work as peace-maker, endeavouring by persuasive eloquence to calm the raging passions around him, although he did fly into the most awful passions himself whenever he deemed it his "business" to do so, and was invariably ill with head-ache or violent attack of cold after each squall.

By the time we had arrived at Assouan his rage with the Reïs had reached its climax; and the governor, with whom the Reïs had been repeatedly threatened, and at whose supposed approach he had as frequently repented and promised to keep quiet for the future, at length appeared in the persons of his 'agent,' the chief magistrate of the place, and a rich merchant, who came probably as witness to the proceedings. On our return from a delightful row on the river one day just after sunset, Selina and I found these three dignitaries assembled, and seated on the divan opposite to 'Cousin Phil.' They were supposed to be honouring him with a visit, and he had had the pleasure of looking at them in silence for one hour, while Ali brought them coffee, lemonade, and pipes in succession. Selina and I joined the silent assembly, though silent they soon ceased to be.

The dragoman and dignitaries entered upon business. The Reïs was brought up and sat on the 'quarterdeck,' looking as hard as the rocks around him. Warmer and warmer waxed the discussion; colder and harder looked the Reïs; as first the dragoman, then the agent squatted before him, pulling him first by one shoulder, then by the other, as though they would try gently to shake a little reason into him. It was all of no use, and the peace-making dragoman's wrath was kindled; he poured forth a volume of Arabic, in which 'il contrato, il contrato' (the contract), held a very prominent position. He started to his feet, called "my man, Ali;" and the leathern bag containing the precious document was brought forth and submitted to the magistrate, who spelt it carefully through while the others stormed on. So long and fiercely did this debate continue, that we were obliged to retire to the saloon, and leave the Arabs to fight it out by themselves, 'Cousin Phil' first giving a very decided order to the magistrate, that this affair should be concluded, and peace restored before he left the dahabëëh,—a peace such as might last till our return to Cairo. The same message was conveyed to the obstreperous Reïs; and with a wholesome awe of "the Rajah from the London Parliament," or "Exhibition," by which high titles Mohamed indiscriminately endeavoured to express 'Cousin Phil's' importance, we left them all in possession of the 'quarterdeck.' By eight P.M. the business was "finished," as Mohamed expressed it, by a washing of his hands and gestures which would seem to indicate that the tiresome Reïs was blown away to the winds! He had promised good-behaviour for the future; his conduct was reported by letter to his master at Cairo; and a paper was drawn out by the magistrate, whereby on the next offence he might be displaced, and another Reïs taken in his stead.

The Reïs was thus silenced, but quarrelling is contagious, and the spirit had spread so far that there was further wrangling at Gerf Hossayn, and to our dismay this morning the culprit was the steersman El Abiad, the quietest man in the boat, whom we had even wished to carry away with us to Europe on account of his good looks and gentlemanly deportment. El Abiad (the white) was coal-black, but we fancied he had looked blacker by several shades for the last few days; the quarrel, however, was brought to an end by a strange ceremony which the Nubian pilot beckoned us privately to witness, as he stood with his black eyes twinkling up at us, to see how we should enjoy the fun. The parties were assembled in a hollow at a little distance, and both Reïs and steersman were made to kiss the dragoman's head. It was a ludicrous solemnity, as each one was almost forced to give the token of peace and good-will, a friendly hand literally pushing the unwilling penitents to touch the turban with their lips. The dragoman sat rather moodily, twisting a bit of palm-leaf in his fingers during the act of homage, and looking as if he were trying to keep down a spark of superior intelligence which told him that he ought to have been above the proceeding. All parties looked greatly relieved when it was over, but they hung down their heads, prayed, and then by slow degrees conversation recommenced. In the evening the deck was enlivened by the 'tom-tom' and other musical instruments pealing forth with redoubled energy, the dragoman himself joining the circle and clapping his hands to beat time along with the crew. The song was long and loud, and the whole village turned out on the bank to hear.

By this curious process peace was effectually restored, and Mohamed said it would be sealed again on the morrow by joint prayer in the mosque. Thus passed Christmas-eve, not unsuitably, though unwittingly so perhaps on the part of the Arabs; and when we expressed our hope that all the fighting was over, Mohamed replied with astonishment, "Fighting—no! these people never fight! Only Egyptians you know! Egyptians all mad!"

Be that as it may, Christmas-day 1860 dawned in peace on the Nile, and the rising sun dawned upon me, on one of the rocky eminences as far away in the desert as I could penetrate by that early hour. The Christmas hymns were sung in this wildly grand scene; grand in its extent of barrenness; the hoo-poo sang too on the porch of the ruined heathen temple, bobbing its pretty crested head on its striped breast, singing its peculiar note, "Hoo, hoo, hoo! Hoo, hoo, hoo!" A small black bird with snow-white head came near to listen, without any fear of harm; and these with my companion 'El Abiad,' were the only living things in sight, throughout the desert waste.

Breakfast came in due time, Christmas greetings and good wishes along with it, and thoughts and talk of the parties assembled at home, when in came our faithful dragoman, with a beaming countenance, a hearty shake of the hands, and "Good morning, sir!" to each of us in turn, irrespective of sex. He had, for some time past, looked forward eagerly to the arrival of this day, and now, having hoisted three additional flags, had determined to celebrate it in proper style. Off he goes; and presently the stillness is broken by a loud burst of voices, shouting "Hōōp, hōōp, hōōp, hōōr-rōōh!" three times repeated. The picked musicians of the crew are found assembled in a circle at the door of the cabin. Mohamed, dressed in his best, his back to the cabin-door, bends forward, and all the other heads follow the lead; each eye is fixed on the mouth of its opposite neighbour, and every muscle shows the most earnest desire that the cheer shall be simultaneous. The "three times three" over, the chief singer starts the song which the chivalrous crew had composed in honour of Selina, "The best of the flowers in the garden! The sun of the sultan!" Another cheer, three times repeated, and then comes the song for me, "The rising moon! The light of the house!" A concluding cheer, louder than ever, and then the full band squat on the deck, and music and singing continue uninterruptedly, whilst breakfast goes forward with extra good fare on the table. It was a noisy way of ushering in the solemnity of Christmas morning; but we were very much pleased with our new style of "English Christmas," as Mohamed called it; and I doubt whether it had not the desired effect in making us feel much more Christmas-like at the end of the outburst from the good-natured Arabs than before. 'Cousin Phil' gave a sheep to the crew for their Christmas dinner, and a present in money to the dragoman, Ali, and the cook, the latter coming by his own request at dinner-time, to lay his Christmas pudding on the table with his own hands. He bowed, kissed hands, and, with a delighted countenance, placed before us a castellated elevation of almond 'hard-bake,' extremely nice for young teeth, but, from its hardness, not quite so universal a Christmas pudding as that in which our friends at home, old as well as young, will have indulged. The dinner was as princely as the Nile and the dahabëëh could make it, albeit the characteristics were almonds and 'mishmish,' instead of roast beef and plum-pudding. The real plum-pudding had appeared two days before, as though by anticipation, in the form of an extremely plain and heavy manufacture, but all flaming in Christmas fire; not, however, considered by cook or dragoman in any way so suitable to Christmas-day as their almond castle.

The tropic had resumed its natural heat, and the thermometer pointed to 85° in the shade, and 110° in the sun. The flies would not be behindhand; they imprinted their Christmas wishes more perseveringly than ever in the corners of the eyes of every one of us. The fly-flap waved incessantly this way and that, while 'Cousin Phil' read the Christmas services in the little saloon; and then, as we sallied forth to the temple again, to sketch the shattered gods, we thought with gratitude how the lowly and miraculous birth which we commemorate this day had destroyed their heathen worship; and we breathed a heartfelt prayer for that blessed time when the Light which shone forth from the manger in Bethlehem, shall shine freely and unobscured in the Moslem land.

The day was closed with a row on the river, and a visit to a small village, whose wild inhabitants looked wilder than any we had yet seen as they grinned at us, with their rows of white teeth, very much as if, in their own minds, they would return to us the compliment which we were inwardly paying to them.

Wednesday, Dec. 26th.—The 'Cairo' sailed away again. We had much enjoyed the delightful air of Gerf Hossayn, and looked out for more such on our way. The thermometer pointed the same as yesterday; the wind was fair, so that the awning, happily for us, was left up, and the ladies, with sketch-book, novel, and needle-work, 'Cousin Phil' with Herodotus and the flies, passed the hours of the tropical day very pleasantly.

The breeze was refreshing, the sky of the brightest blue, the desert sand on either side a brilliant buff colour, and one bank of this sand so clearly reflected in a sheet of water left on the deposit, that for a long time we could not persuade ourselves that it was a mere reflection. We passed the Temple of Dakke, and stopped for the night at Maharraka, a small village, where the women were grinding corn in bits of a broken vessel, by rolling a stone over it with their hands. Their hair was elaborately plaited, and daubed with castor oil; the children were perfectly naked, and, notwithstanding their black skins, some of them really pretty.

Thursday, Dec. 27th.—We sailed on with a side wind, the thermometer still the same, 85° and 110°, yet the awning was not allowed to be raised. Selina took refuge in the cabin, and, for want of better occupation, sketched its interior; 'Cousin Phil' fell asleep on the divan, inside his umbrella; I sat by, and, having secured the four corners of my writing paper, with some fragments of 'Memnon' and the 'Cataracts,' proceeded to write, with pen in one hand, umbrella in the other, my mother's neutral-tint spectacles to keep off ophthalmia, and a veil closely tucked under my chin, but ineffectual to baffle the undaunted flies. It certainly was writing under difficulties.

Here a Nubian paddled across on a boat made of three bundles of cane, tied together, and floated on the water. We stopped at a small village, to bargain for a calf which was discovered there; but the price was too high for the dragoman's purse; so the calf was allowed to live a little longer, and we to go without the intended veal.

About this time poor Sarah's eyes had begun to show symptoms of ophthalmia, and now she kneels within her cabin-door, with clasped hands and upraised head, to receive into her eyes the dreaded drop of zinc. She looked as if she thought her last hour was at hand, but flinched under the operation even less than Ali, and we began to wonder whether we should be as brave should our turn come round.

At four P.M. the 'Cairo' stopped at Sabooa. The hills on the eastern shore were suffused with a deep, rich purple colour, contrasting beautifully with the bright yellow sand on the western side. A golden sunset soon glowed behind the lions of the temple, and the silver moon, nearly at 'the full,' rose in the clear blue vault above. We did not land this evening, but the crew jumped on shore, and, with amusing avidity, started hopping and jumping matches on the mud-bank, with all the ardour of schoolboys. Even the fat, heavy-looking dragoman surprised the company by the high springs in the air with which he led off the fun. The lines were brought out in the evening, and we tried our luck again at fishing. Alas! my hands generously gave away bait after bait to the hungry fish, who called again and again, and most ungratefully swam away unhurt. Presently Selina's line was pulled with a vigorous grasp. Such an enormous fish bites, that she cannot draw it in by herself. The dragoman pulls, the captured creature pulls; the dragoman chuckles and dances for joy. It cannot be a fish; it must be a crocodile, at the least. Not very digestible food, perhaps; but the excitement and suspense are great. The pilot has taken the small boat, in quest of food, to the opposite shore, whence is heard the sound of a wedding festival—a shrill cry of female voices, irresistible as the song of the syren to our Arab boatmen, who are, therefore, not likely to return in a hurry to help us—so Selina and her monster play at cup and ball for some little time, while the bark of a wolf adds to the novelty of the scene, and, finally, the creature relinquishes its hold, and turns out, after all, to be nothing but a large stone.

The cry which reached us from the distant village was made by the women attending a wedding procession, and is called by the Arabs 'zagharit.' It somewhat resembles the sharp note of the fife, but so loud that it seems to pierce the brain. In producing this extraordinary noise the tongue is rolled in the mouth, while the voice is raised to a higher pitch than we could previously have conceived to be possible.

Friday, Dec. 28th.—The broiling appearance of Saboon had well-nigh frightened us away, despite the eulogium which Mohamed had made on the bracing qualities of its atmosphere; but we did remain, and spent one very pleasant day there after all. First I took my morning constitutional, and enjoyed the lovely moon and the sunrise, the Arab who attended me helping me over every stone and up every hill, by clutching at my left shoulder in a most lop-sided fashion, which we could call by no other name than 'pinioning.' Close by the temple the sand lies so thick that the whole of a lady's boot will disappear at each step. Further on, the walk was a rough one; and the trophy of the morning's excursion was the jaw-bone of a camel, which lay bleaching on one of the rocks, little thinking that it was destined to take a journey into Europe. The chair and our whole party set out after breakfast to see the temple. The bank was extremely steep, and Selina was mounted on high, and carried up by the pilot and steersman. The dragoman had perceived the injurious effect upon her health of all these steep climbings, and had decreed that, for the future, she was to be carried as well as 'pa-pa.' Of course she made a fuss about it, as young ladies will do; but this was all the more fun for Mohamed. He always carried her himself, when he could be spared to do so; and it was very amusing to see how cautiously he now assembled his forces. Two pair of strong arms seized the lady and raised her aloft, just as she was quietly lifting her foot, in the expectation of re-plunging it into the dust from which she should have been so thankful to escape. Gratitude came only when the top of the hill was reached, and the bearers were repaid with most gracious smiles, and assurances that she could walk quite well by herself. The faithful bearers were notwithstanding, ever at hand; and it is but fair to state, that each man in the dahabëëh was always ready to fulfil any little duty for any one of our party, in the most good-natured and good-tempered manner.

The temple of Sabooa is of the time of Rameses

the Great. In front, at some distance from it, are two lions, and two pillars with hieroglyphics upon them. Portions of the other lions or sphinxes, which probably led as an avenue to the temple, lie scattered about on the sand. The temple is built of sandstone, with the exception of the adytum, which is hewn in the rock. All but the towers and the tops of a few of the columns, is filled in with drifted sand, which is here remarkably clean, and of a very brilliant colour. We sat upon its sloping surface in the small extent of shade thrown by the towers, shifting our position along with it, until the noontide rays drove us back into the dahabëéh. The heat here was so intense, and the sand so burning hot as we stepped into it, that I felt convinced an egg might be baked in it. The Arabs said no, and, true to their nature, could not be prevailed upon to try. I, true to mine, of course did try, and popped one in; but, if the sand was not sufficiently hot to bake the egg, the sun proceeded to bake me so thoroughly for my obstinacy, that I was obliged to relinquish the experiment. Mohamed said that two months later the egg would have been baked at once.

The natives here were quite black. One of the women was spinning, with a very small spindle, some of the long brown wool, destined to make the loose garments worn by all the women here, in place of the blue cotton seen further north. The material is very thick and heavy, but, no doubt, serves better to keep off the burning rays of the tropical sun than a lighter one.

A stuffed hyena was brought to the boat in the course of the day by a party of wild-looking individuals, in the hope of gaining a little 'baksheesh' by letting us have a look at the creature. He looked very fierce, and as if he had done service as a show for many years. Mohamed, however, summarily dismissed him, and would have nothing to say to him. He and his owners contentedly seated themselves on the bank, determined at least to have a sight of us; and we had thus a full opportunity of examining his long fangs and striped white and black coat. The men sat the whole day long with the crew, evidently having nothing whatever to do. It seemed strange at first, but, after all, what can they have to do in this barren desert home of theirs?

A chameleon was next offered for sale, which claimed greater attention, and amused us for some days with its curious changes of colour. On its first appearance it was of a very pretty grass green shade, which became darker and lighter by turns. Brown spots, passing into every shade of yellow, and back to brown again, appeared and disappeared all over its body; the tail was at times black and then became green again. The shores of the Nile from hence to Derr, abound with these little creatures. They are a species of the lizard tribe. The head is very large and curiously hooded, and their prettily striped, globular eyes, turn every way, so that the chameleon enjoys the faculty so often, and so foolishly envied by man, of having eyes in the back of its head, as well as in the front. The effect upon our captive was evidently to make it frightfully timid. It apprehended danger on all sides, and like all the others which were brought to us, refused either to eat or drink a single thing, passing by even the flies and the ants, and looking so unhappy that we let it loose at Derr. The Arabs marvelled to see us take so much interest in what they regarded as an unclean beast. The dragoman would hardly look at it when we held it in our hands, and all showed a strong aversion to touching it. The fall of a crane and of two pretty turtle-doves under Thomas's gun on the opposite shore, together with a row to the village, closed the sport and the 'Natural History' of the last four-and-twenty hours. The inhabitants of the village were at first terrified at the appearance of the Europeans. When coaxed by the dragoman into fetching eggs for sale, they stared in mute amazement at the strangers, and finally resuming the natural powers of their tongues, talked so loudly and in such shrill tones, that while within reach of the bright steel axes, which the men carried on their shoulders for breaking up the soil, and under the savage influence of their sparkling eyes and grinning white teeth, it required some little amount of nerve to exhibit entire pleasure in their society. Their noise was, however, perfectly harmless: a little pumpkin dish with a crocodile ingeniously represented upon it, was filled with eggs which we purchased; and the boat pushed off again while the villagers rushed away to catch all their poultry, and returned yelling, to offer it for sale. The women wore brown woollen dresses, but they were not very particular about covering themselves with them; the children wore no clothing at all, the men hardly any.

Saturday, Dec. 29th.—At sunrise I trudged up the sand again, to finish my sketch of the temple. Little black Mohamed attended me. Of his own accord he placed himself so as to intercept the rays, which even at this early hour were inconvenient to me. When his services in that way were not needed he skipped to the other side, squatted down and insisted on relieving me of the weight of my paint-box. He was a most active little fellow, and always ready to do anything, even before he was asked; but we were summoned to the boat, the milk for breakfast was procured, and at eight A.M. the 'Cairo' resumed her course. There was but little wind, and that little was contrary, so that 'tracking' was again the only means of proceeding. So it continued for several days, and we were long in reaching Korosko; but as we draw nearer to the town, the belt of vegetation increases, the palm-trees become more numerous and very fine, while small gardens are perceived here and there, if I may call them gardens, when a very few green leaves of cucumbers, onions, or lupines, are all the produce they can boast.

The first of these 'tracking' days was enlivened and shortened by a long pause at a small village to take in stores. The crew, as was their wont, had helped themselves as they went along to some fine branches of acacia which were lying on the bank, to use for fuel. The villagers rushed down, and by the noise and clatter which ensued, it might have been supposed that they were threatening all the terrors of the law upon the marauders. They were only bargaining for the payment. Mohamed sat dignified and satisfied on a chair on the deck, whilst branches, eggs, chickens, milk, a goat and dried dates for the crew as hard as walnuts, were offered, bargained for, rejected on the one side, walked away with on the other, and as regularly brought back again and delivered over for the originally proffered price. The wild and savage dignity of some of the women, as they walked away with their babies on one arm, shoulder, or hip; their bowl full of eggs or milk, on their heads; and the bundle of unfortunate chickens or pigeons pinioned by the other hand, was very striking; whilst their shrill voices pierced our brains as they rattled out their abuse no doubt, of our stinginess. There was one ugly creature in particular who clamoured for herself and for the whole of the population of the village, men, women, and children, better, we feel sure, than any virago of any complexion, ever has done before her, or we trust ever will do again. How she kept up her voice to its extraordinary pitch, for such a length of time we were at a loss to imagine; for we could hear it still as we 'tracked' along, when she was far out of sight. It was on the whole a fiendish scene, in which the weaker sex showed themselves by no means behind the stronger. Half the noise was caused by the unwillingness of the villagers to hand over their property, until the payment was placed in their hands, and the determination of our dragoman to receive the goods first, and to pay for them afterwards.

The succeeding calm was agreeable, and we stopped for the night under some of the desert hills. Sarah and I proceeded, unattended, to ascend the high rock, to see what was to be seen at the top, but we were quickly made to retrace our steps. There are snakes on those rocky hills whose bite is so venomous as sometimes to cause instantaneous death. A man of the village produced one immediately, which he had shot that morning on this very hill. It was about one and a half feet long, of a light pinkish colour. The pilot said his mother had died some time since from the bite of a similar snake, surviving only a few days. We could not find that they were aware of any antidote for this poison.

Sunday, Dec. 30th.—Our Church Service was almost undisturbed by flies to-day, a rare event, and no small relief to all parties. The bank along which the 'trackers' walked and clambered was prettily wooded with the 'sont,' which is used for building the Nile boats. The Egyptian jessamine, its leaves a bright yellow-green, hung in rich clusters over every stone and stump, like the clematis at home; but there was no flower upon it. This was succeeded by a large quantity of the 'sensitive mimosa,' growing like a luxuriant briar all over the bank. It folded up its leaves quite tightly, on the slightest touch of our hands; and even as we stood by, talking about it, our breath produced the same effect, and very soon the whole shrub was withered up. The leaves and branches which we gathered did not revive in water, but shrivelled up and became quite dry and crisp, nor would the water soak into a small branch which was plunged in and left there for a long time; the drops rolled off like balls of quicksilver. Some of our crew were acquainted with the plant, and called it by the name of one of the Pashas. The dragoman and the greater number of them had never observed it before; and his nerves were decidedly shaken by a contemplation of its supernatural qualities.

Monday, Dec. 31st.—The last of the year had come round again and we tracked it out. The wind was still contrary, and, as if to remind us of the season in our own homes, the tropical climate assumed a chilling temperature. The thermometer fell to 17° at sunrise, 75° in the shade at noonday, and to 96° in the sun. Yesterday it had pointed to 112°. Rocks in the bed of the river, and numerous mud-banks, impeded the progress of the dahabëéh. A strong wind at times blew us close upon them, and the skill of the Nubian pilot was in constant requisition. In one or two places, where the current was strong, we were reminded of the passage of the cataracts. We could not manage to reach Korosko, but moored again within a mile and a half of the town. The distance from Saboon might with a fair wind have been accomplished in a few hours: this was our third day, and we had not reached it yet. Time had not, however, hung heavily on our hands, and by way of lightening the burthen still further we had begun a series of portraits of our dark companions, to their immense satisfaction. The art with us was quite in its infancy, but they were good subjects to practise upon, and we thought it fortunate that they were so easily pleased as to discover striking likenesses in every picture which we produced. Most of them were young men, and had smooth faces, but those who possessed beards or mustachios were very particular that not one hair less than they could boast should be depicted on the paper.

CHAPTER VI.

FROM KOROSKO TO WADEE HALFEH.

At 8 A.M. on New-year's morning, *Jan. 1st*, 1861, the shout of arrival of the crew, sounding rather like "A happy new year to you all!" announced that the 'Cairo' had at length reached Korosko. Korosko is very prettily situated in the midst of a range of hills, upon which a beautiful purple shade was now resting. It is a halting-place for the caravans from the interior, and hearing that there was one now actually resting on the hills, we deemed ourselves fortunate in having so interesting an object for our first expedition in the new year. There were no donkeys waiting to be hired, but the pilot applied to the sheikh, and two were produced, totally devoid of accoutrements. Our side-saddles were placed on their backs, on the top of the scarfs of some of the crew, which they lent for the purpose, as it was supposed the saddles would not fit without them. A bit of rope was tied to the donkeys' heads; Mohamed cries, "Trust to me," and away we go, following the "Rajah's chair," which is carried by four of the crew, chanting as they go. One donkey-boy leads our steeds by the hair of their heads, and another insists on holding us on behind, which very nearly pulls us off. A large and black company follow in our train; and thus one caravan winds along to see the other.

Alas! the gum Arabic, the ivory, and the wax, had already been disposed of in cargo-boats, for further transport by water, and we did not see so much as we had expected. The road was extremely picturesque and striking, lying over huge blocks of stone and heaps of dust, through a ravine in the rocky hills. There are many such ravines in this neighbourhood, down which the tropical rains from the interior force their way to the river; sometimes destroying whole villages, and uprooting as many as two or three hundred trees in their course. At this moment, all the camels of the caravan were lying about the ravine in groups. The saddles were arranged in semi-circular heaps among the stones; and water-skins and empty baskets were scattered all around. It was reported that this caravan consisted of 600 camels. We saw only about 50.

The owners of the camels and the goods drew near, and formed a circle round the strangers. They came from the Khartoum. This word signifies a promontory, or point of land, and was applied to that portion comprised between the streams of the White and the Blue Rivers. After the conquest of Soudan by Mohamed Ali, the seat of government was established there, and a town was built which retains the name of Khartoum.

The greater number of the dark, half-dressed savages wore their hair closely cropped on the crown of the head, whilst on either side it stood out horizontally, and a little bit of stick was passed through it and left there by way of a comb. Some of them plaited it into a number of small tresses, leaving the ends about two inches long, to form an ornamental bushy fringe all round; others wore thick plaits across the head, and falling down straight behind. A few had large whiskers, which, in spite of their dark copper-coloured complexions, gave them quite an European appearance. The features of many among them were handsome, and all had an independent bearing, which presented a great and pleasing contrast to the cowed and effeminate looks of the Egyptians, who bear in their countenances all the marks of a conquered people.

The circle pressed closely round, too close to be quite pleasant, and Mohamed asked them to show us their manner of fighting, this being apparently their one accomplishment. Three very large, bright, and sharp swords were immediately drawn and passed round, as each Khartoum man in his turn went through a series of sword-cuts and high jumps and springs, pointing the terrible blades systematically at 'Cousin Phil,' and thrusting them constantly within a few inches of his chair. He smiled at the enemy and thoroughly enjoyed the performance; the ladies did not half like the fun, and trembled just a very little at the spectacle. The war-cry was given by striking the lips quickly with the fingers, and at the same time uttering a loud, high-pitched sound with the voice. The mimic war gave great satisfaction to the performers, who would have carried it on for any length of time, but when we had witnessed it for about a quarter of an hour, we judged it prudent to retire. Mohamed gave them 'baksheesh.' After some clamouring they went off, but to our dismay returned in half a minute. It appeared that they had two sheikhs, who ought to have divided the spoil among their men; but one of them had kept the whole, and the other now came to beg for more. Their eyes glared so fiercely, that we looked up at Mohamed's countenance, expecting to see there that this was another case in which "we be afraid certainly." But Mohamed apparently understood the nature of his own race better than that of snakes or crocodiles, and he was never afraid of them. He gave them no more, and they went quietly away. He said they would fight it out among themselves, but would not dare to say a word to him. We were delighted to hear it, although it appeared to us rather unaccountable; and though glad to have made acquaintance with our Khartoum friends, their aspect had frightened us sufficiently to make us very thankful that we were safe out of their reach.

On our return, we passed by the graves of three

Austrians, lying in the wild ravine. One of them has a head-stone with the following inscription upon it: "The Rev. D. Würnitz, Miss. Cen. Afr. died Feb. 4th, 1856." It seemed dreary that the poor missionary should lie there with his companions in the wild desert waste, so far from his home; but their graves were evidently as much respected as they could have been in a Christian land, though surrounded only by small bits of stone to mark the spot, just like the Moslem graves. It was touching to see in the desert land, proofs that the tenderest feelings of our nature may be shared alike by savage as by civilised man, and evinced by exactly similar acts. Just as the Christian will strew the loveliest flowers over the graves of those he has loved on earth, so here, in many small villages, the Moslem had gathered smooth round pebbles from the sandy plain and scattered them over the resting-places of his lost ones. A striking expression, too, we thought it, of the deadness of his faith, compared to the life-giving faith of the Christian.

It is a curious feature in the rocky desert, where hill rises behind hill as far as the eye can reach, that there frequently intervenes a perfectly flat plain of fine sand, strewn all over with smooth yellow pebbles, such as we are accustomed to see only on the sea-shore: and from these the bereaved Nubian gathers, as it were, the flowers for his graves.

The wind was very cold. The thermometer fell to 46°, and did not rise above 64° in the sun. Yesterday, towards evening, a thick mist enveloped the whole landscape. We should have called it a fog, could we have supposed such a thing as fog to rise in the clear air of Egypt. Mohamed scouted the idea, and said again that it was wind. We found that a mist rises frequently in this part of the valley of the Nile, caused by a wind from the desert. It felt very unnatural and very unpleasant, but this was the only occasion on which we were inconvenienced by it. At Korosko, we had an opportunity of making a sketch of a woman grinding at a mill. She was a Nubian, and was slightly covered with a dust-coloured garment, and wore bracelets of bone on her arms. She sat on the ground with her mill-stone, in front of her mud-dwelling, and ground all day and all night for our crew, without any respite or assistance. The supply of bread, notwithstanding the assertions of the troublesome Reïs, was likely already to prove insufficient, and the crew were obliged to procure what they could here. It was mixed barley and Indian corn. This they made into a kind of pancake, which they fried with a little oil. The Pilot, Reïs, Dragoman, &c., each made their own cakes and ate them quite hot, for had they been allowed to grow cold, they would have become too hard even for the masticating powers of the Arabs. When the crew had them for breakfast, they were broken up into pieces, in the large wooden bowl, and soaked in the boiling lentile soup, seasoned with fried onions. It was a savoury mess; too much so for our olfactory nerves, and a decided come-down from the usual fare. The men missed the good brown bread made of the whole wheat meal; the Reïs, Ali, and the cook, missed the small brown loaves of a finer quality with which they always provided themselves; and the dragoman missed the fine white French flour, which he indulged in with his masters, because, as he said, he had "very weak stomach!" They were, however, very good-humoured about it, and having scolded the Reïs, one and all appeared to find the coarse pancakes extremely good, for, until we reached Girgeh again, they knew they could get nothing better.

A dahabëéh arrived here on its return homewards. Cards were immediately exchanged, with inquiries for letters from Thebes on the one side, and the favour of posting at Thebes on the other. "Any letters from Thebes?" on the Nile answers to "Fine weather this morning!" at home, and serves as the commencement to many a sociable chat; and a sociable chat with white faces and warm hearts brightens up the Nile scenery, as well as any other scenery, considerably. Mr. R—— had come to Egypt for his health, but he said he did not return benefited. Neither he nor his wife had ever left home before, and so great were its charms for them, that they considered the valley of the Rhone ugly; and, unlike the roving spirits of the day, they seemed quite unhappy at being so far away from England. They willingly undertook to post our letters, and thus afforded us the unexpected satisfaction of being able to forward new year wishes to our friends on new year's day itself; albeit they would not reach their destination quite so soon as by the London Penny Post. Every dahabëëh on its way home inquires for letters and news from those coming up the river; although no one would run the risk of taking letters up for another party, unless a previous arrangement to that effect had been made. In any case there is danger of missing them, and we came across one instance of this in which the night-watch had overlooked the returning dahabëëh, and had either passed on themselves, or suffered the other to pass by without hailing it; so that the letters made the journey up to the second Cataracts, and all the way back again as far as Cairo, before they reached their unfortunate owner.

Wednesday, Jan. 2nd.—We left Korosko. The weather began to resume its tropical temperature, and the thermometer rose considerably; but Selina shivered, for the wind was contrary and very keen, notwithstanding the heat of the sun. The 'trackers' tracked on till four P.M., and then we were obliged to stop. The hills which rise all round this spot are very beautiful, and of most peculiar forms; the greater number exhibiting much the same outline as the high-pitched roofs of European houses, while some bear a strange resemblance to the Pyramids. May they not have suggested the form of these interesting piles to their ingenious architects, who seem to have copied nature in most of their works.

We landed, and Selina sat down on a stone, enchanted with the gorgeous sunset. 'Cousin Phil' walked and sat by turns, Mohamed at his side, making very ungallant exclamations on the women who came forward to admire the strangers. "Ugh! how ugly!" exclaims the Arab, so frequently that polite 'Cousin Phil' forgets himself, and exclaims, turning round to Selina, "Pooh, the castor oil! My dear, I think these people can never require a dose of it!" The 'fair sex' here were ugly indeed, and smelt of the castor oil with which their hair was bedaubed to such an extent, that it was impossible for any but a Nubian nose to endure their near approach.

I walked out with El Abiad to one of the curious-looking hills, but dinner-time, inexorable dinner-time, obliged me to return without climbing it. Next morning, El Abiad and I started again before sunrise. He could not understand my pleasure in climbing these hard rocks, and wanted to carry me all the way himself. He would soon have changed his mind, had I allowed him to try, but he helped me along most gallantly, and looked at me with unfeigned astonishment when he saw me at the top of the hill which I had pointed to as the object of my ambition. There I enjoyed the wildest, most extensive, and characteristic view of desert land that I had yet seen. A vast extent of curiously-shaped rocky hills and mounds of sand, intermingled with the smooth pebbly plains mentioned above, was stretched before and around me. The narrow tracks along which the caravans from the interior wend their burning way could be traced on all sides, and looked parched and uninviting indeed, and the eye rested with pleasure on the blue line of water, and the gaily painted 'Cairo' in the distance. At eight A.M. we were off again, as soon as the milk for breakfast had arrived; we reached Derr at four P.M., passing by refreshing green plantations of beans, lupines, wheat, the castor-oil plant, and remarkably fine specimens of the date-palm. This district abounds in date-trees, and between Korosko and Derr it is reckoned that 20,000 of them are taxed; this being one of the regular taxes of the country.

Derr is quite a comfortable-looking town. It is the capital of Nubia, and is worthy the distinction, for the houses are much larger and better built than in any of its other towns. They all have doors, and at least the appearance of cleanliness. The streets, though three or four inches thick in unavoidable dust, are also very clean. There are large open spaces, 'squares' we might call them, planted round with date-trees, which Mohamed said were used for the meetings of the 'Parliament,' by which grand title he designated any meeting of any kind, in village or town. The date-trees are all protected by little mud walls to the height of four or five feet, and in the centre of one of the squares is a large 'Egyptian fig-tree,' (a species of sycamore). Some of the fruit was brought to us to taste. It was the size of a very small fig, only half-ripe, and full of an extraordinary blight of small black flies, which, despite their well-formed wings, the Arab refused to see, and we have reason to believe that he afterwards devoured figs, flies and all, and thought us very silly for allowing him the chance.

Close on the river's bank is a Roman ruin, overshadowed by one of these large trees, and now inhabited by some of the grandees of Derr. It is a picturesque object, and is backed by a large grove of beautiful palm-trees, all equally protected with walls like those in the square. Under one of them we observed a small mud trough with three circular holes in it, quite black with the castor-oil mixture which had been manufactured in it by the 'belles' of Derr. The population of Derr is of every shade of colour, but the generality of the people are much fairer than in other Nubian towns. Some of them seemed to be really white, but they were not pretty in our eyes, although they were white. They are the descendants of some Bosnian soldiers; they pride themselves on their fair complexions, and are far better dressed than their neighbours. The women in general wear a dark-blue checked cotton dress, and cover their faces carefully ; the men wear light sky blue calico robes, and handsome white turbans, and even the children are all covered in one way or another. Ivory bracelets, necklaces, and a few ornaments in the plaits of their hair, are worn by all the women, and some had silver anklets, but this ornament is chiefly confined to the children. As we sat in our dahabëëh, we watched the women coming down to fetch water from the river. The water-pitchers here are of a globular form; they are carried on a small cushion on the head, supported very slightly with one hand, or frequently balanced without any support at all. The women came down to the river in groups and pairs, and when they had filled their vessels, which they accomplished by means of a small pumpkin dish, one of the girls would place one burden on her companion's head, then hand her a second, which she, though laden herself, placed on the head of the other, and then, hand in hand, they walked up the bank together. The tall figures, the well-poised jars, the flowing drapery, though draggle-tailed to the greatest extent, had an extremely elegant effect; but the features of the women were unfortunately plain.

Our walk through the streets of Derr was very amusing. The whole population of the place turned out to see us. About every ten minutes or so, they were put to flight by a servant of the magistrate who had joined our party. He flourished a long wand in his hand, and shouted in Arabic, that all the ladies should retire on the approach of the "great Rajah!" The first shout set them all flying straight into their houses. Many of them, true to the customs of their country, closed their doors, and did not even peep through. Whether those who did peep were emboldened by the benign looks of the 'Rajah,' and the evident amusement of the whole party, or that with them, as with their still more pale-faced sisters, curiosity could gain the day, we cannot say, but certain it is that the greater number came forth again, and at every corner a little crowd was assembled, closely packed in rows rising one behind the other on the raised seats against the walls of the houses, to have a look at us, The women carefully covered their mouths with their hands, and stood almost with one foot in the air, ready to take flight again on the slightest alarm. Some of the best dressed among them, when they perceived that they were individually objects of attention, turned with a dignified, queenly air, and walked away into their houses, as though they would have said, "How very rude you are! How dare you look at me?"

On our return we found that another dahabëéh had arrived. It was Mr. H——'s. He was looking all the better for his trip, and was now on his way home. We had by this time decided on remaining four months on the river instead of three, so that we took it more leisurely than our neighbours, who were, for the most part, satisfied with three months or less. We compared watches, and found that there was a difference of one hour between us; of course, neither party could be persuaded that they were wrong, and so we continued keeping our own time. Mr. H—— was to dine with us. The sudden announcement of a guest to dinner caused some very long faces in the kitchen department. Mohamed, on his usual plan of being first in everything, did not think he could provide food enough for this one guest under twenty-four hours' notice. He heaped upon the kitchen fire as much food as if the whole British army were coming to dine with us; and he put on the table as much of it as the table would hold. It was fortunate, in the eyes of the excited dragoman, that the mutton was that of a Korosko sheep; a very large and handsome kind, which surprised us so much on their first appearance on the bank, that we could not determine at once whether they were sheep or no. They were nearly as tall as a young calf, of a pretty fawn colour, with long pendent ears like goats, and apparently covered with hair instead of wool, but the natives said that their wool was not yet grown. The mutton was as truly superior to that of the poor black creatures, that had hitherto graced our table, as was the whole living appearance of the animal. Mr. H—— had not tasted such mutton for a long time; neither, perhaps, had he seen such tightly-packed dishes for an equally long period; but quantity, not quality, was our dragoman's notion of style, and we could not persuade him that it was not ours also. He looked as pleased as possible, and chuckled within himself, in full confidence that his dinner would far surpass that which Mr. H——'s dragoman could produce on the morrow, when we were to dine with him.

Alas, for Mohamed! Suliman's table produced 'soupe à la Julienne;' salmon, with shrimp sauce; roast beef of old England, and, to crown all, an English plum-pudding.

Mohamed positively trembled; he had worried his brains with fruitless attempts at this latter dish, till, finally, it was discovered that the *currants* had been forgotten, and with a very small allowance of raisins, a quantity of stone pines, and very bad suet, the Arab cook could hardly be expected to turn out a rich Buckingham pudding. With this discovery, and the conviction that the chickens and pigeons of his beloved Nile were better far, and far more wholesome, than all the potted dishes of Fortnum and Mason, and that no cook could surpass our cook, Mohamed rocked himself into a quiet resignation to his fate. The 'Cairo' was first in everything but plum-pudding; and seeing that we did not take this too much to heart, the dragoman preserved his high opinion of himself, and the plum-pudding was forgotten.

But we must not forget the Temple. The Temple of Derr is of the time of Rameses the Great, and, like that of Gerf Hossayn, is hewn in the solid rock. It has but two side-chambers, and the hall is so encumbered with fallen masses from the roof, that it is difficult to explore it. It has two rows of columns, without figures upon them, but with more hieroglyphics than at Gerf Hossayn. Behind, on the hill, there are several small chambers excavated in the rock, but apparently unconnected with the temple.

Saturday, Jan. 5th.—We were still at Derr. This was a broiling day; the thermometer, though not above 79° in the shade, rose to 112° in the sun. We made two rowing expeditions, and walked with 'Cousin Phil' on a fine dry bank on the opposite side of the river. Mohamed here suddenly proposed that he, with his own good hand, should try the effect of 'shampooing' upon 'Cousin Phil.' "In eight days," declares the enthusiastic Arab, "you walk upright." He asserts it, promises it, will make a contract to that effect, and pay one hundred pounds if his words do not come true. Shampooing, like Nile water, is infallible in his eyes, and suiting the action to the word, he shows on his own supple limbs how each limb is to be rubbed, and each joint 'cracked,' in order to make 'the blood flow every way.' His rough hand next assails 'Cousin Phil's' hand. He said, quietly, that it was enough to rub the skin off, but he gave Mohamed leave to try. The dragoman's zeal kept up for some days: he would not be asked any questions on the subject, lest, like those regarding the wind, they should 'spoil it all.' But gradually he perceived that shampooing was not likely to produce the magical effect anticipated, and so his zeal cooled down, the mornings became too cold and the experiment died a natural death, though nothing more was heard of the hundred-pound forfeit.

Mr. H—— now showed us the collection of 'Scarabeus' which he had procured at Karnak. The ancient Egyptians were fond of using the form of the scarabeus (beetle) for their amulets and rings; it was carved on stones or bits of bright blue and green porcelain. On the under side of those that belonged to the kings, the royal monogram and the date of the king's reign are inscribed in hieroglyphics; they are frequently dug up in mummy-cases, and are highly valued by antiquarians. They may be set as brooches, bracelets, or even as necklaces; but we saw plainly that there would be none left for us at Karnak. Mr. H—— had bought them up, and tantalised us much by describing the beautiful ornaments they would make. He had been sufficiently knowing to visit Karnak on the way up the river, and so got the first choice. These treasures may be obtained from the Bedouins for a few piastres; but when once they pass into the hands of those who know the value set upon them by the lovers of antiquity, they fetch a fabulous price.

Sunday, Jan. 6th.—The two dahabëéhs moved on their respective ways. The morning of the Epiphany shone bright and tropical,—75° in the shade, 113° in the sun. A very large crocodile appeared basking on a bank close by; on the report of a gun it raised its huge body in full view, and plunged deliberately into the water. Our pilot pronounced it to be sixty feet in length; but since we had heard from our attendants that Adam, when he was created in Paradise, was "eighty yards long," "Eve about seventy-five yards," and that "two millions of men had died in the opening of one of the cataracts," we were not so much startled at the Arab computation as might have been expected. I do not know that any crocodiles have ever been seen on the Nile exceeding twenty-five feet, and this one must have been about that length. The oil of these creatures is valued by the natives as a cure for rheumatism. In Cairo and Alexandria they are frequently seen dried and stuffed, fixed on the walls or over the doors of houses as an ornament; probably also as a proof of the skill of the sportsman in obtaining them.

This was another hard day's 'tracking,' with very little sailing to relieve it. There were 'saghi' within fifty yards of one another, and the hum and groan of their wheels were incessant and painful, though the effect of their work was apparent in the brilliant green patches which they watered. They were very annoying to the crew, owing to the deep cuts made in the bank for them, which obliged the trackers to jump so frequently into the water, that they finally returned to the dahabëëh and worked her along by means of the boat-poles. One of these dropped into the river, and was carried along by the current. Hassan jumped in immediately and swam after it, till suddenly the shout of 'Temsah!' (crocodile) was heard among the crew, and fear and dread were imprinted on the countenances of his companions, who quickly lowered the boat to fetch him and his pole back again, lest he should become a prey to the hungry monster.

At length we reached the fortress of Ibreem, situated on the summit of a high cliff, sloping down to the water's edge but little out of the perpendicular. There are but few remains of the ancient building, or of the Roman epoch. The wall is said to be the work of the Romans. Ibreem was made a station for troops by Sultan Selim (1617). These troops were expelled by the Memlooks in 1811. The fortress can be ascended only from the inland side, and that ascent is steep. The range of hills, for some distance, is very fine. On many of them there are traces of unfinished figures carved on the rock; but the natural rock here frequently assumes a form so nearly approaching the human form, that it seems as though Nature herself had again come forward to suggest to the ancients their taste in this matter. Our curiosity in the matter of crocodiles was now in a fair way of being satisfied. A whispered "Temsah! Temsah!" (crocodile) was perpetually heard, and we saw five of these monsters basking in the sun on one bank in the middle of the river, and later in the day seven others on another bank. After these, no object of interest was to be seen on either side, till we came upon a portion of the bank very beautifully covered with a creeper in flower, which was probably the Egyptian jessamine; and a little further on a large bed of the sensitive mimosa, which greatly impeded the progress of the 'trackers.'

Tuesday, Jan. 8th.—During the four following days the thermometer rose to 84° in the shade, and 120° in the sun. We got out of the dahabëéh and walked along the shore, through a small village, in which the women were carrying on their various occupations in most primitive style. Several of them were spinning cotton on their tiny spindles; a mother was plaiting her daughter's hair into innumerably small plaits, and plastering it well down with castor oil, both seated on the ground outside their little mud-dwelling; another group were making a very rude kind of pottery, by kneading a red clay with their hands, and forming it into round bowls and dishes. The small mud oven in which they were to be baked, stood at a little distance in the centre of the village. Our road lay beyond, under fine date, dôm, and sont-trees. We sat sketching under one of them until the dahabëéh overtook us, when we re-embarked, after descending a rather precipitous bank.

'Aboo Simbel,' with its approaching temples, was now the topic of conversation. Mohamed, tired out by four days' calm, disobeyed orders, and allowed the anxious pilot and crew to take advantage of a rising breath of fair wind, and to make the attempt to pass it during the night. Suddenly, in the still hours, the sailing shout, and a very unusually soft, "Hayléc-Haylée-sah!" (the boatman's chant, 'God help us!') struck upon our ear, and we perceived that we were moving. We had no notion of being "done" in this quiet way, and immediately put a stop to the proceeding, saying that we had not come up the Nile to pass Aboo Simbel in the dark. Mohamed was crest-fallen, not so much at having displeased us, as at being found out; but he considerably upset our gravity when the reproof being ended, he patted Selina patronisingly on the back, saying in a beseeching tone, "Finished now? Very well!"

The wind would not blow for us the next morning, and the Arab world evidently thought us duly punished for our obstinacy of the last night, as we were obliged to stop against a mud-bank during six daylight hours. But it was to us a sort of prize bank, so dry, extensive and smooth, that 'Cousin Phil' enjoyed the luxury of an unusually long walk, whilst Selina and I gained an unlooked-for opportunity for sketching our boat-home.

At one P.M. a slight breeze arose. We started again, and at length drew near to Aboo Simbel. Its colossal figures looked grandly and benignly upon us as we sailed quickly by, though they seemed disappointingly embedded in the sand, which it is frequently necessary to clear away from the entrances. A second temple is hewn in the rock adjoining the great temple, and a little further down is a small figure in a niche, which the Arabs called "the measurer," and said that he weighed with his balances all the wheat on the Nile.

To disturb the romance of the scene, Mohamed came up with the abrupt announcement, "The alum is all used, sir;" "No more clean water to be had for the remainder of the journey." Alarming intelligence indeed, recalling to our minds the red tea, the pea-soup bath of Boulak! We were rather puzzled, for the store of alum which Mohamed had provided, we knew was ample. Nevertheless, the assertion was constantly adhered to, "It *is* all gone, sir." Evening drew on, the wind sprang up afresh, and another petition for sailing was proffered. Few of us can say 'No' for ever; and having gained our point yesterday, we thought it might be wiser not to try the Arab temper too far; therefore, although we knew that the hills in these parts were extremely fine and picturesque, and also that we should not sleep, as soon as the rudder began to groan, we said, 'Teieb, Teieb!' (Very good, Very good). The permission given, the Arabs were satisfied; we all slept soundly, and awoke the following morning to discover that the dahabĕĕh and the hills were both in the same relative position to one another, for we had not stirred from our moorings.

Two of these hills are called 'Gebel e' Shems' (the Hills of the Sun); but Mohamed, in his present irritated frame of mind, stoutly refused them the title. He fought it out with the Nubian pilot, and though Sir G. Wilkinson was his great oracle on all ordinary occasions, he declared that neither Wilkinson himself, nor all the Wilkinsons in the world, should ever make him believe this. Both pilot and dragoman were finally driven nearly crazy by our asking them the probable height of the hills. They looked quite scared, and apparently thought that we were meddling with things far beyond the reach of the human understanding, and into which it was presumptuous to dive. "Nobody ever asked such very curious questions;" "Nobody, anywhere, could know or answer that!"

But the 'Hills of the Sun' are fine in spite of Mohamed; and though not very lofty compared to mountain scenery, they appear so here. They rise suddenly and precipitously from the level sand in forms of house-roofs and cones; each one detached from the other, as though they had accidentally dropped into their places, without any order or plan. It is a most striking spot, and the lights and shades of evening on these hills make it well worth the traveller's while to pause near them for a time.

Sarah tried to joke Mohamed out of his ill-humour with the wind; for I really believe it was the wind with which he was so angry, though he vented his wrath upon us. It would not do; the Great Mogul was in no humour for a joke, and Sarah only came in for her share of abuse. Sarah wanted a bit of soap; she was refused downright. "The soap is all used, ma'am." Sarah was extravagantly clean; she used soap to wash the cabin floor. Ten pieces each time, and the Arabs fourteen pieces at every wash. No store could stand that, it was certain. Ali was so slovenly in his work, that our good Sarah did wash the cabin-floor of her own accord once a-week; but vainly we tried to prove to Mohamed that his statements were wide of the truth; that the soap had not been wasted; and that therefore it must be somewhere. The Arab blood was boiling, and it boiled over now. "What I do with soap?" screamed the dragoman. ('Very little indeed,' thought we.) "Soap not to eat, I sell it perhaps!" This last suggestion was uttered in an awful passion. It was a new idea to us, but the quietly returned answer was, "Very likely; but then you should not have sold it." The squall was ended as if by magic. Mohamed walked about the vessel, speaking to this one and that, his anger cooling down wonderfully; and from various signs in this strange comedy we inferred, though we could not understand a word, that soap and alum were both lying quietly in their accustomed places; and so they were.

At breakfast-time this morning, some common cups and saucers had made their appearance on the table in place of the usual fine white and gold set: Mohamed stated that he "hoped we should not mind it, but the whole set had been broken, cups, saucers, and all." No crash had been heard; no scolding had taken place; no answer was ready as to who had broken them. The story excited our curiosity, and we continued the conversation, when Mohamed, perceiving our incredulity, first admitted that there were three cups in the boat which had escaped the general fracture, but that they had no saucers ; and, finally, the whole set, cups, saucers, and all, reappeared as sound as ever. Mohamed himself had broken one solitary cup, and in dread, no doubt, of losing all his 'best set' before the trip was out, he had fabricated the rest of the story. At dinner-time he came in, and very civilly inquired if we would be contented with having potatoes on our table only every second day, and taking beans and other vegetables in turn with them, as potatoes were difficult to procure, and the supply was running short.

'Cousin Phil' was no epicure, and we agreed immediately ; and what was the result ? From that day forth, to the end of the four months, potatoes in greater abundance than ever graced our table. Fried potatoes for breakfast, boiled potatoes for dinner; potato puddings, and potato garnishes ! Alum found its way daily into the filter ; and soap into the soap-dishes. Was it that dissimulation is so integral a part of the Arab composition, that he must make means for exercising it, when none seem to present themselves naturally, even though they may tell against himself in his professional capacity, and risk losing the recommendation of a 'great gentleman,' like 'Cousin Phil,' which Mohamed emphatically declared, one morning, was of more value to him than a "thousand pounds?" Or was it that this Arab, apparently gifted with but little power of memory at all times, was occasionally, by fits and starts, liable to lose it all, and to contradict himself involuntarily about three times in the course of five minutes? Whatever the cause, Mohamed, at this point of our journey, was an enigma to us which we found it difficult to solve.

In the evening, the men lighted fires on the bank, and rare fun went on amongst them, in jumping over and literally through, the flames. The black, half-clothed figures, the grinning white teeth, the lurid flames, the yells of savage delight, were, to say the least, novel; and we looked on in astonishment as the players concluded their wild sport, by setting fire to a solitary dôm palm-tree growing in the sand. Something will rouse every one of us, and this roused quiet Thomas. Such lawless destruction of property, whether public or private, his careful nature could not brook, and finding his gestures of disapprobation of no avail, he waited his opportunity; and when the excited Arabs were in full fling at another fire, he stole up, and with some trouble succeeded in putting out the tree.

Night came on, and with it one more attempt at sailing made by the troublesome pilot, as we soon discovered by the noise on deck, and the alarming bumping and scraping over hard rocks which ensued and drove me out of my bed to put a stop to the proceeding. A little lecture in the morning brought

Möhamed quite round again. "I do something wrong? Then take my handkerchief (producing the handkerchief), tie it round my neck, and hang me up," was the astonishing sequel to a promise of future good behaviour on the part of the dragoman. The honour was declined; but Mohamed, who recovered his temper as the wind rose, was seriously alarmed, and very penitent for having displeased "the good lady, who never said a hard word to me all the way from Cairo to Assouan." A hearty shake of the hand concluded the solemn and curious interview. Mohamed was the good dragoman once more in every way, and we had had only a very slight experience of the trouble which these strange individuals sometimes give. Their knowledge of English raises them above their fellow-countrymen, and they consider themselves quite on a par with their masters, if not above them. Mohamed thought much of 'Cousin Phil,' but, on the whole, rather more of himself, and he evidently looked upon Selina and me as two very charming children—of a superior class, no doubt, for he was gallant in the extreme; but he clearly thought he must use a little tact to keep us in order. If 'Cousin Phil' managed Mohamed, Mohamed thought he perceived that we managed 'Cousin Phil,' and he endeavoured to frame his policy accordingly. His occasional irritability was caused, in great measure, by the trouble he had in managing our Reïs, who turned out to be a very inefficient one, whilst, in essentials, Mohamed never failed; and we have no hesitation in pronouncing him the best of the dragomen we met on the Nile. At the end of our journey we felt grateful to him for the tender care he had invariably shown towards the invalids, and the trouble which he never spared himself, in order to enable them to see all the objects of interest on the journey, very many of which would ordinarily have been considered quite beyond their reach.

Many Roman ruins lie between Aboo Simbel and Wadée Halfeh. That called 'Kalat Adde' is the most remarkable. It is situated on a cone-shaped hill, and behind, on the further hills, are a large number of tombs—the Necropolis of Kalat Adde. They are clay-built, and each one is surmounted by a small dome, having an open archway, through which the light of day is seen, making a very curious effect.

At this point of our journey the medical skill of the Europeans was called into play, and, happily, with the greatest success. Mohamed appeared one day, with a very long face, saying, "Abdallah very sick. I think he is going to be killed." It was hard to restrain a smile at the strangely-worded announcement, although the fact was alarming. The faculty went out to see the patient, whom they found writhing in agony, standing in the hold, his head and shoulders only appearing above deck. The disease was decreed to be the effect of eating too many dates. Belladonna was administered every twenty minutes. In the course of a few hours Abdallah was convalescent, slept soundly, and next morning was quite himself again.

A few days later Mohamed appeared, leading an unfortunate man by the collar, with features doleful and lengthened out to a ludicrous extent. "Rádee got very bad headache; he *very hot*. After been carrying 'pa-pa,' he take swim in the river; so now he sick."

Poor Rádee, in consequence, got but little pity, and was promised medicine only on the assurance that he would never do such things again. It was almost impossible, we thought, that the tiny globules could take effect on such rough-looking creatures; but four globules of aconite were administered, and at one P.M. Rádee was rowing and singing as merrily as ever. The most obstinate cases brought before us were two of tooth-ache. The first yielded, in the course of twenty-four hours, to the administration of mercurius; but the victim, Awoodallah, who had been in extreme pain for some time, not getting quite such speedy relief as his neighbours, looked mournful and despairing, and glanced reproachfully at the kind doctresses whenever they drew near. At the end of the twenty-four hours, however, Awoodallah was leading the band as usual, and had no return of his tooth-ache, which was perpetually troubling him before. The second case was that of our favourite, 'El Abiad,' the steersman. He went first to the barber of a small village, who broke his tooth, and tortured him as much as might have been expected. 'El Abiad' was in a sad state; he could scarcely open his mouth, either to eat or to speak, but he apparently thought that the barber was the only remedy provided by Heaven for him, and that, if the barber failed, he must patiently resign himself to his destiny. At the next village he went to another barber, and allowed him to have a try at the unfortunate mouth, and, naturally enough, he returned worse. He shook his head at the idea of there being now any cure for him on this side the grave. But Mohamed applied to us in his behalf. Our skill was greatly taxed, but we found at last that 'bryonia' was the medicine required. The pain gradually left him, and poor 'El Abiad's' gratitude was unbounded when he sat down as usual with his companions to the smoking lentil porridge. Due honour to homœopathy and to the preparation of zinc! Before the end of our journey there was not a man in the boat who had not asked for globules or a drop of the magic cure for ophthalmia. They were all, more or less, attacked with this disease, and the zinc invariably cured them. Our reputation as M.D.'s was spread far and wide, and we were truly thankful that all serious illness had been kept from our little world during this trip, when no physician's aid could have been procured had it been ever so much needed.

By *Saturday, Jan. 12th*, 1861, the dahabëéh had reached the village of 'Wadee Halfeh,' the term of her journey. There were we, in latitude $22\frac{1}{2}°$ north, and some of us complaining bitterly of the cold. For some little time a strong north and north-easterly wind had been blowing, and it was now so keen that it was impossible for Selina to remain on deck. This high wind continued to blow during our stay at Wadee Halfeh, and was as uncongenial to those who had come here for the sake of the warm tropical breezes as it was refreshing to their more healthy companions. The thermometer varied at sunrise from 42° to 47°; and, although the heat at midday was great on shore, it never exceeded 73° or 76° on the deck of the dahabëéh.

The village of Wadee Halfeh is a straggling one, shaded by very fine date-palms, but rejoicing in such a quantity of dust, and castor-oily inhabitants as to afford little temptation to frequent visits. The sand-bank against which our boat was moored was far more enjoyable. It was a very extensive one, covered with white sand, like sea-sand; and by careful picking and choosing, we could find a firm footing upon it even for the crutches, so that 'Cousin Phil' turned out for a constitutional regularly twice a-day. A small dahabëéh was moored here belonging to four young men who had forsaken their boat at Assouan, and gone on camels into the desert to Dongola. They suffered much inconvenience from not having taken with them a sufficient supply of water; but they returned in safety, and we met them afterwards at Thebes. The other vessels at

Wadee Halfeh, on our arrival there, were cargo-boats, near which bales of goods were being constantly deposited from the backs of kneeling camels that had come down in long files from the interior.

Two chameleons were brought to us this morning, which we purchased for the price of one piastre. One of them was a great beauty, of a large size, and when angry exhibited the most brilliant shades of yellow, green, and black, forming a pattern very much like that on a tiger-skin. He was very fierce, and flew at his smaller companion whenever he had the opportunity, seizing it by the throat with his large open jaw, and holding it so tight that the victim turned quite black, and would no doubt have expired had not some friendly hand released him. This was no very easy matter, for the finger-like claws of these little creatures cling with a most tenacious grasp to anything which they lay hold of. This chameleon was about twelve inches long, from the head to the tip of the tail. We prized it very much, and to the amusement of the Arabs made a little house for it to live in, and at night brought it into the cabin and allowed it to run about there. But neither care nor flattery were of avail. Both chameleons refused to taste any food, though we tempted them with everything, from their proper diet of flies, to dates, sugar, and roast chicken. The idea that they live upon air seems, however, to be a fallacy, for both pined away; one died, and the beauty either made its escape or was stolen.

Towards evening the report of a gun announced the arrival of a dahabëéh. It carried the American flag, and was moored on the opposite shore. Two lamps appeared at the mast-head by way of illumination. Mohamed chuckled, and immediately hoisted up his eleven. The American was not to be outdone, even by the 'Cairo ;' and up went all his lantern property. Thirteen lamps in all glittered before our eleven. Was Mahomed out-done at last? Not he! There were but eight lamps opposite according to his calculation, and he strutted about as self-satisfied as ever. It mattered little to us what the number really was ; the illumination was extremely pretty on both sides ; and it is much to be hoped that this custom will not be allowed to die out as that of saluting is doing, at least on the part of the English. It was formerly the custom to fire off a gun on arriving at any new place, for every boat that was found lying there, as much as to say "How do you, sir?" and if the boats thus saluted were polite, they shouldered a musket in their turn, and replied in like manner, "Very glad to see you, sir." Last year the popping had been so continual that a reaction ensued, and it was voted ridiculous by the English ; few of them honoured us with the compliment, but when they did we were not so uncivil as not to return it. Mohamed's great delight would have been to fire away all day long, and he evidently thought it slow in us not to take an equal pleasure in the amusement. He finally relieved himself one day, with the exclamation, "Don't know what's come to English this year. All English, always fired before. But now—none."

As night closes in, another report from the energetic 'American,' announced the arrival of a third vessel. Selina and I, though very sociably disposed in general, became alarmed, for we agreed that the charm and romance of sailing on the Nile would be destroyed rather than enhanced by the constant presence of other parties. The feeling that other modern European families are floating alongside, will, in spite of oneself, distract one's thoughts from the ancient world in which they are for the time roaming and revelling; and we were better pleased to drink it all in undisturbed. Our alarm was, however, needless, for the boats never do keep together unless an agreement is made to that effect; and now even our romantic turn of mind hailed the arrival of the new-comers with pleasure when we found that they were some of our Cairo friends. The glimpses we had of them, "few and far between," were a comforting assurance that creatures of our own kind still existed somewhere, and they formed a link which proved that the chain of the old home associations was not quite snapped asunder.

Poor Mr. M—— was sadly altered since we had parted. More than once he and his wife had been on the point of returning, when he rallied again, and hoped so much from the effects of the air of Nubia, that they had persevered and reached thus far; Mrs. M—— keeping up her spirits wonderfully for the sake of her invalid husband. They were accompanied by Capt. and Mrs. N——, who shared the dahabëëh with them. Capt. N—— had lost his arm at Delhi, and was also travelling hither in search of health. Mrs. N—— was full of life and spirits, and thought the climate of Egypt perfection, though her heart seemed much more alive to the sad tidings which had reached her through some American vessels, of the opening of hostilities in the New World, than to the ancient landmarks now before her: yet how little did either of us then think of the years of war and bloodshed which were to devastate our unhappy sister country, and bring misery, almost untold before, to our own.

On *Sunday, Jan. 13th*, a grand cleaning out of the vessel took place. Mohamed was very busy. The hold was emptied, and all the stores were gradually spread out on the bank; affording us an opportunity of seeing all the good things which still remained untouched, and to what extent the others had diminished. The review was satisfactory; nothing was likely to fall short unless it were a day or two of candle-light, in which case we must retire early to bed, and think ourselves fortunate that our three months' store had lasted so nearly for four: whilst canisters of white pepper, black pepper, and mustard, appeared in such amusing quantities, that Mohamed himself was amused. We might have covered every morsel we ate with one or other of these stimulants, and there would still have been plenty remaining.

After our Sunday service in the saloon, the same turn-out took place within the dahabëéh, and it was extremely satisfactory to see the piles of dust and rubbish which were removed from the lower deck pantry and cupboards, and tumbled overboard. The dahabëéh assumed a new form: all unnecessary articles were stowed away out of sight, the filter was removed to the neighbourhood of the kitchen, and the cook-boy's original little fire-box changed sides. The flooring planks were taken up on either side the deck, six of them only being left at regular intervals as seats for the rowers. The loose planks were piled three or four upon each seat; the men's rough brown woollen coats, which they sleep in, were tied on the top, and upon these twelve of the crew were to sit at the oars with their feet in the hold. At night the hold contained them all, huddled together for their rest. What must not its lower atmosphere have been!

A central walk remained for communication between kitchen and cabin, up and down which the domestics made their way between the twelve large oars. The servants' dinner-table took its place on the upper deck, and Sarah and her needlework were promoted to the parlour.

The expedition now in prospect was the ascent of the Second Cataracts. The small row-boat belonging to the dahabëéh, is generally used for this trip, but many travellers prefer going by land, either riding on donkeys, or walking on their own good legs. Of course we went by water as being the easiest, and to our minds the most interesting way. The row-boat was too small for our cumbersome party, so Mohamed hired a small 'cangia' for the trip. The cangia is a cargo-boat, of somewhat the same shape as the dahabëéh, but it has a sharply pointed instead of a rounded stern. They were formerly much used for the trip up the Nile, but have now been almost entirely replaced by the more commodious dahabëéh. The cangia which Mohamed had hired was a small and roughly built one. Under its low, covered-in cabin, he had intended that our party should crowd, sitting Turkish fashion on the matting, and of course seeing nothing; but in spite of his strong disapproval, we finally had the cabin cover removed, and then we furnished the open space with the divans from the 'Cairo,' a table for luncheon, two chairs for Thomas and Sarah, and a canvas awning fastened, impromptu, on two rude poles of a sufficient height.

Monday, Jan. 14th.—We set sail at about eleven A.M. The wind soon failed, and the oars were obliged to do the greater part of the work. The pretty-looking island of 'Manenty,' with its ruined village and Christian church, and another smaller island called by the Arabs 'Mayee,' are the first objects seen on approaching the Second Cataracts.

The rocks increase in number till they form a succession of narrow passages, out of which there is no apparent exit.

The row-boat which accompanied the 'cangia' was put off, with two men in it, taking with them one end of a long rope which was fastened to the dahabëéh, and by which they were to tow the larger vessel along, when they had tied it to some of the rocks. The grisly Reïs of these Cataracts rose at the bow of the vessel, and directed his men by voice and hand. One man, in Nubian costume, jumped into the water, swam with the end of another rope between his teeth, and then jumping from point to point, fastened it to the rocks, and pulled upon it with all his might to help us up. On a smaller scale, the whole scene of the First Cataracts was re-enacted, till the 'cangia' was safely moored in a sheltered nook, under the famous rock of 'Abousir.' We had been four hours on our journey, and before proceeding any further, it was necessary to strengthen ourselves with some of the substantial luncheon which Mohamed had prepared for us. Sandwiches, that is to say, a small flat loaf of bread, slashed up into thick slices, radiating from one point like a fan, between each of which was placed a supply of cold turkey, the remains of our now regularly established Sunday dinner; dates, dried figs, wine, "soft biscuits for pa-pa,"—which latter 'Cousin Phil' pronounced uncommonly hard,—formed the repast.

And now we left the boat. The rock of Abousir

rose almost perpendicularly on the bank overlooking the black and green porphyry rocks of the Cataracts. How was it possible that 'Cousin Phil,' or even Selina, could mount it? I looked first at the rock, then at the invalids, in dismay; but on all such occasions, the word 'impossible' was a word unknown in either of their vocabularies. Two pair of strong arms interlaced to form a sedan, raised each of them from the ground; and after a few halts for breathing-time to bearers and burdens, they were safely landed on the top of the rock of Abousir. I scrambled up, with a lively little "Blackey" skipping beside me, taking great delight in the "Araby" lady's power of climbing, and aiding me at every high step with such zeal, that I was frequently well-nigh overbalanced and sent tumbling down again.

We stood then at last on the rock of Abousir with the Second Cataracts of the Nile at our feet. From left to right, as far as the eye can reach, it follows the thickly studded groups of black or dark green porphyry rocks, with which the bed of the river is broken up. The blue water winds and rushes in rapids and eddies, in and out and round them all, making a low, roaring, splashing sound, which, when the river is full, is heard at a great distance. In the far horizon, a silver line of light marks where the Nile again pursues a placid course, until it shows again its turbulent career in the Third Cataracts at Semneh.

THE 2ND CATARACTS AND ROCK OF ABOUSIR

Vessels of moderate size may pass the Second Cataracts at the time of the high Nile,—in the months of August and September; but later in the year this barrier is impassable, so that all further explorations must then be made by land on dromedaries. The points of two hills in the far distance reminded us strongly of the Pyramids of Geezeh; a few camels, like specks in the distance, trod the burning sand; one solitary swallow flew over our heads, but no other sound or sign of life was there, till 'Cousin Phil,' hat in hand, led a loud "hurrah;" in which the whole party most cordially joined making the rocks resound again.

On ascending, we had looked about with interest for the name of Belzoni and other travellers mentioned in the "Crescent and the Cross," as carved on this rock. But when we reached the top, where the names really are, the beauty and rare character of the scene before us, with the thoughts which the vast solitude inspired, completely drove away the remembrance of the celebrated travellers from our brains. Not till the end of the following day did Belzoni's name return to our minds, with a regret that we had not seen it at Abousir, after all. Due honour to Mohamed and his crew! A hammer and chisel had been provided by them, with the intention of inscribing the names of our memorable expedition. They had been treasured all the way from Cairo as almost the most important part of the whole expedition; and now, on the spot itself, the very Arabs were so wrapped in the scene before them, that hammer and chisel remained quietly in their berths, and never entered the rock at all.

We gazed on, endeavouring, with the aid of pencil and brush, to carry away a hasty, though lasting impression of the view before us. But thoughts which are free could not be confined to pencil and brush, and giving them free scope, we were soon lost in such deep reverie, that it became hard to determine whether our present position were plain matter of fact, or but "the offspring of an idle brain," "begot of nothing but vain fantasy."

Five o'clock drew near, and warned us that we must depart lest night and cold should overtake us, and with reluctant feet and lingering glances, we slowly left the spot which none of our party were likely ever to visit again. The term of our journey had been reached, and we could not fail to look back with thankful hearts on the safety and comfort in which it had all been accomplished.

It was owing to the lack of wind, and the strength of the current, that we had been so long in getting up the 'Cataracts;' we returned in less than an hour and a quarter, and at half-past six o'clock assembled again for dinner in the little saloon, pretty well fatigued by the day's excursion, and feeling as though we had done great things.

An instance of the discipline enforced among our crew occurred on this expedition.

The dahabëëhs, like royal courts in olden times,

are, in general, provided with one member who acts in the character of 'fool' to the rest of the party, in order to keep them alive and in good humour; 'Hassan the Comic,' who was thus designated on account of the tricks and buffoonery with which he was for ever amusing the company, seemed to stand in this position to our crew. His voice had not been heard for some time, when we suddenly discovered him, lying comfortably in the small boat alongside, with a magnificent turban twisted round his head, and composed of the strip of carpet which formed our divan. There he lay, with a most comic expression of grandeur and independence, waiting till we should turn round to have a look at him. Poor fellow! he had certainly forgotten himself, and, in the eyes of the dragoman, had exceeded even the bounds of 'foolery.' Mohamed ordered him and his turban off, with a reprimand, when, to our regret and astonishment, a small stick was produced, and the 'bastinado' was inflicted. The culprit was ordered to hold up his naked feet, which he did instantly, sitting on the side of the boat, and two sharp strokes were laid across the soles, which must have been extremely painful, though not a muscle in his countenance betrayed it. We remarked upon what we considered unnecessary severity; but Mohamed said, "No, he never remember only words." And as Mohamed, though passionate, was certainly tender-hearted, we believe he may have been right.

The poor feet were rubbed for an instant by a sympathising hand, but no other sign of feeling was shown upon the subject by either party.

We were to remain two or three days at Wadee Halfeh, and Mohamed had engaged the 'cangia' for that time, so that we might have made several excursions up the Cataracts to Abousir again; but our boundary line had been reached in every way, and this once the word 'impossible' did step in. The feat once performed was fully as much as, and more than most invalids could have accomplished.

Selina and I, therefore, used the 'cangia' next day for a quiet sail in the direction of the Cataracts, with Mrs. M——, and landed on the island of Manenty, whence she could obtain a partial view of them.

'Cousin Phil' sat meanwhile on the denuded deck of the 'Cairo,' amusing himself with the ingenious contrivances of the pilot, Reïs, and crew, for lowering and fixing the huge yard of the mainmast in every way but the right one for our downward trip. This is an operation of general interest, and causes, in most instances, some little opposition between the passengers and the authorities in the boat. The yard should be slung up out of the way and rested on the awning pole, but our Reïs deemed that this could not be done. First, he wished to lay the heavy beam flat along the deck, thus filling up a large portion of it, and making a high bridge all along from bow to stern, which must have been crossed before any one could reach the opposite side of the vessel. We had at times longed for a little exercise, it was true, but vaulting was not quite the thing for either of us, so that this could not be allowed. The Reïs then laid the yard on the top of the skylight, thus necessarily dooming us to darkness and closeness below in the saloon for two months to come; whilst the barrier on deck would be even worse than the former, for it was neither high enough to allow of our passing under, nor low enough for the objectionable vaulting over it. We had had a week's previous conversation with Mohamed on the subject, and even now we barely succeeded in arranging that some clumsy contrivance should be made for raising the yard at the stern end only, and that but just high enough to allow of 'Cousin Phil's' passing under it. As to the other end,—no, that was not to be; the yard was too heavy, the boat would break, in fact it could not be done. We began to despair of getting rid of it, but truth came to the rescue at last. With all the good-will which the Arabs brought to bear upon their work in the soul-inspiring idea of getting their own way, the wrong way would not prove the shortest. So long were they about it, that we had time to perceive Mr. M——'s dahabëëh turning out in correct style. I went thither for instructions how to decide the knotty point, and learnt that a dialogue of half-an-hour's length to the following effect would in all probability be necessary before the battle were won; but that it would ensure success.

Gentleman. "Hassan, what are you doing with the yard? It must be fastened from mast to mast, and rested on the awning pole in the centre of the boat."

Hassan. "Can't do it, sir. Yard too heavy. Boat upset."

G. "It *must* be done, Hassan."

H. "Break the cabin, sir."

G. "Can't help that, Hassan, but it must be done," (gentleman continues reading; Hassan retires; then returns again.)

H. "The Reïs can't do it, sir. The awning pole is not strong enough: it will break with the weight of the yard."

G. "Then you must get two sticks that *are* strong enough; place them crosswise, at each end of the boat, and put the yard between them. Won't that do, Hassan?"

H. "Oh yes, sir, certainly. That will do."

G. "Then why did not you do so before?"

Hassan retires again, for perhaps the third or fourth time, and all is arranged as comfortably as possible.

This evening 'Cousin Phil' went through a similar dialogue with Mohamed, and with like success. The extra heavy yard of the 'Cairo' was found light after all, and was slung up as it ought to be. The deck was made more spacious than ever by the new arrangements, and Mohamed, feeling duly impressed with the idea that we were "very particular," our very particular ideas were fully satisfied. The yard when fixed extended from the stern some way beyond the bow, so that it must have measured over one hundred feet, and it was a very clumsy and massive one, yet it retained its position in perfect safety. Both Tuesday and Wednesday were occupied with the fixing of the yard, and the re-furnishing of our deck. Messengers were despatched in all directions for provisions, but, to Mohamed's dismay, nothing could be obtained in the villages. A letter from the Governor at Assouan had, he was told, stopped the sale of chickens, eggs, butter, everything for "that English lord." The English lord turned out to be a Swedish prince with his retinue, who was reported to be coming up immediately. He was decreed to be "very greedy" by the enraged Mohamed, and certainly it did seem arbitrary. The fleet did not arrive whilst we were at Wadee Halfeh, so that the prince neither purchased for himself, nor allowed others to perchase before him. As far as we could judge, our stores of food were ample all the time, and there was probably more truth in the high price of the market here, than in the alleged prohibition, for we heard Mohamed exclaim emphatically, "I *hate* Wadee Halfeh. Everything so dear! Always the same here!"

During our stay at Wadee Halfeh, another small

vessel came up, bearing the Sardinian flag. It contained the expedition sent out by the Viceroy to discover the source of the Nile. 'Miani' was its chief, who on a former occasion had penetrated as far as the second degree of north latitude in pursuit of the same object. A Frenchman, whose name we did not hear, and Mr. James, an English photographer, accompanied him. Their goods were accumulated on the shore, and the dromedaries on which they were to pursue their journey came down to be tried. The rider mounted on one of them, but the creature did not like its load, and after a little trotting up and down, set up the most unearthly grunt that ever was heard, and deliberately shook its master from his lofty seat. The sand was soft, and he was not hurt, but the descent must have been far from pleasant. How diminutive and helpless the man looked at that moment, compared with the beast; but when after a minute or two he recovered himself and went up to his uncivil steed, and the gaunt creature knelt quietly down again, and submitted without opposition to its rider, it gave a striking illustration of that wonderful miracle passing daily and hourly before our eyes, whereby man is made lord over the most powerful of the brute creation, and they obedient and subservient to all his wants and wishes.

The men of science carried with them two chronometers, by which our time was proved to be one hour too slow; this did not exactly suit our feelings.

but we were bound to alter our watches, and to rise an hour earlier on the morrow.

Mohamed's heart had for some time been set upon taking me out for a serenade in the small boat with "music on the water," as he termed it. At Wadee Halfeh, I agreed to go. The full band, with tom-tom, tambourines, drums, and fifes, were packed as tightly as they could be packed, in the further end of the boat; and there was but just room enough for me, and Sarah who attended me, to sit in the stern. How astonished my friends at home would have been could they have seen me and my companions. There was only a half-moon, so that it was not a light night, and only a portion of the outlines of the figures of the dark musicians, their sparkling eyes and shining teeth when they opened their mouths to sing, the ornamental portions of their instruments upon which the light of the moon struck, and the dancing reflection on the waters, were perceptible in the surrounding dimness. The men were in high spirits, delighted with their own noise, and with the honour conferred upon them. They sang in full chorus as we rowed along, saluting every dahabëëh on our road so lustily, that their inmates rushed to the deck or the windows, to see what could be going on. The wild sounds nearly deafened us, and the pale moon looked down again from above in silent amaze, I am sure, at the savage din which dared thus to cross her reflection on the still waters. The Arabs went through the whole of their catalogue of songs in succession with unabated vigour to the end, and hardly would they allow us to escape, when we returned to the dahabëéh, having had enough and to spare of their serenading.

A sudden gust of wind blew in the night, so cold and so strong as to waken most of the sleepers at Wadee Halfeh. It lasted for about twenty minutes and went down again in an equally sudden manner. The Arabs complained bitterly of the cold both day and night, and rolled themselves up, heads and all, in their thick woollen cloaks, lying about in all directions on the bank, like so many logs. But the invalids were suffering, also from the cold winds, it was advisable to make no unnecessary delay, and we agreed to start at once.

CHAPTER VII.

DOWN THE NILE.

Thursday, Jan. 17*th*.—Just after Mohamed had indulged in a warm eulogium on Lord Nelson, and given us a very lucid account of the battle of the Nile, which, he said, his mother remembered well, we bid adieu to our friends, and left Wadee Halfeh. Mohamed's notion of the tactics and prowess of the English admiral was this. He said that Lord Nelson got into a small boat, hoisted the French flag at the mast-head, sailed into the midst of the French fleet, and then fired away at them before they had discovered who he was; and Lord Nelson was, consequently, in his eyes the greatest hero that ever lived.

At ten A.M. the 'Cairo' started on her way home. She would be some time about this said journey home; still the sound was pleasant to the ear, and whatever the rest of the party, out of respect to antiquity perhaps, or from any other cause, may have hidden each in their own bosom, there was one face whose features decidedly shortened, and one pair of feet that skimmed the deck for joy at the thought of returning to the civilised world again; and they were those of honest Sarah. Visions of civilised society, European hotels, and no more ironing days in the scorching sun, with the true English home drawing gradually nearer, floated before her brain as she sat watching the newly-arranged scenery of the dahabëéh.

The twelve rowers sat at the oars, and pulled with hearty good-will, for they were going home too. Their manner of rowing is very curious and picturesque. They rise from their seats at every stroke, stand upright on the deck as they dip the oars in the water, re-seat themselves, letting the left foot return into the hold, while the right rests still on the deck, and pull a long double stroke, singing in chorus as they row. They have several different 'pulls,' as Mohamed called them, and a particular song or chant is adapted to each of them. That with which we started from Wadee Halfeh, he proudly announced as "the oldest 'pull' of all! Three hundred years for this song!" In one, they prolong the stroke so much, and pull with such vigour, that they literally throw themselves flat upon their backs on the deck before lifting the oars out of the water; and there was one very quiet and still longer stroke, with a peculiarly low and solemn chant belonging to it, which they called 'The man-of-war pull,' and which was used now and then as a show-off, but the men did not enjoy it much. When there is a gentle or a fair wind they will row all day long, stopping only three times to take their meals and to rest. It is hard work, but in general they show no signs of fatigue, and will, on an emergency, continue rowing all night for a little extra 'baksheesh.' The wind, however, is so constantly contrary, that they have much idle time on their hands, to make up for the hard days of rowing. At such times the oars are laid aside, and the dahabëëh drifts down with the stream; the deck is immediately covered with sleeping forms, lying about it in all directions; or, should the men find the weather cold, they pop down each into his hole, and either disappearing altogether, or, leaving a head and pair of shoulders only visible above, they begin munching leeks and onions. A breath of fair wind springs up, the steersman shouts, and a few of the sleeping forms start up to unfurl the small sail at the bow, to furl it again perhaps in the course of ten minutes, and to disappear once more into the hold, until another shout brings them suddenly back again, to row with might and main till the pilot orders them to cease, when down they all tumble as before.

The high wind of Wadee Halfeh continued blowing against us, and impeding our progress very seriously. From shore to shore we floated, or rowed alternately, making a few yards only at each turn, so that every stone and tree might have been learnt by heart, and by night-fall we had only reached the village of Serra.

Friday, Jan. 18th.—We remained at Serra for

half a day. The wind was contrary, so that we did not lose time by this proceeding, and it suited Selina and me very well. We had, much to 'Cousin Phil's' entertainment, a craving for a true desert ride in which no other object but the desert should be visible. He thought we had had enough of that by this time; but the Nubian pilot had decreed this to be the best place for the purpose, so the chair and the donkeys were prepared. The chair was carried by four of the crew, four others being in attendance to relieve them. The air was so pure and delicious, we thought for an instant that we could have enjoyed a life spent there; but soon the burning rays waxing hotter and hotter, reminded us that verdure with air a degree less pure would be far preferable. We rode on for nearly two hours, and succeeded in seeing nothing around but the sandy plain, relieved by groups of extremely picturesque rocky hills on all sides. A flock of gazelles started up at our approach, and fled like arrows shot from a bow. We picked up a few pretty, transparent pebbles of a deep red colour, and two curious pieces of highly-polished petrified wood. We enjoyed our excursion extremely; 'Cousin Phil' thought we might be satisfied, and so we were, so was he we fully believe, and so were the Arabs, who clearly saw no fun in a walk in heavy sand without even a temple to repay them at the end.

In this happy state of universal satisfaction, we returned to the dahabëéh, proceeded on our way, and stopped at Farras for the night, where our friends overtook us. The heat was extreme, but the ride to the temple ruins very enjoyable. The rocky hills rising in striking forms from the sand, were covered with different kinds of tamarisk growing luxuriantly in the dry desert air. The bright blue shade of these shrubs, the deep brown of the curiously projecting summits of the rocky hills, and the brilliant yellow of the sand, formed a most pleasing combination of colours. The ruins of Farras lie not very far from the river. There are many scattered blocks about, the remains, it is supposed, of some ancient Roman town. The grotto is a series of tombs excavated in the rock, and containing mummy pits. The invalids could not go in, but I explored the low chambers as far as Mohamed's fear of the bats would allow me. We saw no hieroglyphics, but I believe we ought to have found some of the time of Remeses II. At noon, the dahabëéh was off again, once more on her way to Aboo-Simbel. 'Cousin Phil' arrived there in her at about five P.M.; but Selina and I got out, and rowed with the dragoman to the temple of Ferayg. It is hewn in the rock which rises so perpendicularly from the water that the ascent is difficult. The temple is cruciform. It has a hall with four columns, two side chambers, and the adytum, the most holy place into which none but the priests were permitted to enter. It is a pretty little temple, and it interested us chiefly on account of a picture of the Saviour, and another probably of St. John the Baptist, which are painted on the roof. They are very badly executed, but still they are memorials of the Christian worship and faith once acknowledged there. The hieroglyphics on the walls show the original temple to have been "of the time of the successor of Amunoph III. about B.C. 1350." This temple with those of Ibreem and Derr, are the only three on the eastern bank of the Nile.

Sunday, Jan. 20th.—After the Church service had been offered up, we proceeded to ascend the steepest sand slope we had yet attempted, in order to visit the great temple of Aboo-Simbel at the top. Our friends thought it impossible, that any one could be carried up such an inclined plain as that now before us; but to their astonishment, up went 'Cousin Phil' and Selina, on the arms of the Arabs, as comfortably as possible. The strong ones climbed up as best they might, sinking deep in the beautifully fine sand, like the snail who took two steps forward and one step back, till he reached the top of his pole. This sand is so remarkably fine, it is said that every particle would pass through the hole of an hour-glass.

The colossal figures seated on thrones attached to the rock, at the entrance of the great temple, are considered the most beautiful of any of the Egyptian colossi found in the temples. They represent Remeses II. The expression of calmness and benignity which sits on the countenances of all the colossi of

Egypt is very striking. They are all exactly alike, and convey the idea of quiet self-satisfaction, rather than that of great warriors, animated as their realities are reported to have been, by all the fiercest passions of human nature. The thick lips and heavy eyes are characteristic features of their descendants to the present day; and the sleepy, listless moderns look fully as well satisfied with themselves,—as though they also had achieved the conquests attributed to these great ancestors of theirs. The colossi outside the temple, are measured sixty-six feet in height, without the pedestal. Those on the pillars of the grand hall within, about twenty feet. There is a second hall with pillars, and we counted eight chambers opening into the grand hall, in some of which there are seats projecting from the wall. In the centre of the adytum, is an altar, and at the further end four statues in relief, one of which represents 'Re' (the Sun) to whom this temple was dedicated. There is another statue of Re over the entrance, to whom the king is offering a figure of truth. We did not make him out very well: it was such hot work to look up at him. The hieroglyphics on the walls are extremely interesting, representing the triumphs of Remeses the Great. The light of the 'mashal' is necessary to make them out at all, and it would take many hours, or days rather, to trace the story all through. In some of the chambers, there are figures with ornaments painted black on their necks and arms, the colour remaining perfectly distinct. The whole excavation of this temple is about 200 feet. We spent some time in it, and were very much fatigued by the foul air, the heat and smoke of the 'mashals,' and the burning sun outside; but as we were not likely to see Aboo-Simbel again, we resolved to go through it all bravely, and Sarah and I concluded our excursion by an extra climb up the burning, sandy hill. One step forward, and very nearly one step back, it was this time, but we persevered, reached the head of the giant Remeses, and seated ourselves most comfortably on the tip of this very small man's ear, which is said to measure three feet five inches. From thence we read the names and date of one of the expeditions to the source of the Nile, written, with very bad taste it must be confessed, in large black characters along the bridge of the giant's nose. Why not have recorded them on the rock at his side, instead of thus defacing the interesting ruins?

We went back to the dahabëéh, rested a little and suffered the sun to dip a little lower before we dared again to meet his rays. Then we paid our respects to the smaller temple. Its façade is also adorned with figures in high relief, with buttress-like projections between them covered with hieroglyphics. This temple is dedicated to Athor, and her head surmounts all the pillars of the hall. Her emblem, the sacred cow, we did not see in the adytum, but found it in the sculptures on the wall.

We then rowed in the small boat to see the figure

in the niche lower down, but owing to the strength of the current, could not get near enough to distinguish it well. The larger temple was opened by Belzoni and his companions in 1817. They worked for a fortnight, eight hours each day, the heat of the thermometer varying from 112° to 116° in the shade. The sand closed the temple again, but it remained comparatively easy to future travellers to re-open it.

The crew of the two dahabëëhs spent the night in the smaller temple. Their talking and laughing resounded strangely and wildly through the hewn rock, and into the surrounding stillness, and led our thoughts back to the midnight orgies held by their pagan ancestors within those very walls. The stars towards morning were magnificent; each one appearing three times as large as those we see at home.

Monday, Jan. 21st.—Between regret at not taking another look at these beautiful temples, and satisfaction at escaping the foul air within them and the extremely dusty return which another visit would inevitably entail upon us, we and our friends sailed from Aboo-Simbel at seven A.M., playing at 'touch last' with each other during the whole day. The milkman had to go such a long journey before he could find any fresh milk that we waited till ten o'clock for our breakfast. This was a rare occurrence, but not so the high wind which blew so constantly this and the following day, that poor

Selina was again doomed to the cabin, only rushing up now and then at the cry of 'Temsah, Temsah!' Two dahabëéhs passed on their way up the river, one bearing the American, the other the Russian flag; we exchanged cards with the former, and the latest news from the Northern world was sent to us.

Wednesday, Jan. 23rd.—The wind blew fair, and we passed our old friends 'Ibreem' and 'Derr;' and visited the temple of 'Amada,' situated on the bank just below. This portion of the bank seemed really perpendicular, and it was covered with tufts of grass growing in loose dry soil, yet 'Cousin Phil' ascended it supported by a living ladder of Arabs: a most ingenious contrivance, whereby two carried him, while six others pushed them up to the middle of the bank, where another six met and conveyed them to the top. Selina being a lighter weight, required only two men to carry her up. When half-way, she took it into her head that she would like to try her powers of climbing, and endeavoured to put her feet to the ground, but quick as thought the devoted and merry Arabs loosened each one hand from its hold, and tucked her feet up under her, so that she was rendered helpless, shouting, "La, la! Sitte," (No, no, lady), to the immense delight of the whole party. The temple is deeply embedded in the sand; the entrance open only about three feet above the surface: here we thought we must rest on our oars; but no, nothing could daunt Mohamed, and under his able directions the bearers crouch down upon the sand, and slide 'Cousin Phil' in. He saw the temple as well as the ablest amongst us. A brave old gentleman trùly; and a most clever dragoman! The temple of 'Amada,' is of the time of Thothmes III., B.C. 1463, and is dedicated to 'Re.' The painted hieroglyphics on the walls are extremely pretty, and, owing to their having been washed over by the early Christians, the colouring in many places is distinctly preserved. The stone of the temple has a reddish hue. We enjoyed this little excursion extremely, descended the bank in the same wonderful manner that we had ascended it, and rowing on, reached Korosko early in the evening and remained there for the night.

Thursday, Jan. 24th.—Before breakfast I took my concertina out on deck as I usually did, and an audience of about thirty of the wild natives, now 'old friends,' squatted down on the bank to listen to my song. Mr. M——'s dahabëéh started before us, and we did not meet again till we arrived at Thebes. 'Cousin Phil' took a walk among the dusty fields of Korosko, whilst Selina and I sketched a group of three of the Khartoum men, who belonged to the caravan we had met here before. The governor politely ordered them to stand for their portraits. They were promised a small 'baksheesh' for this favour, and grinned satisfaction at us the whole time. There was another fuss with the Rëis, about money and bread for the crew. The governor was appealed to, and the Reïs as usual found guilty, and brought to order.

We started from Korosko at two P.M., but the wind being contrary and very high, we were shortly obliged to stop under some fine granite hills, which I clambered up with little 'Blackey.' His poor bare feet suffered so much from the hard pointed rocks, that I begged him to leave me; he would not give in, and I rather think he wanted to try the effect of a lotion of arnica and water on his return. Mid-way up the hill I found a group of Nubian women sitting against the rock spinning cotton, and plaiting date-leaves into large flat baskets. The hopeful son of one of them sat on a rock, munching a bit of bread very much as an English baby would have done, but he wore a tattered rag about his body, and all his hair seemed to stand straight on end. The women were much troubled at my appearance, and one of them began to cry when I sat down to sketch the group. The dragoman came up and assured them that he and all the crew had survived the operation, so they sat still and were presently joined by a fine-looking man, the grandfather of the baby, in a white dress and large high white hat, apparently of some coarsely woven woollen manufacture. The complexion of the party was a kind of slate-black, so nearly resembling the colour of the rocks before them, that it was not easy to distinguish them at any distance. Selina meanwhile hovered between the deck and the cabin, contesting with

Mohamed the correct English term for the present high wind, viz. : "very cold," or "peautiful clean and fresh." Mohamed thought himself as far above us in his knowledge of the English language as in every other thing; and would not have the term 'cold' applied to the wind, though he complained bitterly at times of cold himself.

A dahabëéh returning from Aboo-Simbel now overtook us, and we proceeded together till nine P.M., making but very little way. Another, favoured by the wind which was keeping us back, passed quickly up. Inquiries for the name of the dragoman rang through the hills, and turning out to be a friend of Mohamed's, the latter went off in the small boat to have a little gossip and a cup of coffee or some other equivalent, which whilst we made such slow progress he could easily do; the thermometer was at 56° at breakfast time, and did not rise above 68° or 70° during the day.

Friday, Jan. 25th.—So strong a wind was blowing from the north-west, that having reached Sabooa we could make no way at all, and were forced to stay there the whole day, sheltering on the windward side from the dense clouds of sand which covered the other vessel, whose owners had not yet paid their visit to the temple.

Saturday, Jan. 26th.—We endeavoured to proceed, but the storm was rising, and we were pitched and tossed about as though we had been in the 'Vectis' on the Mediterranean. We were obliged to give in again and stayed near a village, whose inhabitants, about ten in number, were so bedaubed with castor oil, that it was impossible to stand within some few yards of them without being unpleasantly aware of it.

We started again, reached a mud-bank, where we were forced to stay once more, and had the satisfaction of seeing three other dahabëëhs just before us in the same plight. We made about one mile in the course of this day; tacking first to one shore, then back to the other, gaining a step or two at each tack. This may be thought tedious enough, and so it was in one way; but the spirits of the invalids never failed, and between reading aloud, drawing, fidgeting, and marvelling at the climate of Egypt and the draughts in the dahabëëh, these tedious days passed quickly enough. A little extra occupation was also afforded us in prescribing for Thomas, who was taken ill and kept his bed for two days. The windows of our perfect vessel were so far from fitting, that whenever the wind rose at all, we were obliged to stuff the curtains and everything we could think of round them, otherwise it would blow a gale inside as well as out, and all the furniture be thickly covered with sand in a few moments. The thermometer to-day rose to 85° in the sun at mid-day; fell to 63° by six P.M., and to 55° by ten P.M., when we retired to rest; and as it was not a self-registering one, and our night-watch could not read, we had no means of knowing how much lower it fell that night.

Septuagesima Sunday, Jan. 27th.—At length the wind went down, and we reached Oofideneh and Dakke. The first afforded us very picturesque groups of Nubian children, rushing about in high spirits, tossing their long black hair in the wind. Their only garment consisted of bead necklaces round their necks, and a thong apron like a deep fringe, which they tied round their loins; but many of them did not even wear this. One of the little girls was a 'beauty;' and her pretty shy ways, as she dodged about among the ruins to avoid our glances, attracted us much.

The ancient remains at Oofideneh are few. The temple was dedicated to Isis, and is ascribed to the age of Thothmes III. On one of the walls the goddess is represented sitting under the sacred fig-tree. There is a second building near, which is Roman, and with the exception of Ibreem, it is the last found up the river belonging to the times of the Ptolemies or Cæsars. It has been used for Christian worship; and on one of the walls there are traces of a picture apparently of the nativity of our Lord. The temple, though so little of it remains, or is visible above the sand, is very pretty, and the barrenness of its desert approach is relieved by many green spots of the Palma-christi, and small dôm palms, growing like shrubs before it.

We found a dromedary here, on the back of which Mohamed mounted, trotting up and down to show us how well he could ride. I had been very anxious to try the pace of these long-legged creatures myself. The dromedary was accordingly made to kneel down, and I was told to take my seat, which I did; but before I had time to ask how to hold on, or to make any other question, in fact, the moment the animal felt something on his back, up he jumped, and, naturally enough, off jumped I, on to the sand again, in order to avoid the ignominy of being *thrown;* while the tall 'ship of the desert' reared its lofty head in astonishment at finding that its expected burden was gone. "But," said Mohamed, "you must sit like a man, if you please. Every one sits so with this kind." "This kind," meaning the usual man's saddle of the country, with a small pointed wooden projection before and behind to hold on by. It was beyond me to try that, so the experiment was relinquished, Mohamed promising that two charming dromedaries should be found in Cairo, with 'ladies' side-saddles,' on which we might sit and drink a cup of coffee without spilling it. It would have been extremely imprudent for Selina or any one suffering from weakness in the chest, to have attempted any such thing, and the ride never came off; but from what we saw of the backward and forward movement of others thus mounted, it must be a steady hand indeed that could retain the coffee in the cup without long previous training. Some persons enjoy dromedary riding extremely, but to others it is very painful. It looks very inviting, to be perched up, so high above every other living thing that walks the earth ; and the long and stately strides of the animal convey an idea of liberty and freedom most pleasing to the senses ; but whether or not all this pleasing imagination would have been jolted out of us by the reality, remains still to be proved. Towards evening the temple of Dakke came into sight; we read that the oldest part now remaining bears the name of Ergamun, an Ethiopian king; but the original building is supposed to have belonged to the age of Thothmes III. On its walls are the names of several of the Ptolemies and Cæsars, which may be deciphered even by the unlearned traveller with the aid of his guide-books.

The outside of the towers and walls of this temple are quite plain, and the sand-stone of which it is built is of exactly the same shade of colour as the sand in which it is more than half imbedded. On the walls within, the subjects are in relief, in very good preservation, and some of them very curious. Mohamed said he would take off one for us. He squatted down on the ground before it; applied the paper to the wall, drew a long draught from a can of water held to him by little 'Blackey,' inflating his cheeks like a balloon; and then proceeded deliberately to squirt out the water from his mouth with wonderful force and aim, till the whole paper was moistened, and the figures impressed upon it. Selina and I were fairly thrown off our guard by this unlooked-for performance; and we laughed immoderately. 'Blackey' stood by with inquiring gaze, as grave as a judge, wondering what there could be to laugh about; and Mohamed solemnly assured us that there was "no other way to do this kind!" Live and learn, thought we; "fingers were made before forks," and Mohamed's mouth served him fully as well as the more modern contrivance of a bucket of water and a sponge. The dragoman adopted these on a future occasion, but he was not very clever with them, and the impressions he obtained were not good. I believe we did not give them time enough to dry properly before removing them from the stone. The weather had become warmer again; and oh! what a moon and evening star shone forth to-night. So clear was the atmosphere, they seemed truly to float in the open vault of heaven; and the eye wandered, as it were inquiringly, around the shining orbs—a glorious sight—such as to make one exclaim, almost involuntarily with the Psalmist, "The heavens declare the glory of God: and the firmament showeth His handy-work!" Mohamed, who had taken it into his head that it was necessary to make some sort of valedictory preface to the remarks with which he honoured us whenever he entered the saloon, came in this evening with the following request to the assembled company, "Good evening, sir; if you please the 'Sheikh' wants some physic for his eyes!" The Sheikh was from a village at some little distance, but Mohamed added, "They always know English boats have doctors on board." So, to keep up our name, we sent him enough zinc to cure the eyes of the whole village for some time to come.

Monday, Jan. 28th.—The thermometer fell to 43½° at sunrise, but warmed up considerably during the day. Its days were numbered. In the evening unfortunate Thomas let it fall and broke it. The mercury would rise no more. Happily for us we had one other, which had always been kept in Selina's cabin, so we could refer to that; but it was a serious loss, and showed us how necessary it was to include 'a good stock of thermometers' in the list of requisites for travellers on the Nile. It is particularly satisfactory when you feel 'warmed up,' almost to the last bearable point, to be able to turn round and see how much right you have to such feelings, and how much more you may expect; let alone the far juster estimate of the climate of the country which is obtained by this means than by any other.

We reached Dendour at one P.M. This temple stands just within the tropic and is very small. The sculptures are of the time of Augustus. Some of them we copied, for though we were too unlearned to understand their meaning, they interested us by their quaintness. The groups of natives here too were very striking, and not overburdened with clothing.

We reached Kalabshee at six P.M., and remained there for the night. Mohamed was very busy this evening, rolling up small strips of paper with portions of the Korán written upon them, which he was going to have sown up in little bags to wear about his person as charms. He always wore some about him, but these for some reason were to be additional, and he appeared much shocked on detecting our incredulity as to their power.

Tuesday, Jan. 29th.—Another dahabëéh with the American flag was at Kalabshee on its return home. Mr. —— kindly called and gave us information about the temples, which he and his party had already visited. He had heard also that one poor traveller had lost his wife. She came to the Nile in search of health, but it was too late; she died at Korosko and was buried at Derr the following morning.

Mr. —— started almost immediately, and amused us much by the hurry in which he seemed to be. "Oh! yes," he said; "we push on to keep ourselves alive. We find it necessary to take care of the mind as well as the body." So well did they push on the mind, that before they were half way down the river the poor body was burnt out of house and home. The dahabëéh caught fire, the whole of the saloon was destroyed, and the unfortunate party having lost everything they possessed, were fortunate in finding another dahabëéh able to take them in. They had left Sioot long before we arrived, so that we only heard of their misfortune from others. At Kalabshee we saw two women grinding at a mill. They sat opposite each other on the ground, holding, each with one hand, the upright handle which was fixed in the grinding-stone, and turned it round together, singing a most curiously high-pitched song; the same pitiable wail, repeated over and over again, till the grain was all exhausted. We bought some leathern charms from the people at Kalabshee. They were made in the Khartoum, and brought hither by the caravans. They are long chains of plaited leather, having small bags of the same material hanging to them, containing the charms, with a few blue beads strung upon them. These are worn by the women round their necks; they also wear brass nose-rings, ornamented with beads of brass and blue glass. The ring is passed through one nostril, and on their dark skin it looks rather pretty than otherwise. They wear bracelets and bead or brass necklaces, as well as some curious pendants from their hair, composed also of beads and small buttons of very common mother-of-pearl, strung together on leathern thongs. Many of the thong aprons worn by the girls were ornamented with shells. The married women wear a loose garment, so arranged as to leave one shoulder bare. It reaches below the knee, and sometimes they will throw a portion of it over their heads to defend them from the sun, but they do not cover their faces; none of the Nubian women in the small villages do so. The men wear a white cotton shirt, short trousers, and a large scarf passing over the left shoulder and round the waist, the long ends hanging, one before and the other behind, sometimes having very pretty borders of coloured threads woven into them. Their caps are of white cotton, fitting close to the head, and most of them have a knife or small dagger, in a leathern sheath, fastened to the left arm above the elbow, together with some charms like those of the women. Most of the boys wear very substantial, plain silver ear-rings, generally only in one ear. There was one little girl, the daughter of the Sheikh, who was laden with ornaments, on her neck and in her hair, but she wore no further covering than the thong apron ornamented with shells. Her brother, who was somewhat older, was in the full dress of the men. I think it was here that we noticed one boy on the bank with a pair of white gloves, which he was carefully exhibiting on his black hands. When he had worn them for some time, he passed them on to his neighbour, who had been eyeing them with longing glances, this one handing them on in like manner to a third. It seemed to be the amusement of their day, and the proud, happy look which invariably sat upon the face of the wearer was very amusing. Most of the men here wore large sandals made of elephant's hide, brought from the interior, and some had less handsome ones of sheep-skin.

Just as our American friend fired a salute to wish us good-bye, Mohamed, returning laden with curiosities purchased from the group assembled on the bank, had a somewhat tragic fall from the plank which was placed as a landing slip. The poor fellow was hurt, and laid up for the day, but he acted the dying man so well as he hung utterly helpless on the shoulders of two of the crew who carried him on board, that he almost succeeded in alarming us as much as he was alarmed himself. The Nubian pilot and Ali took his place to escort us to the temple, and very proud indeed the latter was of the temporary promotion.

The larger temple is close to the water's edge. It is the largest in Nubia; built in the reign of Augustus, and supposed to have succeeded to one of the age of Thothmes III.

It has a great many chambers and chapels, a hall, and portico; but they are so choked up with the fallen blocks of the temple, that 'Cousin Phil' and Selina could not go further than the first entrance; and it was a matter of difficulty, even for me, to penetrate through five successive portions, to see the remains of the gilded sculptures, and the Greek inscription in which "Silco, king of the Numadæ, and of all the Ethiopians," details his own victories.

The view from this temple was so pretty we could not avoid sitting some little time to sketch it, while listening to the warbling of the larks in the sky above as on a bright spring day at home. The smaller temple lies higher up, at the top of a steep accumulation of rocks, stones, and rubbish, up which 'Cousin Phil' mounted bravely with the assistance of Ali and his stick. This temple is called 'Bayt el Wellee,' the House of the Saint; it is hewn in the rock, and is very pretty. The sculptures on the walls of the area outside the temple, recount the victories of Remeses the Great. They are extremely interesting. We traced them all through with the assistance of 'Murray,' and I shouted the story to 'Cousin Phil,' and to the benefit of the assembled company, who looked as if they thought it a wonderfully clever performance. Now and then Ali interpreted scraps of it to the other Arabs, who always showed a considerable degree of interest in the ancient monuments of their country. We left at half-past one P.M., and passed the gates of Kalabshee in safety. On our way up we had passed these gates at dark, so that this bit of scenery was new to us, and extremely pretty it is. Groups of rocks appear in the bed of the river resembling those at Assouan, some of them of most fantastic forms. The rocky cliffs on either side rise perpendicularly from the edge of the water, many of them crowned with Roman ruins; while from the bend of the stream the water is at times enclosed on all sides like a lake. The river runs with a strong current round the rocks, making a little disturbance, which Mohamed called "very strong water." Two men swam fearlessly across the current on their log-boats. Towards evening the sky became cloudy and overcast.

We stopped at Tafa and visited its two small temples. One of them has an almanac on the wall, supposed to be of the fourth or fifth century. The other temple is made use of as a dwelling-house by a Nubian family. These buildings have also been used for Christian worship. It is sad to read that the Nubian Christian temples, so late as the seventeenth century, were closed for want of pastors.

If the remains at Tafa were to most travellers not much worth seeing, its group of natives certainly were; with the exception, perhaps, of the Khartoum men, they were quite the most savage specimens of humanity we had come across. The men were armed with swords, knives, spears, and pistols, fastened about their persons. Their chief, who, though a savage, was a very intelligent, fine-looking man, very good-humouredly allowed us to examine all his arms. He talked of "killing men" as a pleasant pastime, and showed a little coal-black child, whom he said he had "caught in the Khartoum," and would "sell" in Cairo for 15*l.* or 20*l.* The men were well clothed, the boys wore, most of them, nothing at all, the girls only the thong apron. Their figures were extremely pretty, and some of their countenances very pleasing, but the old women were frightful. We proceeded to within one mile of Gertasse, and remained there for the night.

Wednesday, Jan. 30th.—The crew tried hard to reach Dabôd and Philæ to-day, but the wind was extremely high, and it was contrary. To begin with, the vessel struck on a bank, from which she did not get loose for an hour and a half, and then only with the assistance of eight men from another dahabëëh which overtook us, and kindly lent their assistance; and yet every one of our men had been working hard all the time. We sailed on again, but at three P.M. were obliged to stop, on account of the wind, at a small village on the eastern bank, numbering about twenty inhabitants. We landed, and took a walk along a fine avenue of palm-trees. It was the first avenue we had seen, for these trees appear generally to be planted in clumps or small plantations. The sand from the opposite shore blew up in thick clouds. Nothing but white dust was to be seen all around; a dreary, uncomfortable scene, and we began to think our "warm winter" was coming to an untimely end. 'Cousin Phil's' active mind saw no fun in remaining here, and he thought that if the Arabs were not impressed with the idea of 'destiny,' they might still do battle with the elements. The dragoman evidently thought it very audacious of the 'English gentleman,' to think that he knew better than him, or the pilot, or the Reïs and crew all put together. They did try, whether their best or not we cannot say, but they soon satisfactorily proved that we were going *up* the river instead of *down*, and we gave in accordingly in despair. A cargo-boat passed up in the evening and communicated the sad intelligence of the death of a young Englishman, in a rash attempt to swim the cataracts near Philæ, in the passage by which the boats ascend the river. The Nubian natives perform this feat very expertly for the amusement of travellers, and to gain a little 'baksheesh.' They plunge from a rock into the midst of the rapid, with a log of wood upon which they rest, or sometimes even without it. They are shot down in an instant, apparently powerless, but in another moment they reappear in the smoother water below, and swim in safety to shore. It requires long training even for the natives to be able to perform this feat, and the poor young Englishman was instantly overpowered by the current, and disappeared. His friend, whom we met at Assouan, watched anxiously for the body till, on the tenth following morning, when he was about to give up in despair, it rose in the very spot where it had gone down. It was buried at Assouan. This was an awful incident, and it cast a gloom for a long time over all the parties travelling on the Nile.

Thursday, *Jan.* 31*st.*—The cold this morning was trying. When I put my hands into the cold water, my fingers tingled all over as on a frosty day at home. The thermometer inside the cabins at 8 A.M. was not higher than 48°, and did not rise above 64° in the sun during the day.

The temple of Dabôd had but a short visit in consequence. I went to see it first before breakfast. There was a thick haze all round, and a strong wind was blowing from the north-west. The wind I did not object to, it was rather refreshing than otherwise, but the clouds of sand and dust blown into one's eyes, made it almost impossible to see at all. The report which I brought back did not give much encouragement to my companions. After breakfast they landed, looked at the temple with one eye, shivered, pronounced it very ugly, and dived again into the saloon. I made a rapid sketch and followed them. The three pylons (gateways) which succeed each other in front of the temple, are almost all that is visible of the building. Within the portico is a sculpture, which represents the pouring, alternately, of the emblems of Life and Purity over Tiberius, supposed to refer to the ceremony of anointing him king. The temple is ascribed to an Ethiopian monarch of the time of Ptolemy Philadelphus, the sculptures being added by Augustus and Tiberius. The Arabs also pointed out the remains of the stone quay, which had a staircase leading to the river.

We proceeded, but at four P.M. were obliged again to stop on a bank. The wind abated a little, and we went on, and once more reached our admired Philæ at ten P.M. This afternoon, whilst the high wind kept us all idle, and we had nothing better to do, we fetched the mercury from the broken thermometer and showed it to the Arabs. Their astonishment at its liveliness was unbounded; at first they showed a degree of alarm at its power of dividing into separate globules, and re-uniting again into one, Mohamed at last becoming quite excited over it. He could not understand why he could not catch and hold it in his hand; and with a determination not to be conquered by the quicksilver any more than by anything else, he continued his efforts most perseveringly. The absurd struggle was vigorous and long; all the powers of mind and body were brought into play, and in the space of one hour and a half Mohamed triumphantly brought up his enemy, reduced to a small grey powder, and he was satisfied. To our astonishment he now begged for a portion of this powder for Ali "to wash his head with it," declaring that it was sold expressly for this purpose "to ladies." The boy did use it, with what advantage or disadvantage we never heard.

Friday, Feb. 1*st.*—The wind continued still in the same direction, blowing so hard that it would have been impossible to descend the Cataracts; but we were not sorry to see a little more of Philæ, although it was too cold to be quite enjoyable to the invalids, the thermometer not rising above 63° in the heat of the day. The natives said the winds were unusually high this year; but there are always high winds at this season. We moored opposite the island, close under 'Pharaoh's Bed,' this being the warmer side, and also because it afforded a good walk for 'Cousin Phil.' Here, for two days, Selina and I amused ourselves very well with excursions to the island, rambles among the ruins, observations on the groups of natives, and conversations with Mohamed on the Bible histories, compared with those of the Korán. The histories of Moses, Joseph, and all the Egyptian Pharaohs, were so jumbled together in the dragoman's brains, that there was no making head or tail of them, and they were intermingled with the most ridiculous traditions. He listened with much interest to the Bible story of the life of Joseph, saying at every portion which he recognised, "Yes, that's right, that's right," and at the conclusion he admitted that my story was better than his. Among other extraordinary ideas he said, that the Jews in Alexandria watched every Saturday night by the river side, expecting to see Moses rise out of the water. He fully believed that Moses did appear there, and his not having seen him, as yet, did not in the smallest degree shake his belief in the fact. We wished much that our dragoman could read the Bible for himself, for there was a great deal of intelligence in him ; and it seemed at times as though he were ready to embrace the light of truth. On our return we began teaching him to read, and he was so very clever at it, and learnt so quickly, that we could not but regret that we had not begun from the first. Four months would have gone a great way towards teaching him, but it was late now ; and our lessons were well-nigh brought to a tragical end when the Mussulman discovered that, in order to reach the envied point of spelling his own name, it was absolutely necessary that his lips should frame the unclean word *ham* — Mo-ham-ed !

At five P.M. of Saturday, Feb. 2nd, the wind abated a little, and we removed to the village of Shellāl, the starting-point for the Cataracts, bidding a last adieu to the lovely island, with its surrounding groups of rocks : and it was arranged with the Reïs of the Cataracts, that he should take us down at eight o'clock the following morning. He had wished us to go at three o'clock A.M., but whatever people in health might have done, it was clearly impossible for our invalids to witness the scene at such an hour without risk; neither were they inclined to lie quietly in their beds, and to pass the alarming and picturesque passage blindfold. Eight o'clock then was agreed to, and after ordering a cup of warm coffee to be prepared for our early breakfast, we retired to rest.

Sunday, Feb. 3rd.—At seven A.M. Bedlam seemed to have broken loose. All the wild 'Reïs' and their retinue appeared on the bank, the chief was ready, and we must go now, or not at all. They chattered, and shouted, and screamed, and tumbled ropes and other necessaries into the boat. Mohamed was bewildered, rushed down perpetually to the cabin entreating us to come up. 'Cousin Phil' was dressing, quietly unconscious of the uproar; Selina was just out of bed: we replied that we should come as quickly as we could, but start before we were all on deck, they must not. When we did appear, still before the appointed hour, they said the wind had risen, and that we could not go, either now, or at any hour of the day, even supposing the wind should fall. They must have had some private reason for all this; but 'Cousin Phil' took it very quietly. We preferred waiting any number of days to passing the Cataracts without seeing the descent, and we knew that they could not take any other boat down before us. Each vessel must be taken in its proper turn, or the pilots are liable to a heavy fine. As long as they said the wind blew, we were obliged to remain, whether it did blow or not, for the 'Cairo' was too large and heavy for us to risk any responsibility in persuading them to start. Mohamed was extremely anxious about it, and I believe he fully expected some catastrophe. Another dahabëéh had been so much damaged on its way, that its journey was delayed several days for repairs. And we learnt afterwards that the 'Cairo' last year had had three planks damaged in the descent of the Cataracts, which accounted somewhat for the anxiety of the Reïs and the dragoman.

Sunday, then, was spent at Shellāl. Selina and I rode on donkeys to Assouan to see what boats were there. All our friends were gone. They had reached Shellāl before the high winds had set in with so much force, and had proceeded at once.

Monday, Feb. 4th.—This time we were ready before our pilots. The wind was favourable, but though seven A.M. was the appointed hour, they did not appear; and it was 'Cousin Phil's' turn now to complain. We watched anxiously, and Mohamed was very wroth. Two other vessels had arrived, one bearing the French, the other the English flag; a photographer and a pretty gazelle were on board, the latter doomed to be exported, and to die of cold in England. Yet its ways are so winning it is not surprising that travellers should be tempted to carry the gazelle away from its native soil, and I almost coveted the pretty, bright-eyed creature. The wind would continue to rise—what should we do? "Oh, no fear," said Mohamed, "it is *Monday* to-day!" His superstitions were always ready to suit the occasion—he wanted to keep us quiet, though he was far from quiet himself.

Down they came at last, the whole of the wild party,—four grisly chiefs with their retinue. In another instant, the Frenchman's dragoman had gone up to them, and they were all squatted composedly on the ground for a parley. This was too much; Mohamed went up to them, bribed them, and threatened them with the anger of the Rajah, and other dreadful calamities; but we did not gain our point until we walked determinately towards the French dahabëëh, to request that the gentleman would withdraw his dragoman. On this Mohamed made renewed exertions, and literally dragged the tardy pilots on board the 'Cairo.'

At a few minutes before eight A.M. we succeed in starting. The four pilots take their stations in various parts of the boat, one at the helm in the place of 'El Abiad,' while twenty-four new rowers replace our own twelve, two to each oar. The whole direction of the boat is handed over to the new-comers, and our men look on, whilst a Nubian is perched on the edge of the quarter-deck, holding a long rosary of beads in his hands.

They row the boat silently through rocky passages, where it has only just room enough to pass, till we arrive at the entrance of the great Cataracts. A narrow pass, indeed, for a boat like ours. The water is boiling, foaming, and whirling within it, over a hard bed of rocks; and rocks enclose it on either side. It certainly does look formidable. The excitement of the Reïs increases; anxiety is depicted on every one of the Arab countenances; the rowers raise their oars, and sit immovably in their seats; the rosary-man begins repeating the Korán, as fast as his lips can move. We are all ordered to be seated. Mohamed, fearing that Selina and I may tumble overboard, makes a dart at us, squats down on the deck beside us, catches hold of our dresses with both hands, to hold us fast, and with every muscle in his face hard at work, he calls on "E Seïde! E Seïde!" (the Saint of the Cataracts,) to protect our passage. The poor Reïs, the 'old man,' is wild with anxiety now, for there is a very sharp turn at the end of the passage, and the length of the 'Cairo' is against her. He stands at the helm, and in we dash; we strike against one rock mid-way, and we feel another rock under us; but in scarcely more than a minute and a half the dreaded corner is turned in safety. 'Cousin Phil' was delighted with the skill of the old Reïs, and the manner in which he had steered the vessel through. The rock had made a small hole in one of the planks, but the Arabs all maintained that we broke the rock; not the rock us! Shaking of hands and congratulations now went round, the men resumed their oars, and we wound once again between the picturesque rocky islands towards Assouan. The pilots resumed their equanimity, together with their pipes, taking snatches at them and at the helm by turns, while the handsome cook-boy carried his original coffee-pot round, and served out its contents to the strangers.

The mixture of the sublime and the ridiculous in the whole scene was so absurd, that it kept down fear in our minds. The intense and novel excitement, added to the suppressed expectation of approaching danger, brought on hysterical fits of laughing, and the tears rolled copiously from our eyes. The passage *down* the Cataracts far exceeded our expectations, and was universally acknowledged the crowning scene of the Nile trip.

We thought that we might be much more alarmed were we to attempt it a second time, when the novelty would have passed away, and the danger be more apparent. The cleverness of the native pilots, however, is so great, that there is no reason to avoid the Cataracts from fear of danger; and it is a sight well worth seeing, in which opinion both Thomas and Sarah warmly agreed with us. Twelve guineas, or thereabouts, is the sum paid for taking a large vessel through the Cataracts, besides a 'bakhsheesh,' over and above, of about 2*l.* Half the sum is paid going up, the other half coming down; but prices have increased during the last few years, and therefore may do so still. Mohamed told us that the money collected by the pilots during the season is put aside in a common purse, till no more dahabëéhs are expected. It is then divided; one portion between the pilots, the rest between the other men who form the population of the village of Shellāl, the whole company being one and the same family. A good thing they must make of it, for certainly their mode of housekeeping is not extravagant.

CHAPTER VIII.

ASSOUAN, KARNAK, DENDERAH.

We reached Assouan in about an hour from the moment of starting, and sat down to breakfast at ten A.M., mooring against the island of Elephantine. The name of this island is represented in hieroglyphics by the form of an elephant. A portion of the staircase that served for the ancient Nilometer is still in existence, but I cannot say that we saw it, though Mohamed showed the spot, and one of our men got out of the boat, and groped into an opening in the rock to point it out. Mohamed afterwards said it was still under water. As we could do no more, we were content to believe that it either was or ought to be there, and the curious hieroglyphics on the surrounding stones, together with a few traces of building, were at any rate proofs of something having once stood there, which was no doubt the veritable Nilometer.

At Assouan there is a manufactory of the red and black pottery of the ancient Egyptians. It has been kept up from the old times in this town and at

Sioot. The pottery is extremely pretty. It is made of a clay which is found near this town, formed on a very simple lathe, coloured before it is baked, and engraved with curious devices by means of a pointed iron tool. We purchased some vases, small crocodiles, and birds, in this ware, the flat bases of which were scored all over, and intended to be used as a flesh-brush after a Turkish bath. A father and his two sons were the manufacturers. We did not see a very large assortment of goods, for other travellers had purchased them before our arrival.

Mr. M——n's dahabëëh was at Assouan. He dined with us twice, and kindly lent us an English translation of the Korán to look at. Perhaps it was the curiosity natural to our sex that made Selina and me so anxious to look into it, for 'Cousin Phil' did not in the least care to see it; he said he "could not see why people should not be satisfied with the Bible." And we were soon satisfied that no book in the world could be more full of vain repetitions and absurd stories than the Korán.

The dust had blown up in most unpleasant clouds during our stay at Assouan, and we were anxious to be off. Our Reïs had gone to pay a visit to his home; the charcoal was a long time coming in; and half the men were away amusing themselves. There was some trouble in collecting them all; indeed they did not come until they saw that preparations were making for starting without them.

Wednesday, Feb. 6th.—We left Assouan: the

Reïs was to join us in a few hours, but the Reïs came not. The wind was high and contrary. We had nearly reached the home of little 'Blackey,' which, had the Reïs been on the boat, he would have been allowed to visit. The hours pass by; the boat makes little progress, and the sad face of the young Arab attracts our attention. He cannot prevail with the dragoman, and with tears in his eyes he appeals to us. "Sitte, sitte! Ana! (Lady, lady! I, home! home!") pointing first to himself, then to the shore, and ejaculating the last word in a tone which told that he thought that the key which would most surely unlock our hearts. He was right; the appeal was irresistible, and we spoke for him. He was packed off with his three dollars for his mother, who was a widow, and a promise of "twenty sticks" if he were not back by dinner-time. It was almost an impossibility that he should be back by that time, but, happily for him, his mother saw the boat in the distance, and came to meet him. Poor 'Blackey!' when she came she only scolded him for not bringing her more money; and when he returned to the boat with the bread she had brought for him, she sat down on the ground to cry. The son's heart was moved to compassion; he undressed, and threw to her, for his little brother, the white waist-coat which he had put on for his 'best.' I fear our friend was not faultless. By the law of the Korán a son is bound to give half his wages to support a widowed mother; and this son, it appears, should have had much more than three dollars to give on the present occasion.

Thursday, Feb. 7th.—The truant Reïs arrived at last. He never should have been allowed to go, and, to our astonishment, he came in smiling and bowing, and was greeted by dragoman and crew with the usual number of friendly 'salaams' and good wishes. When all this was duly over, he received a good 'set down' from Mohamed.

'El Abiad' was next allowed to go home, with a solemn promise of returning by sunset, which he did. He was supposed to be 'engaged' to a Nubian 'belle' in these parts, to whom he was to be married in the course of the summer, when English people were out of the way. 'El Abiad' was very sad indeed about the long delay of his wedding. Mohamed said it was because he was going to be married that he always said double the number of prayers of any other man in the boat; and certain it was that the steersman, from the date of this visit, whenever his duties permitted him, was always upon his knees.

At one P.M. we reached Kom Ombo. The temple, though deeply embedded in the sand, is very interesting and pretty. It is dedicated to the crocodile-headed god, 'Savah,' whose figure occurs on the walls. On some parts of the roof of the portico the figures were left unfinished, and furnish an example of the Egyptian practice of drawing them in squares when the pictures were begun. It is supposed that

THE TEMPLE OF KOM OMBO & THE DAHABEĖH 'CAIRO

this was only practised when the artist was copying from another drawing.

A second building towers over the river; it is covered with hieroglyphics, and large masses which have fallen from it lie on the bank, as though ready to slip into the water. Both are of the times of the Ptolemies; but there is another gateway here which bears the name of Thothmes III. and Amun-nou-Het, who erected the great obelisks of Karnak. Many parts of the crude brick wall which enclosed the temple are visible above the sand. Beyond it is a cemetery, but the heat was so extreme it would not have been prudent to venture further, and we returned to the boat.

This evening we reached the hills, 'Aboo Moolar,' which Mohamed amusingly recalled to our minds by saying, in a high-pitched note, "Don't you remember the echo, when you called 'Se-lie-e-na?'"

The Reïs was troublesome again. Mohamed could not manage him alone, so he came into the saloon, saying, "If you please, tell 'Pa-pa' to come with me to the Governor at Esneh, with the Reïs. He will make the boat go at night, and I can't stop him." 'Cousin Phil' shouted out, in the voice of a 'Commander-in-chief,' for the benefit of the said Reïs on deck, "I will not go at night, and I will not go before seven o'clock in the morning!" Mohamed looked terrified, and began an apologetic "La, la." But 'Cousin Phil' continued, "And you may tell the

Reïs that I am ready to go to the Governor, or any body else you please, with him." Mohamed's fear was turned into joy; he scarcely waited to hear the end, but patted 'Cousin Phil' on the back, with a "Thank you, sir, thank you, sir; that's right!" and away he went. The Reïs never tried going at night any more. 'Cousin Phil' remarked, "That's the only way to do it," and we continued our game at back-gammon.

About this time the noise which the rudder made during the night, from not being properly tied up, was so great as to prevent our sleeping. We had a great deal of trouble about it, and only succeeded at last by getting up in the middle of the night, and rousing Mohamed to have it set to rights. He was very angry, but still it required two nights' disturbance of his sleep to secure our own. He then took fright, thinking we were displeased with him, and one day came up, looking greatly agitated, and, counting on his fingers, said, "Well, there's Philæ, one; the rudder, two; the Reïs, three: well, that's not much; three in three months; good ladies, good heart, you know, not think about this?" He spoke in most imploring accents, casting all the time the most beseeching looks at us. It was hard to look grave at so absurd an appeal, yet it was melancholy to see a character spoilt, as Mohamed's was, and as, indeed, is that of most Mussulmen, by the cringing dread of the displeasure of their superiors. The whole people seem to be cowed down, bearing in every way the look of a conquered nation fulfilling the prophecies of Scripture concerning them.

Friday, Feb. 8th.—We reached the quarries and grottoes of Silsilis at three P.M. This evening was devoted to the western side. The principal grotto was commenced by Horus, B C. 1337. We hunted out his oval on the wall, as also the picture which represents him pursuing his conquered enemy Cush, the Ethiopians. The subjects are difficult to make out, for there is not much light within, and the walls are blackened by the 'mashals.' The grotto is cut in the rock, with five openings in front like doorways. There are figures on the rocky pillars left between them, and hieroglyphics all over. The chief scientific interest of these grottoes consists in the mention, among the hieroglyphics, of some assemblies held during the reign of Remeses the Great. There are other smaller grottoes and niches further up on the edge of the river. In one of them we noticed a bed of the alluvial deposit left there by the inundation of this season. The first Cataracts were originally here, till a fall of the rocks removed them to Assouan.

The natives of Silsilis all carry guns. They hunt the gazelle, and brought us some of the meat for sale. Mohamed called it delicious. Without saying that it was bad, we did not discover its excellence.

The corn was in ear on the bank at Silsilis, and

the cracks in the soil made by the heat of the sun were so deep and wide as to make it quite a matter of difficulty for 'Cousin Phil' to walk upon it.

Saturday, Feb. 9th.—Selina and I went with our guides to see the quarries on the opposite shore. They are far more extensive than those on the western side, and marvellous in their gigantic proportions. They may be compared to a town, with streets leading down to the river, and large open squares in all directions. The walls rise to the height of sixty feet, perpendicularly hewn on the rock, and blocks, large and small, lie strewn about on the ground. The marks of the wedges and tools used in cutting the stone are seen on many portions of it, and every cut is so clean and dry, no sign of age having accumulated upon the pale-coloured sandstone, that one is apt to look round inquiringly for the multitude who worked the gigantic works. Were they but now suddenly swept away, leaving their unfinished labour behind them, and whither were they gone?

The quarries extend a long way. Those furthest to the south are the most remarkable, but they were too far off for us, and we were obliged to leave them and return to the boat. I think we enjoyed these quarries as much as anything we had seen, and, curiously enough, here we picked up the best specimen of 'pudding-stone' that we had ever come across. It was sandstone like the rest, and, put in a plate on table, it might have been mistaken for a real bit of plum-pudding.

Little progress could still be made on account of the contrary wind, and at half-past seven P.M. we moored under the shelter of the bank.

Sunday, Feb. 10th.—Proofs of having left Nubia behind us were accumulating fast: a larger number of sails appeared on the water; birds again were flying overhead; the natives wore more clothing—the fields were more green; mosquitoes again claimed our attention, but the flies did not tease, and gave us a temporary rest.

At noon we reached Edfoo. Its temple is very remarkable; it is preserved almost entire, and thus gives a good idea of what the Egyptian temples originally were. Their massive structure has more the appearance of a fortress than of a building appropriated for sacred worship. The richness of the sculptures on every portion of the walls astonishes the eye, but they are far from possessing any beauty of form. The towers, courts, pillars, chambers, and enclosing walls, remain in the temple at Edfoo,—a model more or less of what all its neighbours were. It is of the date of the Ptolemies. Among the sculptures are sailing-boats; fishing-nets, from the absence of perspective apparently full of every kind of creature; the spearing of the hippopotamus in the water; chiefs cutting off the heads of fifteen prisoners at one stroke, &c. &c. Two hundred steps, each two inches high, lead in a gentle incline to the tops of the towers, whence an extensive view is obtained. We spent three hours in this temple; and when Mohamed had made a purchase of thirty chickens, we started again, and rowed till ten P.M. A great number of wild geese congregate here, and the pigeon-houses at Edfoo are on an elaborate scale.

Monday, Feb. 11th.—At half-past twelve we reached El Rab. The wind was so high, and the dust blew in our faces in such thick clouds, that we almost gave up the expedition to the grottoes; but we did go, and reached them in safety, veiled and spectacled, though on extremely unsafe donkeys. The grottoes are hewn in succession along the side of the hill. These tombs are extremely interesting, from the remains of the painted subjects on their walls. They are so mutilated that it takes some time to decipher them; but we did succeed in finding out, on one side, the harvest-labours of the ancients, from the reaping of the corn to the baking of the bread in the oven. On the opposite wall of the grotto is the banquet, over which the master of the house and his wife preside, sitting on a throne at one end of the apartment, she having her right arm thrown round his neck, and at the further end the death and funeral ceremony of the owner of the tomb is depicted.

The grottoes date from the sixteenth century

before Christ, and the name of a king of the sixth dynasty (about 2030 B.C.) is found on a rock in the valley by those who know how to read it.

The temples are small, and were beyond our reach; but we noticed the enclosing crude brick wall of the old town of Eleithyias: substantial it is still, and is said to have been thirty feet broad. We resumed our way. The wind blew the vessel against the shore, so that we were obliged to stop till its violence abated. At five P.M. we proceeded again, but did not reach Esneh till the following morning. Though the wind was so high, it was gradually becoming warmer, and the thermometer pointed to 94° in the sun.

Tuesday, Feb. 12th.—We reached Esneh. The city appeared to us now far more worthy the name than before. Had our ideas expanded or contracted? What we deemed only a mud village on the way up the river we now saw clearly to be a town of some importance. The streets, which we had called alleys, appeared spacious; and, alas for the force of habit, what had appeared to us dirty in the extreme, was now pronounced to be, on the contrary, rather clean. Excepting in this latter point, at which we were naturally grieved, we decided that the change in our ideas was on the side of expansion. The entire novelty had worn away, and we could, no doubt, form a more just estimate of the various objects around us than was contained in the first sweeping condemnations of poor, small, narrow, low, &c. &c.

—everything, with the exception of filthy, which all here really is, and, so long as Turks and Arabs exist as such, ever will be. We took another look at the beautiful portico, and walked through the bazaar. On our return we found that some misunderstanding had been going on between the Reïs and the crew. They were all assembled before the Governor of Esneh, and we thought we should never get them back again. The explanation of the affair given to us was as follows:—The Reïs was condemned to receive '150 sticks,' laid across the feet. The company of Reïs on the Nile all hold together as 'brothers.' When such a judgment is pronounced on one of them, if another is in the way, he steps forward to redeem the punishment: he lies down on the ground by the side of the culprit, draws across his own feet the chain which had been placed on those of the delinquent, and claims the awarded blows in lieu of his 'brother.' The punishment is then remitted; but the accusers are satisfied, because the humiliation is esteemed equal to the actual strokes.

We did not see the proceeding, and were rather sceptical as to the truth of the statement; and, having mentioned it on our return to several persons acquainted with the country, we found that they had never heard of such a custom. Yet certain it is that something lasted more than two hours; that every man in the boat was summoned; that the Reïs of Lord H——'s dahabëéh, which we found at Esneh, was called in; that our Reïs returned when all was over, looking alarmingly scowling; that he did not speak one word to any man in the boat for some days, and remained on sulky terms with the dragoman to the last; and that our 'fool' (Hassan the 'Comic'), who had been reprimanded at Silsilis about his dress, or rather undress, and had been rather sulky ever since, ended his 'fooleries' here, in so far as we were concerned, by turning out in a very smart suit, which transformed him from a very ugly into a handsome man, and deserting our service. We saw him, a few weeks later, in one of the towns further north, looking quite like a gentleman, with a walking-stick in one hand, and leading an equally well-dressed child by the other. When Hassan had been one of our crew, he had frequently pleaded poverty to excuse the rag with which he covered himself. Fortunately for us, our boat was so well manned that it was not necessary to take in another pair of hands.

We left Esneh at four P.M., and rowed till ten P.M. This was an extremely warm evening: the thermometer rose to 80° in the cabins.

Wednesday, Feb. 13th (Ash-Wednesday).—The sun was extremely hot, yet the wind was so high that the awning could not be kept up, and we were forced to take refuge below.

Some of our 'antiquities' were so fragrant with mummy-perfume, that we amused ourselves with giving them a good washing. I fear this was not a very scientific proceeding, and that it did not increase the antique appearance of our treasures; but though we might have deteriorated a little in our ideas of cleanliness, the natural instinct had not quite disappeared, and we voted that, '*coûte-qui-coûte*,' the virtue should extend to our treasures: into the tub they all went, to the immense satisfaction of Mohamed, who walked in immediately with a lemon, and asked leave to assist in perfecting the process.

We passed by Erment without landing; and on Thursday, Feb. 14th, at eight A.M., the ruins of Luxor again came into view. Thebes was now a harbour full of floating dahabëëhs, at whose mast-heads were waving the flags of almost every European nation. Including the 'Cairo,' there were twelve such vessels, whose gaily-painted sides, the costumes of the various crews, together with the waving banners and pennants, formed a very gay scene. All was not gay, however, within. The dahabëëhs were, for the most part, the houses of so many invalids; and amongst them were Mr. and Mrs. M——, only waiting for a steamer to take them in all haste back to Cairo. Mr. H—— was also here, and the "four young gentlemen" (as Mohamed called them) from the Desert, who had chosen a 'crinoline' for their ensign.

Letters again were the first thought, and eagerly I dived into the Consul's box and collected a large budget of them, and of newspapers, which had accumulated there during the past two months and a half. How anxiously we opened them, one after the other, for who could tell what time might have accomplished in that space? Some friends had passed from this world to their rest, but our own immediate belongings had been preserved well and happy; and with thankful hearts we sat down to answer the budget, before proceeding to any further investigations into antiquity.

The Consul, Mustapha Agra, paid us a conveniently short visit, which was most inconveniently lengthened out by Mohamed, who actually sent him back again, that he might receive the indispensable cup of coffee. The Consul can boast of no personal attractions, but he behaved himself very politely, and inquired anxiously if Mohamed had performed his duties satisfactorily. He appeared quite ready to take him to task, had he not done so. Mustapha was formerly in the service of an English family settled in Alexandria. He removed with them to England, remained there some years, and returned again with them to Alexandria. When he left their service he was made Consul at Luxor, his native place. He is an intelligent man, and knows how to make a little money out of the ancient inhabitants of his birthplace. A few days ago he dug up two large mummy-cases, very brilliantly painted. He generally sells them before they are opened, so that the purchaser takes the chance of treasure or no treasure within. One of the visitors at Luxor bought these two for 70*l.*, and found nothing within but a few gilt figures. We were told, on good authority, that a mummy is rarely worth more than 5*l.* or 6*l.* The Consul showed us two rolls of papyrus, which would have tempted us much more. He asked 10*l.* for one, and 12*l.* for the other. They were between two and three inches wide, and of considerable length. He unrolled a portion of one to show us the writing upon it; it was written all over in small characters; the other had figures of men, horses, &c. The papyrus must be wetted with water before it can be unrolled. It has the appearance of a sheet of bark, of a pale yellow colour. There is but one spot where it is said still to grow. (Isa. xix. 7.)

The first greeting a stranger receives on arriving at Thebes is from the donkey-boys, and up to a late hour in the evening the cry was heard, up and down the bank, "Karnak glorious! Karnak mag-ni-fi-cent! To-morrow, Karnak, lady! Very good donkey! Donkey go like steam-boat, lady! *Ex*-qui-site donkey-boy! Every gentleman give donkey-boy baksheesh! plenty! &c. &c."

The donkey-boys are right—Karnak is glorious; it is magnificent! Some of the donkeys do go "like steam-boats," and it is a hard matter to make them go slowly, with their "*ex*quisite" attendants behind them, urging them on with the points of their sticks, accompanied by the most inhuman sounds that human throat ever uttered, but which apparently are well understood by the donkey tribe. Some of the little Arabs were very clever and amusing, and had a considerable English vocabulary on the tip of their tongues; others were very dull and stupid.

Karnak would occupy many a day without weariness, and we gave as much time to it as strength would allow. The view of the ruins from the south is very fine indeed, and the general idea of the extent of the great temple of Amun thus obtained, is perhaps more pleasing than the inspection of any one particular portion. Its five or six gateways, the obelisks, the columns of the Great Hall, those of numberless other courts and avenues, the colossi broken and scattered about, the four avenues of sphinxes which led to it on four sides, the two lakes, one of which is said to be extremely salt, may all be seen from thence. It was a striking and beautiful picture. The surrounding country was bright with the rising corn, the stately palm-trees rose against the clear blue sky, and the brilliant sunshine gave an exquisite colouring to everything. The wonders of the "Great Hall of Columns," 134 in number; the subjects of the sculptures within; the battle-scenes without; the chamber surrounded with lion-headed statues in black granite, the sphinxes, and androsphinxes; the name of Shishak, King of Egypt, who was cotemporary with Solomon; the representation of the captives taken by him at Jerusalem, when he went up against it in the reign of Rehoboam (2 Chron. xii.)—are all full of interest; and with the assistance of Murray's Hand-book may be traced out to a considerable extent.

The original buildings, of which a very few remains are to be found, date from Osirtasen I., about 2020 B.C. The greater number of the existing ruins are of the age of Amunoph I., 1498 B.C., and many of his successors. The temples of Thebes were destroyed or defaced in the invasion of Cambyses, 525 B.C.; but Karnak, it is said, suffered more particularly in the second century before Christ, at the hands of Ptolemy Lathyrus.

Our second expedition was to the Tombs of the Kings, on the opposite side. They are now called 'Biban el Moluk,' the Gates of the Kings. Well might those who chose the spot have thought themselves safe from disturbance by the hand of man. A ride of an hour and a half over barren rock and sand, down a ravine flanked on either side by perpendicular cliffs or huge boulders, brings the traveller to these abodes of the dead. The principal tomb is that which was opened by Belzoni, and bears his name. Three flights of steps, all but perpendicular, lead down to its subterranean halls and chambers, each of which is sculptured and painted all over in colours as bright as though they had but just been laid on. The scenes relate chiefly to the death and burial of the owner of the tomb. In one chamber, where the paintings are unfinished, the figures are drawn first with a red line, and then apparently corrected with a black one, supposed to be that of the master. They are drawn without squares. A few patches of colouring were begun, but left unfinished. The entire length of this tomb exceeds 320 feet., and its depth 90 feet. The descent appeared perilous in the extreme, but down we all went, and we came up again in safety.

This was as much as 'Cousin Phil' could accomplish; but Selina and I visited Bruce's tomb, which contains the representation of the two Harpists first given in "Bruce's Travels." They are drawn with striking expression and elegance on the walls of one of the small chambers which line either side of the long passage at the entrance of the tomb. The drawing of the subjects represented on the walls of these chambers is remarkable and interesting, as showing the household occupations, the articles of furniture for their houses, the arms, the ships, and the agricultural customs of the ancient Egyptians.

Examining into all these had well-nigh exhausted Selina's remaining strength, and Sarah alone accompanied me with the guides into the third principal tomb, called Memnon's tomb. Our time was short, and we could do barely more than rush through; yet we saw enough of the long processions on the walls and vaulted roofs of the chambers, painted in brilliant yellow on a black ground, to make us wish we could have remained much longer.

Time would not wait for us, even in Egypt; evening was drawing on, and considerably fatigued, both in mind and body, from the interest and length of the expedition, our cavalcade set out again, the donkey-boys picking up a few fossils for us on the way, or offering a hand or some other portion of a disinterred mummy for sale. It was revolting to see them handle these latter, for surely no curiosity or love of antiquity should overcome the feeling of respect and reverence which ought ever to be shown to the remains of the dead, even though they come before us in the forms of Egyptian mummies.

Sunday intervened before the third expedition at Thebes, and gave us a day of rest, though not a public service, on the deck of one of the dahabéèhs, as we had hoped. All the travellers assembled on shore in expectation of it; but, through some mistake, the missionary did not offer it; so that, after waiting for some time, we had our private assembly for Church service as usual. In the afternoon some horsemen were sent down on the bank by the Governor or Consul, to play the 'Gereet' for our entertainment. The 'Crinoline' party set up a tent, and offered cake and champagne to their guests, kindly inviting us to join them and see the 'Gereet.' There were not many horsemen present, and they seemed to play without much distinctive plan; but they threw their long lances or sticks in the air and caught them again with much skill, while the horses were going at full gallop. It was a graceful game, and we regretted to hear that it is fast dying out in Egypt.

Monday, *Feb.* 18*th*, was devoted to visiting the temple-palace of Medeénet Hâboo. This must have been a splendid building. The halls and columns still remaining, strike the spectator with astonishment. The sculptures on the interior of the walls are full of interest. On one we traced out the coronation procession of the king, and the carrier-pigeons which were to fly to the four corners of the world, to announce his coronation to the gods of the south, north, east, and west. On the outer walls many battle-scenes are delineated, but provokingly interrupted by the heaps of rubbish thrown up against the walls in clearing out the ruins. Among the sculptures describing the victories of the king, heaps of the amputated hands of the slain are piled before the conqueror; an officer counts them one by one, and a scribe notes them down, 3000 in each heap. We took our luncheon among the ruins, and some Arabs came again for a sale of '*antiques*,' which are sure to meet one at every ruin. We bid adieu to this side of the wonderful city with regret, for we were to leave Thebes to-morrow.

To-morrow came and we did not start, but paid one more visit to Karnak, and underwent a considerable 'baking' in so doing. In the afternoon we went to see a collection of curiosities, "the manufactory of antiquities," as it is called; the owner enjoying a high reputation for skill in his art. They were extremely curious, and in many, no doubt, we might have been easily deceived; but there were some in which even our inexperienced eyes could detect the signs of modern workmanship. The Arab guides are supposed to be adepts at pointing out the distinction to strangers; and the best plan for the uninitiated is to trust to them in this matter, and be content if among a lot of rubbish they bring home one or two articles of some value.

Wednesday, Feb. 20th.—Mohamed was so long in his preparations for departure, that we did not start till half-past three P.M. The donkey-boys, to the number of forty, were assembled on the bank, shouting "Good-bye, lady! baksheesh! me! lady, me!" at the highest pitch of their voice. We threw them some coppers, and a sudden silence and scramble ensued as we rowed off, the crew raising their usual shout and chant. All the vessels that we had found at Thebes had left, and a new set had replaced them there.

We reached the palace of the Sheikh whom we had promised to visit on our return, so late, that we were obliged to give up both the visit and the 'Gereet play' which he had promised us. We rowed past and Mohamed landed, returning with "a jar of honey (treacle), a couple of turkeys, and a quantity of charcoal, presents from my friend." He had made the Sheikh several presents on his former visit, and this was his return.

Thursday, Feb. 21st.—At Negádeh our cook went on shore, and returned with a large stock of the cotton Maláiat for his family. These cloths are manufactured here and exported to the other towns. They are very like blue-checked French cotton, and some have red silk borders, which look extremely well. A little further on, at 'Ballas,' is the manufactory of large water-jars, called 'Ballásee,' the rafts of which we saw constantly floating down. The crew did not seem inclined to their work to-day. Their long holiday at Thebes had made them lazy, and there was some trouble in getting them to row us as far as Ghench. The thermometer rose to 100° in the sun.

Friday, Feb. 22nd.—It was at Ghench that the donkey-chair and our whole cavalcade had first appeared on the scene, and we recalled with amusement the impressions of our first expedition, as the chair and the donkeys were ferried across to convey us to the temple of Denderah, on the western side of the river: we were getting quite used to it all now.

The ride on this second visit occupied three-quarters of an hour. A portion of the road lay below the telegraph wires, between two railway-like embankments, modern and unromantic-looking in the extreme, and little in accordance with the train of thought and anticipation suggested by a visit to the renowned 'Temple of Venus.' The embankment ceased in due time, and nature appeared again clothed in fields of green corn, with peas and beans in variously-coloured blossoms, among which we found a very fine specimen of the wild hyacinth. We had raised our minds to the highest pitch of pleasurable anticipation as we drew near the temple. Perhaps this was the reason of the reaction that ensued; but, when we entered the great portico,—

shall I confess it?—we exclaimed simultaneously, with mingled feelings of disappointment and surprise, "How ugly!"

The sound of our own words startled us, and we almost expected the ancient gods and goddesses around to start into life and rebuke us; still the effect was the same. Heavy, grotesque, the portico appeared, though still a grand and perfect specimen of the architecture of the age. The hall beyond has much greater pretension to beauty and elegance, but it is sadly defaced, and so blackened that we could hardly make out anything. The atmosphere in this and in the succeeding chambers was so impure, that we could do little more than poke our heads in, cough, and come out again into the portico, to study its massiveness and perfect preservation, if our taste would still refuse to perceive any beauty in the style.

The portico was added to the temple by the Emperor Tiberius; the oldest names occurring on the building are those of Julius Cæsar, the beautiful Cleopatra, and their son Cæsarion, or Neo-Cæsar, whose portraits are found on one of the outer walls. It was extremely hot, and I had a great deal of trouble in finding out these figures, not knowing exactly where to look for them. I did find them, however, and thought that either Cleopatra could hardly have felt flattered by her portrait, did she ever see it, or the ideas of beauty in that age were no more in accordance with modern taste than was the temple of Denderah with our own.

The portico has twenty-four columns, six across the front, closed half way up by screens. Each pillar is surmounted by a woman's head, four times repeated, so that it faces you every way ; and these are again crowned with a large square block of stone, sculptured with hieroglyphics, and conveying the impression of a far greater weight than the four heads together are calculated to support. The winged globes all along the centre of the roof have a curious effect. At the risk of breaking our necks, we traced out a great portion of the zodiac, painted up there ; it has been proved, like the rest of the temple, to be of Roman origin, although, both here and at Esneh, the sign *Cancer* is represented by a scarabeus, and not a crab. There was an avenue of sphinxes leading to the portico, and extending to a gateway, which stands at some distance. The ruins of various other chapels or temples are to be seen at short distances from the Great Temple. On these we could only cast a passing glance, and peep at the ugly giant-monster Typhon represented upon one of them.

We returned to Gheneh, and made an expedition in the afternoon to procure some of the celebrated dates from the Hegâz, which are sold here in drums. We paid twenty-five piastres a drum. They were quite the best, but may frequently be had for a lower price. Mohamed invested in so large a stock of 'goolleh' for his own private use (four large crates full), besides oranges and limes for our refreshment, that we were delayed for some time. Moreover, the Reïs took the opportunity of dismissing two of the crew, who had absented themselves without leave. This was rather serious, for it was not so easy to procure others to replace them. Happily the men were not anxious to leave; and the Reïs, making a virtue of necessity, remitted their sentence to that of corporal punishment, which I believe was never executed.

At seven P.M. we started, leaving Denderah and its pretty hills behind us. The people of Denderah were the professed enemies of the crocodile. It appears that, instead of worshipping it, like the inhabitants of Kom Ombo, they attacked, killed, and ate it, without fear; on which account the two people waged a long and vigorous war.

No crocodiles disturbed us, but an army of rats was gaining daily, or rather nightly, strength, so that we welcomed with joy the arrival of a second cat on board; and it was with considerable satisfaction that we saw her instantly disappear down the rudder-hole into the body of the boat, where she found work to satisfy her for some days.

No more temples were in store for us for two or three days, but occupation seemed never to fail. The dahabëëh was beginning to assume a much less charming appearance than usual, and now reached such a pitch of uncleanness, that it was necessary to investigate into the cause. It soon appeared that cleanliness was no natural virtue of the Arabs.

Whereas the rule was that the deck should be washed three times a-day (the dragoman's own rule), which had been more or less attended to on the way up the river; and whereas the vessel had undergone a thorough cleaning at Wadee Halfeh, and a second at Luxor, the Arabs considered their duty to be well done, and had put all idea of further cleaning entirely out of their heads. Night after night, on their way home, they would lay themselves down to sleep contentedly in the hold after their day's rowing, and neither wash themselves, their clothes, nor their own portion of the boat, till they reached Cairo again. But the consequences naturally became too apparent to last, and a hue and cry was raised on the subject.

The men took it most good-humouredly, and we breathed more freely as bucket after bucket poured upon the deck, and washed away the thick coating of accumulated dirt. Twice every day now, to the end of the journey, the deck was washed by two men in turn; and it was not more than it needed. The fact is, that far more care in this respect is requisite on coming down the river than on going up, when the crew are kept clean, as it were in spite of themselves, by their frequent immersions in the water, necessitated by the constant 'tracking.' The men, no doubt, found the benefit of our strictness on the subject; for gradually they were seen dipping their clothes in the stream of their own accord, and even begging a bit of soap to restore their colour. Mohamed, too, walked about the deck picking up every little shred of sugar-cane or onion, haranguing and scolding as though he himself were the very essence of cleanliness. Alas, Mohamed! more than once a hint had been thrown to you about your own attire. But "all's well that ends well," and in a few days the 'Cairo' and her crew resumed their character for cleanliness amongst the dahabëëh fleet of the season.

From the night of the 23rd till the 26th the wind was so high and contrary that we made but little way. The crew sank into the hold, rose out of it again for a few moments' work, then back they went again. On the 24th we passed Farshoot, with its tall chimneys. The engineer and his family turned out to see us pass, and we bestowed some pity upon them, for their isolation from their own kindred, which pity may possibly have been very ill placed, but we judged by our own feelings on the subject. On the 25th, backwards and forwards trudged the 'Cairo,' from one side of the river to the other, making the least possible way along; now she was driven by the wind straight against the bank, now thrust off again with some trouble, by means of the long poles, and finally obliged to give it up, and to stop at an early hour.

Tuesday, Feb. 26th.—We reached Ballianeh, the nearest point for visiting Abydus. It involved a ride of upwards of two hours. Selina was fatigued, after all our excursions, and could not undertake it. 'Cousin Phil' and I started sorrowfully without her, to see the remains of this famous city, once one of the most important in Upper Egypt. The heat was excessive, but it was truly refreshing to see the rich, luxuriant plains, stretching all around, covered with waving crops of wheat, barley, beans, peas and lentils in flower, with the brilliant yellow 'Semga' (coleseed), cultivated in large quantities for its oil; and the white clover blossom, which our strange-headed dragoman would insist with me was called *in English* grass, not clover.

Thought went back to the time when Joseph and his brethren came down to Egypt, because there was much corn there: if the present crops appeared so luxuriant that the valley seemed to laugh and sing, what must they not have been in those seven years of miraculous plenty which succeeded the famine? The present beauty of the landscape was no doubt enhanced to us by our long stay in the barren land of Nubia, where only one narrow line of green meets the parched-up eye, and beyond this valley we soon arrived again at the white, barren, burning desert exactly in the heat of the day.

The temple is almost buried in the sand, but a sufficient portion is visible to show its original grandeur. It is of the time of Osiris and Remeses the Great. The city enjoyed the fame of being the true burial-place of the king, for which reason many noble, ancient families sought a tomb here, that they might lie in the same spot with Osiris. The Hall of

Columns is very handsome. The wall seems to be of alabaster, very beautifully sculptured, and the colours are still in many places quite bright. There is a succession of chambers, remarkable for the construction of their vaulted roofs, covered with sculptured ovals, containing the names of the kings; that of Osiris, to whom the temple was dedicated, being constantly repeated.

The second temple stood at a little distance. A few fragments only are visible, but there is a portion of a wall lined with alabaster, sculptured and painted in brilliant colours; also, on a bit of granite, some of the lovely blue colour which it is said cannot be imitated now. There were very handsome blocks of red and blue granite scattered about. The whole of this building is said to have been lined with alabaster.

The heat soon drove me back again to 'Cousin Phil,' who sat comfortably sheltered in his wonderful chair. By half-past four o'clock we had rejoined Selina, with a large nosegay of wild flowers, whose brilliant colours adorned our deck for many days; they were as precious in our eyes as the handsomest roses or geraniums in our more favoured land. Mohamed, who had nearly wept at leaving Selina behind, expecting, I fully believe, to see her sob violently on the subject, now came forward with assurances of, "You do quite right to-day. I myself finished altogether; and quite tight!" We discovered afterwards that 'tight,' in Mohamed's vocabulary, meant 'tired.'

Selina had occupied her time in sketching pigeon-houses, while Sarah had become so expert in the customs of the country as to seize a palm-branch from a little Arab who passed by, in order to brush the flies out of her lady's eyes.

The hero of the 20,000 wild geese was here at this time, and sent some of his superabundant stock to our boat. A rare feast for the crew, for we found these birds so fishy and tough that we could not touch them. As a specimen of Arab exaggeration, the sportsman's dragoman, of whom Mohamed had often told us, in a significant manner, that he was clothed, by the liberality of his master, in suits of apparel innumerable, together with "watches and gold chains," now appeared in our dahabëëh to beg some of his "brother's" wardrobe—which, of course, he did not get.

Late in the evening Girgeh came in sight. We scarcely recognised it again, and attributed the improvement to the fancies of an approach by moonlight, but morning dawn showed Girgeh still to be no inconsiderable town. It was at one time the capital of Upper Egypt, and now ranks second after Sioot.

The crew made their purchases; the kitchen utensils were sent on shore to undergo a thorough cleaning with the rough brown fibre of the date-tree. It was the second time they had been submitted to this process, and they returned looking quite bright and new. Whatever might be said of other departments in the dahabëëh 'Cairo,' certainly the cooking establishment was consolingly clean.

We walked through the bazaar, and captured an excellent specimen of a spindle, which a youth of eighteen or twenty years of age was carrying, spinning the brown woollen thread as he went along. The poor lad did not wish to part with it, and I begged the dragoman to leave it to him; but Mohamed understood no such ways of acting. He told the boy the lady wanted it, and that he would give him three piastres for it. Suiting the action to the word, he takes the spindle, wool and all, out of the owner's hand, and deposits it in 'Blackey's,' desiring him to keep it. 'Blackey' struts on before us, tucking the spindle under his arm as composedly as if it had been his own all the days of his life. The owner makes not the slightest resistance, but walks along with Mohamed, bargaining about the price. Two "Egyptian gentlemen" passing by, are attracted by what they consider a very amusing scene, and Mohamed, summoning them as umpires, yields so far as to give five piastres, and to keep the spindle. I brought it home with me, but always look upon it rather in the light of stolen goods.

Girgeh is famed for its honey. Some samples were brought to us, but it was so strongly flavoured with orange, that we did not like it, and considered it no better than what we get much nearer home. The bee-hives along the coast are very curious. We only saw them in the distance as we passed on, for they are outside the town. They were apparently composed of cylindrical tubes of unburnt clay, piled in rows one over the other, terminating in a single one at the top. The bees were buzzing about the open ends, in great excitement.

This evening we reached Ekhmim.

Thursday, Feb. 28th.—Before starting again, I took an early walk, and saw a most refreshing sight. It was nothing more nor less than a large tract of poppies all in bloom. The snowy-white, waving field, sprinkled here and there with pink and lilac, the fresh green of the leaves peeping out between the flowers, were refreshing as a shower to the parched-up land, and I enjoyed it for some time in silent admiration, to the astonishment of my guides, who immediately asked permission of the owners to gather a few to add to our nosegay. They are cultivated for the sake of the opium which they yield. Ekhmim, traditionally said to have been one of the oldest cities of Egypt, was completely destroyed at the time of the Arab invasion, so that no ruins are left here.

Near the tomb of the patron saint of the town of Ekhmim is a tree, which is studded with nails, driven into it by the sick, in expectation of a cure. Mohamed spoke of it with reverence, but we were to start at seven A.M., and I had stood so long looking at the poppies that we could not reach it in time. The tomb is also hung with offerings to the Saint, called 'Shekh Abou'l Kasim.'

Sunday, March 3rd.—We had passed the convents, called the 'red' and the 'white,' from the colour of the stone or brick of which they are built, the Gebel Shekh Herécdee, the woods of acacia where large quantities of charcoal were preparing for sale, and we now beheld Sioot, the capital of Upper Egypt, for the first time, having passed it at night on our way up the river.

Sioot is a true city, rising with mosques and minarets among clumps of tall date-trees. It has a population of about 20,000 inhabitants. The houses are of mud, with the exception of the Governor's palace and one or two others; but the immense length of the Bazaar, and its well-furnished shops, reminded us of Cairo itself. There were a number of very handsome red leather saddles, embroidered with gold, which attracted our attention, as well as the large pipe-bowls which are sold as samples of the ancient Egyptian ware, red and black, which is still manufactured here, as at Assouan. There was also a small fruit resembling the 'Siberian Crab,' but having a stone within, like the stone of a cherry or small plum. The natives call it 'Nebk.' The taste is that of an insipid apple. Sunday is market-day at Sioot, and the streets were crowded.

A ride across a beautiful tract of cultivated land, like the vale of Abydus, but of greater extent, brought us to the catacombs on the hills. They are very extensive, and have been called the "Cities of the Dead." The largest is known by the name of 'Stabl Antar.' The ascent is precipitous, but the donkeys climbed it well, chair and all.

The Catacomb is very large; but the sculptures are almost lost. On the roof of the entrance-hall we could just trace some pretty devices, which go by the name of "Greek scrolls." A few figures smelling the lotus were all we could make out on the walls: and in the further chambers nothing at all, the walls are so blackened and defaced.

Here 'Cousin Phil' remained, in view of the lovely landscape; but Selina and I ascended higher, to another grotto, on one of whose walls is depicted a phalanx of soldiers, carrying shields so large as almost entirely to conceal the warriors. This sculpture is interesting, because we read that the shields are the same shape as some mentioned by Xenophon, when speaking of the Egyptian troops in the army of Crœsus. The name of a very ancient king is said to occur in this tomb, but we were not clever at hieroglyphics, and, to say the truth, Selina and I were by this time becoming so well satisfied with the amount of Desert, Temple, and Tomb which we had seen, that a green field of waving corn had, for the moment, far more interest for our eyes and minds. We mounted higher, to feast upon the view of the luxuriant plain. The ascent was steep, so steep that the guides at first said the donkeys could not climb it; but Selina could not mount the hill herself, so the donkey was made to go up, one man pushing him from behind, another supporting the rider in the same manner, at the imminent risk of tumbling her, head-foremost, over the donkey's nose. I climbed up on my own feet, and found the ascent steep certainly, but short. We were soon at the highest point that we could reach, and there the wind blew so strong and fresh, that our expected treat was but a short one. A richly-green plain lay spread before us, in the midst of which rose the city of Sioot. The Nile, and the 'Bahr Yusef,' which enters the Nile a few miles below, wound along in a very circuitous course; two or three bridges thrown across the river looked extremely pretty; and to the left of the city was the modern cemetery, looking like a town of whited buildings, bounded on this side by the arid desert and hills, on that by green fields and the Date-Palm.

We descended the hill and rode to the cemetery, through the streets of closely-packed tombs. They are built of unburnt bricks, and are mostly white-washed. The doors opening into the vaults lie on the ground in front of the tomb, which is sometimes surrounded by a wall, enclosing an open court, rudely painted over the white-wash, in brilliant colours of red, yellow, and green. The wall is crowned with small pinnacles or Vandyke ornament. If there is no open court, the enclosing wall is surmounted by a dome, or oblong vaulted roof. The aloe, accompanied by a pitcher of water, is seen near many of them, and in the walls of some of the principal tombs there is a niche containing a jar of water and a cup, for the refreshment of travellers, of which our dragoman and guides partook and offered some to us. The appearance of this City of Tombs is most curious. It calls to mind the "whited sepulchres" we read of in the Scriptures, but brings with it none of the sacred feelings which we are accustomed to associate with the place of repose of the dead: it speaks of death, but not of life beyond the grave.

As soon as Mohamed could tear himself away from Sioot, we prepared for departure. The excited manner of the Arab, during the whole of our stay there, together with the benign and smiling looks which, contrary to his usual customs, he here bestowed on all the ladies of Sioot who passed by, could not but attract our notice; and, remembering his former intimation of coming to this city when he wanted to choose a wife, we began to be seriously afraid that a bridal procession might soon be approaching the 'Cairo,' although we had reason to believe that Mohamed, notwithstanding his assertions to the contrary, was in the happy possession of a wife at the present moment in Alexandria; that he had had two others before her, and had not yet succeeded in gaining Sarah's promise to become No. 4, in case of the death of the third. The excitement, whatever the cause, died away, and at five P.M. we bade 'adieu' to Sioot.

Tuesday, March 5th.—Some small mummy crocodiles were brought for sale to the boat, purporting to come from the cave of Màábdeh, which once served as a place of sepulture for these creatures. We trust these identical small specimens were really regarded as deities by the ancients, since they were so foolish as to regard any of the tribe in that light. We bought them for two piastres a-piece, and carried them away home with us till some learned antiquarian should tell us their real age. The mud banks along the river's edge here were very curiously perforated by the little 'water-wagtails,' that were always paying us visits on the deck. They made their nests now in the bank, and were twittering and flying in and out of them in swarms, like bees about a hive. Two or three very pretty Egyptian swallows, with red breasts and black plumage, flew by, and at Sioot 'Cousin Phil' had noticed a small bright green bird, like a paroquet; but it was the only one of the kind that came in our way.

At Manfaloot the wind rose again. A large assembly of boats were waiting in the harbour in expectation of a storm, and our Reïs was afraid of passing the dreaded hills of Aboolfeydeh. We thought it absurd to wait till the storm did come, and Mohamed, being of the same mind, the Reïs was persuaded to continue his course. The hills were still some miles away, and on we went in safety, experiencing no inconvenience beyond a slight roll or two, though it must be confessed the gusts may have sounded alarmingly wild and furious to such timid navigators as the Arabs appear to be.

Wednesday, March 6th.—The dreaded hills were passed, and all their curious caves and curves left behind us. Towards evening I was attracted by a sudden stir among the crew. The steersman began saying his prayers very devoutly, and after a good deal of solemn muttering among half a dozen of the men, some bits of bread were thrown into the water, in front of a small cavern—for "Sleek Saïd," they said; and Ali assured me that a bird always came and carried it to the saint within the cave. Mohamed said the custom was kept up by all the boats on the Nile, in commemoration of the deliverance of a certain vessel from shipwreck some "hundred years ago," and the grateful offering of the Reīs, who threw a loaf of bread into the river, vowing to do so ever after on passing by that spot. The ceremony was terminated by the crew starting one of their best songs in honour of the saint, while El Abiad prayed again. When two dahabëéhs come alongside of one another, the crews frequently amuse themselves by racing. This happened to-day. There was a sudden silence among the rowers, and we perceived that they were pulling away with all their strength. The excitement depicted on each one of the dark countenances was very amusing. At one time the rival boats were obliged to steer so near to each other, that the oars of the one dipped in between offering themselves cheap to any one who would enjoy a roasting during the summer months. Our luggage was all landed; and the crew, having received a small extra 'baksheesh' for their services in carrying about the invalids, bade us an affectionate farewell; and as we mounted *en voiture*, it felt rather grand to be driving in a cushioned carriage, drawn by a pair of horses, with an individual on the box who at least called himself a coachman, and finally to be stopping at the door of a great hotel swarming with Europeans. A mail from Southampton and one from Suez had just arrived. Many of our fellow-travellers on the Nile were also there, but our meeting was saddened by the first intelligence, that Mr. M—— had died almost immediately on his arrival at Cairo, and that the funeral was to take place that afternoon in the English cemetery a little way out of the city.

Most of the travellers this season who were in the enjoyment of good health continued their route into Syria. It was somewhat of a trial to us that we could not follow them, but Suez and a short trip on the Red Sea, with a few days more to explore the wonders of Cairo, were all that was in store for us, and then we should leave the Oriental world, in all probability for ever.

After the open sky and free ventilation of our boat-life, Shepherd's Hotel was dull, dreary, and dirty; notwithstanding its lofty, spacious rooms, it was difficult to avoid catching colds and sore throats, simply from passing along its cold stone passages.

those of the other. Mohamed said the other steersman had no business there, knew nothing about the river, and was only "following El Abiad." No doubt the neighbour dragoman said the same of our perfect 'El Abiad;' but in a few moments more we left them far behind, and our crew raised a shout of triumph. The two vessels followed close upon each other frequently during the day; at seven P.M. they both stuck upon mud banks.

The river had, of course, fallen considerably since we passed up, in the month of November; the appearance of the banks was completely changed; no more dhourra was to be seen; wheat was now growing on plains which were then under water; the river was at times quite narrow, and flowed through small passages between intervening banks, formed by its rich alluvial deposit, which are no sooner left dry than they are prepared for fresh crops of cucumbers or water-melons. Since our leaving Sioot, these banks had gradually increased in number and size, and careful navigation was required to avoid them. The dragoman's wary eye was never off the water, and now he warned the Reïs, as night drew on, to stop the vessel if he did not "know the water." The Reïs said he "knew the water quite well," and presently, with three considerable lurches, we stuck fast. Mohamed paced the deck or sat upon the steps in a most unenviable frame of mind. I believe he thought we were there for a week; and so we might have been had not assistance come opportunely in our distress. Moreover, Mohamed considered that, although the whole fleet of the Nile should stick once a-week, the "best boat on the Nile" had no business with "sticking" at all.

Every man on board, the Reïs, steersman, and all, got into the water to try and move the heavy weight. At length we floated, but for two minutes only; in we were again, deeper than before. Loud calls upon 'Allah' and 'Mohamed' resounded through the gloom; the men renewed their exertions with almost superhuman force, but it would not do, and there we must have remained had not a cargo-boat passed and lent us the aid of her crew. The rival dahabëëh was set free much about the same time.

Meanwhile the landscape was enlivened by a long line of flame and clouds of white smoke on the horizon; the natives were burning the dry stumps of the sugar-cane, in order to prepare for another similar crop, to be planted when the ground had been ploughed into deep drills.

Our grounding occurred near Mellawee, which we reached by ten P.M., and remained there for the night. The grottoes of 'Tel el Amarna' we had left behind us; they are at some little distance from the river, and as it was calculated that the strength of the enterprising invalids might, with care, just suffice for the two remaining excursions to Beni-Hassan and the Pyramids, we were obliged to give up the interesting subjects recorded on the walls of 'Tel el Amarna.'

CHAPTER IX.

THE LAST EXCURSIONS.

On Thursday, March 7th, we passed by 'Reramoon,' a busy town, where there is a large sugar and rum manufactory. The bank was alive with men, bullock-carts, camels, and boat-loads of chopped straw, going down to Cairo as food for the cattle, when their two months' feast upon green things is over. There was a very elegant-looking tree here, which the natives called 'Suf Saf,' but we were not near enough to inspect it minutely. At one P.M. we reached Beni-Hassan. The heat was so great we determined to wait till the following morning to visit the grottoes. The last 'Cairo' washing-day was come. The whole apparatus, chairs, tables, &c., were turned out on the bank, a guard being stationed to warn off the inhabitants, who bear the character of being great thieves. Some years ago it was considered hardly safe to land here at all. Mohamed was greatly impressed with this fact, and took every precaution in order to make it appear that there was sufficient means of defence in the boat, in case of any thieving being attempted. When the natives saw the ladies, they inquired where were their husbands? Mohamed replied that they were "in the cabin making their guns ready to shoot geese to-morrow!" No matter, he said, when the daylight came; it was only the night he was afraid of; and as evening came on, after three watchmen armed with guns had been duly posted, he turned out all the crew upon shore, and set them to work at their musical instruments, in order to show that there were "plenty of people in the boat."

Before dark we walked through the village. The people assembled there were an unusually lively set, and crowded round us more than was quite pleasant. They were full of talk and fun. The patriarch of the flock jokingly offered one of his daughters for sale: she was half-frightened lest the joke should end in a reality. He asked one hundred piastres for her; and when we asked the price for his wife, he said he would sell her for fifty piastres. Their merriment amused us much, but Mohamed said, "Yes, very lively, but like the things that come up in the soap when you wash. I not trust to these people at all!" If the temper of Beni-Hassan was likened to a soap-bubble, so we soon thought might also be that of the author of the simile. As we sat in the saloon in the evening, listening to the noisy concert outside, the music suddenly ceased, a crash was heard, and a long silence ensued. Mohamed was happy, enjoying the charming sounds of his beloved band, when the Reïs, in a fit of sulkiness, ordered the men into the boat for no purpose at all but, as he said, to "stop that noise." The excitable Arab blood boiled over in less than an instant. Mohamed started to his feet, seized the crockery drums from the hands of the performers, and deliberately broke them to atoms by throwing them on the ground. The tom-tom he would have proceeded to destroy with a hammer, had not the cook rushed forward to save its life by hiding it in his canteen. The dragoman told the story himself the following day without expressing or feeling the least regret for the loss occasioned by his violence. It was, apparently, in his eyes, the just and lawful retribution for the sulkiness of the Reïs; the consequences, a kind of destiny, brought on by the same individual, which he could no more avoid than any other destiny of his life: indeed, his impression seemed rather to be that he would have signally failed in his duty had he not acted in this particular manner, sacrificing what he had most delighted in, because "no man ever teased me like this Reïs!"

Friday, March 8th.—The countenances of the guides and donkey-boys who appeared as our escort to the Grottoes this morning, the longing eyes which they cast on various articles of our property, the cunning way in which they endeavoured to keep one half of the party separated from the other, and from the dragoman, together with the actual disappearance of the luncheon bottle of wine on the road, all bore out the character which is attributed to this village.

As for the donkeys, such donkeys were never seen! Selina was perched upon one, and pitched off in an instant; on again—off again—it was of no use to try! The donkey's back presented a sharp narrow ridge, upon which the saddle swayed from right to left, like a 'see-saw.' An Arab was laid hold of, no matter who, the first at hand, and his large scarf rolled up to make a pad under the saddle, which was at last fixed on the donkey, with Selina on the top. All were mounted, and at length, in similar manner, we started after 'Cousin Phil,' whom the crew had already carried far ahead of us. We had no bridles, but we had become used to that in Nubia. Selina came down again half-way; and as to Sarah, who was not so accustomed to riding as her ladies were, she was positively thrown off when the donkey began to trot, and dragged some steps in the stirrup. Fortunately she was more frightened than hurt, but for the future stoutly declined trusting to any legs but her own. I believe she would have traversed the desert on foot for miles, rather than submit any more to a Beni-Hassan donkey or guide. Let us consider the style of Beni-Hassan; the donkeys walk quietly along, not very well accustomed to their loads; the guides lag behind, singing to themselves and paying little attention to the steeds: suddenly the thought strikes them that the animals are not going fast enough; they make a dart at them, thrust their pointed sticks into the poor creatures' sides, giving violent grunts, like so many pigs. Up go the donkeys' hind legs, and, unless the riders have had the good luck to turn round and perceive the impending shock, naturally enough, off they go. Such was the 'catastrophe' which had dismounted our good Abigail, and reduced her to using her own strength for the remaining portion of the expedition.

We reached the Grottoes at last. They are cut along the side of the hill, at a distance of about two miles from the village. Those to the south pleased us extremely. They are of the oldest style of Egyptian architecture, and very elegant. The columns represent four stems of water-plants, supporting a capital in the form of lotus or papyrus buds. The transverse section of these grottoes is very elegant, and the architecture resembles a depressed pediment, extending over the columns, and resting at either end on a narrow pilaster. The simplicity and elegance of the style and device strike the eye at once. The walls of all the grottoes are covered with various interesting coloured devices. When the eye has become accustomed to the partial light within, these can be gradually made out, and we took great delight in tracing the following subjects:—The tillage of the ground; making of ropes; weaving of linen cloth;

the manufacture of jewellery and pottery; various hunting-scenes; men tending sick cattle; feeding the oryx; fishing-nets; clap-nets; pressing wine in a wine-press; men wrestling; women playing at ball, and performing various feats of agility in a most unwomanlike manner; both sexes receiving the bastinado, the men laid down on the ground, the women sitting; playing the harp; games of Draughts and 'Mora;' a barber shaving a customer; some cranes; a very curious procession of strangers, supposed, from their dress, beards, sandals, and boots, to be some Asiatic people, being presented, probably, to the owner of the tomb, and offering him presents of the produce of their country; finally, boats bearing the dead body to its place of sepulture: these, and many others, we examined with interest, by the assistance of 'Murray's Hand-book' and 'Wilkinson's Ancient Egyptians.' The curious custom is also seen here of writing over the subject represented the name of what it was intended to represent. In one instance, in particular, it appeared very desirable; if the artist did intend in this case to represent kids feeding upon a vine, we should certainly have wished to see written up over them, "This is a vine, and these are kids."

The Grottoes of Beni-Hassan are very ancient. In one of them there is an inscription in hieroglyphics of 222 lines, running all round the tomb underneath the paintings, like a wainscoting, written in perpendicular lines about three feet or four feet in height, and introducing the name of Osirtasen the First and three succeeding kings, as also that of Shofo, a king of the Third Dynasty.

We left the Speos Artemidos (the cave of Diana) with regret; for the thorough inspection we had given to the grottoes was as much as we could accomplish. Luncheon was acceptable, though we were minus the wine, which refreshed Beni-Hassan instead of us. In a shower of rain, the first we had seen since leaving Alexandria, and numbering about twenty welcome drops, our cavalcade returned to the 'Cairo.'

At half-past three P.M. we started, but not before the villagers and guides had clamoured for more pay, and threatened the dragoman, until, fairly frightened by their din, he ordered the boat to start, hiding himself and his money within the cabin, because "those people going to kill me, if I stay out there."

The same evening we reached Minieh, whither 'Derweesh,' the biggest man of the crew, and the cook-boy, the smallest, had gone from Beni-Hassan to see their wives and families.

Saturday, March 9th.—When we had proceeded a little way the small boat was sent out to fetch the two men back again. It was affecting to see the feeling exhibited by these rough-looking creatures. There they stood on the shore, perfectly still, with their hands joined before them, as they watched for some moments the receding forms of their relatives, to whom they had just bid adieu. The women turned every now and then to take a last glance, then the 'strong man' and the 'boy' returned to the boat; the former full of talk for this one and that, in strangely softened and subdued tones; the latter, perfectly silent, set immediately to work to hide his grief. His charmingly clean appearance attracted our notice, and we felt quite sure that the famous bath of Minieh had had the honour of his presence.

The excitement and long walking at Beni-Hassan knocked up both Sarah and Mohamed. The former was seen at her ironing-table as busy as ever, notwithstanding her ailments; while Mohamed, for the next two or three days, got up a little comedy of symptoms, the chief of which he described pathetically as "a stopped-up nose," of which he was like to die!

Sunday, March 10th.—The morning dawns exquisitely calm; the Nile as smooth as a sheet of glass; not a breath stirs the air; the unusual comfort of the awning spread before breakfast awaits me on deck; and the concertina and hymns are undisturbed by hostile sounds. The rowers prepare for a long day's work, and there is no knowing what point we may not reach before evening. Breakfast over, we reappear on deck, when in an instant the whole scene changes. The wind howls violently; down goes the awning in a trice; off flies Selina's hat into the river; quick as thought, 'Awoodallah' jumps in after it, and restores it before it has had time to get wet. We look around in astonishment for the cause of the disturbance. The thermometer is at 80° in the shade, but the storm steadily increases; the vessel is blown against the lee-shore. The sail flaps in the wind and is stripped into ribbons, the obstinate Reïs will not take it down, but insists on repairing it himself at the mast-head. He mounts and perches aloft, his garments floating in the gale, while, needle and thread in hand, with one of the crew catching the flying ribbons and holding them for him, he succeeds beyond all expectation in stitching them together. It is after a fashion, however, which soon yields to the force of the gale. The seams rip up again, and the Reïs is obliged to give in. Yard and sail are lowered and carried on shore; the whole of the crew squat down with needle and thread, and set to work like so many tailors. The repairs occupy two hours, during which time we walk on the bank and gather a few wild flowers. A large flock of grey and black birds, probably herons, fly overhead; and when our sail is repaired we set off again, and gain, with some trouble, the opposite shore, there to remain for the night, the thermometer falling rapidly with the rising gale.

Monday, March 11th.—The storm is still on the increase. The men try a start, and, contrary to the advice of all on board, the Reïs unfurls the sail; the wind catches it again, and we are driven to leeward. Thump we go against the bank; out come all the long poles again; the sail is still up; thump the second is harder than the first; and now we stick fast in the mud; the men are all in the water to shoulder us off, but to no purpose. The storm increases; the Reïs is baffled, flies into a passion, throws down his boat-pole, furls the sail in despair, and gives up. The crew, one by one, wrap themselves in their warm cloaks on the deck, presenting a row of brown bundles, which, gradually decreasing in number, disappear into the hold, to sleep till the storm shall abate. The angry Reïs sinks into the small boat, to sleep away his rage also. The steersman and dragoman alone are left on the look-out. Ever and anon a head rises from its hiding-place, looks inquiringly round at the elements, as much as to say, "Have you finished?" and when the elements answer, "Not yet," the head disappears again, nothing loth to take another nap. Until three P.M. the storm increases, the waves dash over the vessel, clouds of dust hide every object around, save some unfortunate women, who brave it all to fetch water from the river; a few buffaloes strolling down to drink, and even these are hardly discernible till they reach the water's edge. Chairs, seats, sofa-cushions, all but 'Cousin Phil' himself, who sits bravely through the whole, are blown from their places. All the warm wraps that are available are needed; the 'warming up' has truly come to an end for the time being, and Selina is imprisoned below for a season. Suddenly the sleepers are all roused by the voice of the dragoman, and the huge yard is lowered, lest its swaying should capsize the dahabëéh.

Again all sleep till five P.M., when, the wind abating a little, the anchor is ordered out; they will cast it at a little distance and haul upon it till we are set free from the bank. But the anchor is found to be out of order; its ropes are tied up into every knot imaginable or unimaginable, and by the time they are sufficiently untied, the wind blows again as hard as ever. At seven P.M. another vigorous effort is made, and at last the 'Cairo' floats; she regains the opposite bank, where, over-fatigued, no doubt with her long day's sleep, she remains securely for the night.

The storm had lasted two long, tedious days, but they formed a not uninteresting portion of our Nile experiences, and we congratulated ourselves on being now able to bear testimony to the reality of what we had hitherto heard of with some degree of incredulity—a true storm on the Nile.

Thus was ushered in the first day of 'Ramadán,' the great annual Moslem fast. It lasts for thirty days, during which period the devout Mahometan will taste neither food, drink, nor pipe, between the hours of two A.M. and six P.M. At these hours a gun is fired to announce the commencement and termination of the daily privations. Night is turned into day in all the towns of Egypt during the season of Ramadán; the bazaars are open, and buying and selling continue through the greater part of the night; the mosques are also open, and the people assemble in them twice for prayer, making two good meals between the hours of these assemblies. Dragomen employed in the service of Europeans on the Nile are held exempt from observing the fast, but Mohamed was most strict in keeping it. He made a rare meal, it is true, before and after each gun-fire; but it must have been real fasting to go through all the burning heat of our mid-day excursions without partaking of a single morsel of food, or even a drop of water to allay his thirst. He performed this duty apparently without any idea of deriving benefit from it, as an act of self-denial; nor, on the other hand, so far as we could discover, looking upon it as a meritorious act. It was "only a custom," he said, enjoined by the Prophet, and they all enjoyed the nightly feast extremely. Ali pretended to keep Ramadán also, but at eleven A.M. he was discovered in the bow of the boat, behind the kitchen-screen, making an extra good meal on the remains of our breakfast. Some few of the common crew at times observed the fast, but not during the whole season.

Tuesday, March 12th.—A calm succeeded to the storm, and the dahabëéh proceeded quickly and peacefully on her way. At about one P.M. Selina and I, accompanied by Mohamed and some of the crew, got into the small boat and rowed to Benisooéf by a short cut along a canal, leaving the dahabëéh to continue her way down the stream. By this means we had time to visit the town, purchase provisions, and meet the vessel again without causing any great delay.

The bazaar of Benisooéf is not to be despised.

There are some very good shops in it; a few of them even bearing comparison with those at Cairo. At the time of our visit an extensive manufacture of 'Kunafeh,' was going on for the evening meal of the town. Kunafeh is a kind of very small macaroni, made by pouring a liquid paste of flour and water through a perforated vessel, on a large circular copper plate, heated by fire from beneath. The liquid is poured round and round; it falls in long strings on the hot plate, is baked as it touches it, and swept up immediately into heaps, before it cools. It is then made into a mess with treacle, butter, and almonds, to be eaten during 'Ramadán.'

The oranges purchased here were the best we had seen for a long time. Mohamed's chief business was in the meat market. There we left him, and promenaded up and down the bazaar, with 'Awood-allah' stalking before us, keeping the admiring natives at a respectful distance by means of his great stick. The bazaar is of no very great length, and we were much surprised at the speed with which our business was transacted on this occasion. At the end of our first turn we met the sheep which was destined to grace our table; on the second it was hanging up dead, skinned and converted into mutton; on the third and fourth it was cut up, and deposited in joints in a basket with other provisions. A pretty little collection of aubergines, cucumbers, and other vegetables, stood on a counter hard by. Up comes Mohamed with sheep, oranges, spinach,

&c., takes up the little dish, heads the procession, and we follow our own dinner through Benisooéf to the boat, the expedition having occupied about three hours.

There is a Governor's palace at Benisooéf, and a manufactory of silk and cotton stuffs. We reached Zowyeh, and remained there for the night. The army of rats had by this time increased to such an alarming extent, that they had made their way into all the drawers of the saloon, by numberless creeks and holes; riding habits were nibbled; gloves, handkerchiefs, pen-wipers, curiosities, disappeared daily, and re-appeared, tugged and nibbled at, in the most unlikely corners; empty nut-shells were found stowed away in every wardrobe. It was high time to institute proceedings against the marauders, and Mohamed's carpentering powers were fully occupied for two successive days. Ali, in the midst of it all, brought in a young rat which he had just found commencing its career, and assured us, with the greatest delight, that there were "*plenty, plenty, in the hold.*" No sooner, however, was there a question of seizing and destroying them, than Ali's intelligence had flown, and he seemed to be suddenly afflicted with stupidity. It would have involved far too much trouble to the easy-going youth to do any more than recognise the rat as a plaything. The following morning Thomas announced an increase in the family of the dahabëëh; he had found seven young mice comfortably located in the corner of one of the wine-boxes; but, with less scruple than Ali, the demure Scotchman had "heaved them overboard one after the other."

It was time that our trip should draw to a close. Had the 'Cairo' been sunk before starting, we might not have been thus inconvenienced. It had been considered unnecessary, but it would seem that this is never the case, and it would in general be preferable to delay starting, rather than run the risk of such annoyance. Had we been but three months on the river, as was at first intended, the annoyance would have been but slight; as it was, had we remained only a few days longer, we might have lost everything we possessed, while the nightly carousals of the enemy sounded like a charge of cavalry overhead, and, together with the nibbling and gnawing all round us, completely chased away sleep from our eyelids. Happily, then, for us and for our wardrobes, our days on the Nile were numbered.

Wednesday, March 13th.—The matter-of-fact occupation of packing began again. Mohamed, with his usual dexterity and confidence in his own powers, stowed away all the newly-acquired treasures into empty wine-cases, and looked as 'happy as a king.' The weather was very warm. At five P.M. the thermometer pointed to 78° in the shade, 83° in the sun. The Nile was studded with the prettiest little fleet imaginable. The Citadel was in sight, so were the Pyramids. The Arabs became more and more excited ; they laughed, sang, and cracked jokes more than ever. Now a new strain strikes on our ear. The 'solo,' in his most melodious tone, sings, "Where is our village?—where?" The chorus replies enthusiastically, "Our village is quite nigh,—quite nigh." Over and over again peals forth this Arab "Home, sweet home," with unabated energy, for the space of an hour or more, and causing a thrill of delight to pass through our hearts, as we reflected that our "home, sweet home," lay not quite so nigh to this barren scene, enlivened though it was by the first, and now again last, remaining objects of interest in our cruise—the Pyramids of Geezeh.

We stopped this evening at the village of Bedreshayn, and sent a trusty messenger on to Cairo to fetch our budget of letters and to meet us with them at Geezeh the following evening.

Thursday, March 14th.—Our cavalcade started again. The donkeys were so large compared to what we had been riding lately, we seemed to be mounted on horses; and soon they brought us to the plains of the ancient Memphis, where the Pharaohs of old held their court and state. Memphis was the capital of Lower Egypt after the decline of Thebes. It was first reduced by Cambyses, but continued to be the capital until the rise of Alexandria. It is said to have been founded by Menes, the first king of Egypt. The small Arab village of Mitrahenny now marks its site. A number of mounds on all sides cover the ruins of its ancient grandeur, and little remains to be seen besides the colossal granite figure of Remeses the Great, which lies, broken and prostrate, on the ground in a hollow which is filled with water at the high Nile. The face lies downwards; the features are still perfect, and surpass even the colossi at Aboo-Simbel in their soft, placid expression. In the course of our journey we had frequently animadverted on the practice of carrying away the monuments of Egypt from their own to a foreign soil; but in this instance we could not but wish that some means, and permission for transport, should be found, and this interesting statue preserved instead of lying, as it does here, so thoroughly neglected, that it will, in all probability, like Cleopatra's Needle at Alexandria, be eventually lost.

A number of pyramids rise on the plain beyond. Those of Dashoor are the largest; they were beyond our reach, but we managed to get close to the principal one of the Sakkara group. The nearer we approached the smaller it seemed, yet its dimensions are about 351 feet on two sides, and 394 feet on the other two. We could not perceive any entrance; it presents the appearance of five giant steps, its several stories having lost their outer casing. Our guides next directed us to some catacombs at a short distance, concerning which they could tell us nothing more distinct than that "all English, French, and Italian go to see it," and therefore that we must go too. From our guide-books we inferred that we had come upon the celebrated 'Apis Cemetery.' Long underground passages were hewn in the rock, crossing each other at right angles mid-way. On either side were deep recesses, lined like the passages with masonry, and arched over at the top. In each of these was a very large, handsome sarcophagus of black granite, highly polished, and measuring 12 feet 5 inches long, by 7 feet 6½ inches wide, and being 7 feet 8 inches in height without the lid, which is of the same material, coped above, and making the total height 11 feet. These lids were all pushed a little on one side, thus showing the interior of the now empty sarcophagi. The greater number are without any inscriptions, but two or three have hieroglyphics upon them; and there is one, much larger than the others, which is placed, as it were, in a chapel by itself. When 'Cousin Phil' had seen the first of them he returned to the open air; but Selina and I were too much interested not to penetrate to the extremity of the principal passage, and peep into all its recesses. In them we counted twenty-five sarcophagi, and many others remain still bricked up and unopened. There was one very much smaller than the rest, and in one of the recesses near the end were a few fragments of sculptures in sand-stone. Human sarcophagi seemed but common-place in our eyes compared to those of Apis, the actual existence and sight of which now clothed with reality to our minds the strange stories of the honours paid by reasoning human beings to the unreasoning beasts of the field. That such honours were paid to the sacred bulls of Egypt; that the cemetery appropriated to them has been discovered, and is situated somewhere in this neighbourhood; that their sacred remains have been taken out almost entire from their resting places; that we had already seen one of the venerated heads on a drawing-room table in Cairo: all these were undoubted facts, and that this was the actual cemetery must be another, for we cannot deprive our expedition of one of its deepest interests, by acknowledging any doubt on this subject, although we were afterwards told, and on good authority, that the burial-place of the sacred bulls was quite beyond our reach.

We emerged from the sepulchres into the open air under the broiling sun, and finding just sufficient shade to accommodate us beneath the wall of the rocky entrance, we spread our shawls on the sand, and sat down to luncheon. The Arabs would taste nothing, because it was Ramadán: even a little boy to whom an orange was offered put it away till the evening feast.

The degree of heat which we experienced here would in an English climate have induced extreme languor and loss of spirits; but the bracing air of Egypt produced a totally different effect. Although the exposure to it was at times painful, or even dangerous, inducing headaches and burning feverishness in those with whom it did not quite agree, yet we never felt languid during any part of our journey, and we noticed an unusually even flow of spirits in all the travellers on the Nile, not excepting the invalids. It was not often that my companions found the heat of Egypt unpleasantly great; but on this occasion it was agreed on all sides that 'painful' would not be too strong a term to apply to our ride back from Apis to the dahabëéh, although both Apis and Memnon had furnished ample food for thought, and although we passed by many refreshingly green fields of wheat and clover, and large tracts of the brilliant yellow 'selgum.' As a kind caution to future visitors, it may be worth while to mention, that on our return to the dahabëéh it was discovered that some few squadrons of the 'light infantry' of Egypt had returned along with each one of us, collected no doubt from the sand in or near the catacombs. Other bands were evidently making their presence known on the lower deck, as its busy appearance soon testified. The troops of the enemy were fortunately discovered before their intended onslaught had begun, but we warn all travellers to keep the visit to Sakkara for their return from the Cataracts. Although extra ablutions will be found necessary after the shortest excursion on shore (or even without it), had this been our first instead of the last but one, and that one to the Pyramids of Geezeh, from which I believe the whole army of Egypt could not have deterred us, our antiquarian zeal would have suffered materially.

By half-past ten P.M. the dahabëéh had reached the village of Geezeh, and by eleven P.M. the long-expected budget of letters had arrived. What a budget it was—the home news of weeks! 'Calm old age,' though so zealously active by day, as we have seen, reads the directions carefully through; then, making a guess at the contents,—nay, perhaps, not even diving thus far,—quietly tucks the sealed treasures under his pillow and goes to bed, to enjoy and dream, we suppose, of his morning feast; not so restless youth, which, as a matter of course, spends the night in devouring the closely-written pages. Selina, as a precautionary measure, after the fatigues of the day, and with the closing excursion in store for the morrow, has been safely caged for some time behind the mosquito curtains, a light burns outside, and with one eye only open, she plunges into her folio volume. The backgammon-board, which had well-nigh fallen asleep itself in its efforts to keep 'Cousin Phil' awake, was quickly laid aside; and if my eyelids had begun to droop, they now opened wide, as I was launched deep into the modern world. Nile, Pyramids, Sacred Bulls, and all, vanished into nothing before the tale of modern romance, which now unfolded itself. Cupid had invaded our quiet homestead; had sought, won, and well-nigh carried away his prize! There was nothing for it; for better or for worse the deed was done; and as neither we nor the ancients had been taken into the counsels of these impetuous moderns, we magnanimously made up our minds to the fact, and said that a full and free consent to the whole proceeding should be written the following morning, from the summit of the Great Pyramid of Geezeh.

Friday, March 15th, dawned—a brilliant, broiling day; and at ten A.M. our cavalcade started on its final expedition from the dahabëëh. We passed by the village of Geezeh and its potteries, arriving at noonday at the foot of the Great Pyramid of Cheops. The surrounding sand was full of a small, deep, purple crocus, and one or two other wild flowers, growing in clusters about it. These simple flowers were unexpected objects, and, consequently, came in for their full share of admiration; but as we surveyed the long-desired object of our ambition, the Great Pyramid itself, the first feeling was that of disappointment. Imagination, which had been roaming free and unfettered during the past four months, had invested the mysterious piles with superhuman proportions; and I believe nothing short of a mountain would have satisfied that first glance. The nearer we had approached, the smaller the pyramid and its architect appeared to our bewildered minds, until imagination, gradually calming down into sober reality, and taking dimensions in accordance with the various objects around, the Pyramids rose again to their truly gigantic proportions, and we ourselves shrunk into ourselves—the diminutive lookers-on from the modern world.

It is calculated that each side of the base of the Great Pyramid measures 746 feet, occupying a space of above twelve acres, and its perpendicular height is 450 feet 9 inches. It is well known that the Pyramids are supposed to have been used as tombs, and that Cheops, to whom the principal one of this group is attributed, was a king of Egypt, who lived somewhere about 2050 years before the Christian Era. The speculations of the learned on this subject will occupy many a vacant hour; but here we have only to do with what was seen, felt, feared, or admired by the present enterprising party of travellers on the Nile.

A quiet outside survey was all that 'Cousin Phil' or Selina could accomplish; whilst I, accompanied by Thomas and Sarah, did the work for the party. Several Bedouin guides, and other Arabs, took immediate possession of us, and led the way into the Great Pyramid. I had had no previous idea of the possibility of entering it, believing that feat to be reserved entirely for the stronger sex; but Abraham Khattab, our chief guide, assured me that it was quite feasible, that a great number of ladies accomplished it, and that one lady could undoubtedly do what another had done before her. With this incontestable argument, I determined to try. The entrance was appalling to begin with; but ambition whispered that we stood on the threshold of what few of our friends had seen, or were ever likely to see; so I summoned up my smouldering courage, deposited the skirt of my long brown-holland riding-habit at the entrance, exacted a solemn promise from my guide to bring me back in safety, and entered the Pyramid, giving myself up to the tender mercies of the Bedouins, watching their quickly-shortening candles with dread forebodings of being left in darkness in the centre of the pile, begging of Thomas and Sarah to follow closely, and to come to no harm, and assuring them at the same time that no expedition could be easier. The entrance is raised some distance above the present level of the sand; the Arabs took each a lighted candle in one hand, and one of my wrists in the other; the same for Sarah, whom I saw safely started, but saw little enough of afterwards, though I heard her behind me, making sundry exclamations on the impossibility of proceeding. First we went down a steep, slippery passage, and then along some level ones, just wide enough for the group to file through, with footprints slightly cut or worn away in the stone. The constant shout of the guides, "Take care of your head, lady!" making us stoop lower and lower, till at length we arrived at a lofty passage, in which we were allowed to walk upright. The fact was announced by a shout from the Bedouins, which rung through our nerves, as well as through all the windings of this curious structure. The nerves received a still greater shock at the sight of a narrow ledge on the side of the wall to the left of us, sloping upward, with a steep incline: it is only just wide enough for one foot to step upon it, and is rendered more safe by small holes on the inner side, just large enough to admit an inexperienced leg and to break it. The stride up to this charming promenade is almost beyond the power of European legs at all; and I looked up in amazement, when my guide said to me, as a matter of course, "Up here, lady!" I must confess to having unhesitatingly said, "No, I can't go up there!"—and at that moment I should have preferred returning. But the Arab looked so astonished, glancing first at the step, then at me, then at Sarah, saying, quite in a tone of reproach, "You like to say you been in the Queen's Chamber; you not like to go back; you very good lady.—Ah, bravo! — you very strong lady; other lady all right," (though other lady looked certainly much more like "all wrong"), that my courage returned immediately. I thought, indeed, what would they say at home had I turned back here before I had accomplished my task! On we went, then, though how I cannot say, but we did go on, till another unearthly shout ushered us into the King's Chamber. The walls are so thickly encrusted with salt, that the huge blocks of which they are built appear to be one solid mass. The Arabs immediately set to work to knock off portions of the salt, and to clamour for baksheesh, as pay for the sacred relics. We had nothing to give them; and Abraham Khattab, who had received strict orders from Mohamed that we were not to be annoyed, soon silenced them.

In the King's Chamber there is a granite sarcophagus, which our guides told us had been brought down from some chambers above, in which Col. Howard Vyse had discovered fourteen others of very large size, lying side by side. This is an instance of the degree of reliance that may be placed on the guides in these matters, for in the upper chambers opened by Col. Howard Vyse there were no sarcophagi found at all, but only a few hieroglyphics upon separate stones. The ladder leading to these chambers has been removed, the guides said, on account of the danger of the ascent. They took us next to the Queen's Chamber, which is below the King's, though it appeared to me at the time to be on the same level. It would be a hard task to be called upon to draw a plan of the passages along which we passed, being so completely bewildered by the darkness, noise and feats of climbing, together with the anxious endeavour to retain in the memory something of this expedition when it should be over, that it would not be far from the truth to say that I have not now the remotest idea of when we went up or down, to the right or to the left; successively we were led in all these directions, and getting out of the Pyramid was still more difficult than getting into it. The narrow incline had now to be descended; the only stay for our feet being to place them against the naked feet of the guides, which certainly proved as firm and unfeeling as the rock itself, though it was hard for our tender hearts to realise it at the time. Towards the end of the journey there came one step so deep that the only resource was to let the Bedouin take you by the waist and deposit you below after his own fashion. At length the opening to the Pyramid reappeared glimmering in the distance, and never was daylight more welcome. The climbing in itself is hard work for ladies, and it is rendered more so from the intense heat within the Pyramid and the close contact in which you must necessarily be placed with the Bedouin Arabs, who are not the cleanest of human beings, while their unearthly yells increased tenfold the apparent danger of the ups and downs. Our guide, 'Abraham Khattab,' was an excellent one, and deserves recommendation to future travellers. He spoke English, Italian, and French, the latter with a first-rate accent; while within the Pyramid he made no appeal whatever for baksheesh, and when he took me up on the outside his requests were made in the form of the most polite and unobtrusive insinuations.

Fatigued and sunburnt, I rejoined 'Cousin Phil' and Selina, who were stationed at the other side of the Pyramid, under a projecting stone which afforded some little shade as well as a table for luncheon. The marvels of the interior were related, and the flies came buzzing round to hear with so much attentive devotion that we felt far more inclined to make them a present of the cold chicken at once than to struggle with them for the possession. Selina had employed the time in making a sketch; and now Abraham, the guide, stood complacently for his portrait, until advancing day reminded me that my work was not yet over. Thomas and Sarah had had enough of it, and they declined the honour of mounting the Pyramid from the outside. This last feat was reserved for me alone. Three Bedouins accompanied me — Abraham and two companions— one as hearty as himself, the other rather too old for the work, as was soon proved by his remaining behind before we reached the top, so soon as he thought that his services could be dispensed with. For this he incurred considerable raillery from his companions, who spoke of him just as you might speak of a worn-out horse—"old fellow," "good for nothing," &c.

Each of the two first guides seized one of my wrists and held them with so tight a grasp that I was obliged to remonstrate upon the subject and to show them the red marks which were appearing in consequence, upon which they condescended slightly to loosen their hold. They first mounted one of the giant steps themselves, while the third guide, remaining on a level with me, placed two more hands at my waist, and assisted me to a succession of springs varying from three to five feet in height. Thus by a series of jumps the ascent of the Pyramid was accomplished in a far easier manner than I had anticipated. 'Cousin Phil' and Selina moved to a distance to watch me. They said I looked like a doll as I was lifted up by the Bedouins from one giant step to the other; they could not hear the song with which the guides aided their efforts and mine as we proceeded; but here it is set to a kind of boatman's chorus, to which they sang it.

Chorus. Haylée, Haylée, sah!

Solo. 'Plenty baksheesh, lady!'

Chorus. 'Haylée, Haylée, sah!'

Solo. 'To take you up to the top!'

Chorus. 'Haylée, Haylée, sah!'

Solo. 'Custom of every nation!'

Chorus. 'Haylée, Haylée, sah!'

Solo. 'Ah! bravo, bravo, lady!'

Chorus. 'Haylée, Haylée, sah!'

Solo. 'Don't tell this man what you give me!'

Chorus (who do not understand English). 'Haylée, Haylée, sah!'

Solo. 'Give it to me myself!'

Chorus. 'Haylée, Haylée, sah!'

Solo. 'Now stop and take rest, lady!'

Chorus. 'Haylée, Haylée, sah!'

The ascent occupied twenty minutes, and I rested five times on the way, to take breath for the next climb and to look around me and remember where I was. A sixth pause would have been more to my taste, but the wary guide, suspecting signs of approaching fatigue, said, "No, lady, you must go to the top *now*." I felt he was right, though I doubted my powers to proceed. The old guide had halted at the fourth station, and, to say the truth, he was no loss, for although his assistance was of the greatest use at first, he had by this time become fatigued himself, and instead of jumping me up he only assisted in weighing me down. I jumped much better without him now, and the blocks towards the top of the Pyramid are not so high as the lower ones. One last, longish effort then, enlivened by the chattering guide, who well-nigh dispersed the remaining breath that was in me by gravely inquiring if the gentleman down below were my husband and why my Mamma was not here with me, and I stood at the top of the Great Pyramid of Geezeh, with the famous view spread around me, of which I had so often heard and read, and so little dreamed of seeing with my own eyes.

After a few moments to recover breath and my senses, the first objects I sought for were 'Cousin Phil' and Selina. How grand I felt up there, and how very small indeed they looked as they waved their specks of handkerchiefs up in congratulation to me! Yet could I have summoned thither the wand of one of the magicians of old, or some more modern railway contrivance, I would willingly have resigned the honour of the single triumph for the far greater pleasure of sharing it with them. The burning rays of the sun, however, soon recalled me to a more respectful attention to the scene around me. To the south, a maze of pyramids extended to an unlimited distance on the desert plain, having no apparent connexion with one another, save in their outward form. To the west, the Lybian Desert stretched far and wide, grandly solemnising in its barren solitude. To the north and east, the shining river flowed on, nourishing the richly green crops on its banks ; the island of Roda was there, and Cairo, 'Kahirah' (the triumphant), with its citadel and its mosques, rose in the clear blue sky above, backed by the Mokattam hills. A few scattered villages studded the desert plain, whilst close around the Pyramids there were numberless rising hillocks in the sand, suggesting the existence of similar piles still hidden beneath. Lastly, and close by, were the two remaining Pyramids of the group and the Sphinx. The Second Pyramid is attributed to Cephrem, the third to Mycerinus, successors of Cheops. The outer casing of the Great Pyramid, which originally filled in the square blocks, making a smooth sloping surface from top to bottom, has been removed, or the ascent would be next to impossible for any one. It was removed by the Caliphs to serve for buildings in Cairo. The casing of the second pyramid still remains, and the ascent is seldom undertaken even by the natives, though they will sometimes try it for the sake of 'baksheesh.' The Third Pyramid is quite small compared to the other two ; it occupies two acres of ground, and is 203 feet in perpendicular height. Its outer casing was of granite, so that, although the smallest, it must have been by far the handsomest of the group. A portion of the granite still remains at the base. By far the most impressive view of the Sphinx is obtained from the summit of the Great Pyramid, though every one may not care to obtain it at the expense of the climb. Those who do will be well repaid the trouble; indeed, I should not scruple to go up again as often as I had the opportunity, though nothing would induce me to revisit the interior. The summit of the Great Pyramid presents a surface of about 32 feet square, covered with four-sided blocks of stone placed side by side, without any cement or mortar between them.

Fascinating as my position then was, I must of necessity come down again, and the heat soon drove me to do so. The descent was comparatively an easy process. I required but little assistance, stopped only once on the way to rest and to take a last look at the surrounding scenery, and reached the bottom in the course of eight minutes from the time of starting. I was now, and naturally so, nearly as great a wonder as the Pyramids themselves, particularly in the eyes of our dragoman, who would not have gone up, he said, at any hour,—no, not for "thousand pounds," because the heat and exertion would make his "head sick." But time was wearing on; brave as I had been, my own legs would not at that moment have carried me even to the Sphinx, but happily those of a good donkey were at hand, as was also a most refreshing orange. We mounted and rode only a few yards' distance from the Second Pyramid, where sits the majestic Sphinx.

The Sphinx is cut out of a solid piece of rock, a small portion only having been completed with stonemasonry. Stately and majestic still the lion-headed, woman-faced figure sits, half buried in the sand. The cap which it wore on its head is destroyed, the nose is gone, much of one side of the face is broken; but the Sphinx represents an Egyptian beauty still, and its mutilated features still smile benignly upon the spectator. The fore-paws are said to stretch a length of 50 feet. Between them was formerly a sanctuary, in which offerings were made, and religious ceremonies performed in honour of the monster divinity. My donkey seemed rather afraid of it, but I made him take me all round the hill of sand surrounding the cavity in which the Sphinx is excavated, that I might have some idea of the real size of this curious and beautiful monument. It is said to measure 143 feet in length, and 63 feet in height from the base to the top of the head. We left contemplating it with reluctance. Our brains full with all that we had seen, we re-crossed the sandy plain, passed through the village of Geezeh, remarking on the noisy character of its inhabitants, and regained our dahabëéh without once remembering what Mohamed had called "the manufactory of chickens." Up the Nile and down the Nile, our hearts had been set upon seeing the egg-ovens of Geezeh, in which, from time immemorial, chickens have been hatched by artificial heat; we had perpetually charged the dragoman that they should not be forgotten, and now, as with Belzoni's name at Abousir, the Pyramids, Sphinx, and the letters from home, had driven the chickens far away from our minds. Not till two days after the Nile trip had been numbered amongst the things that had been, did it suddenly occur to us that Geezeh, with its "chicken-manufactory," was lost to us for ever. Mohamed's account of the "manufactory" was this: "A Nubian sits upon the eggs, which are placed on the floor, puts his arms out, gathers them all round him, takes them up one by one, calling 'Gloo, gloo, gloo,' to tell the chickens to come out, and sitting there patiently day and night to take care of them." The Nubian, we thought, could hardly represent so aptly the conduct of a hen towards her rising family, but as we did not see we cannot deny the motherly proceeding. Between sailing and rowing we crossed from Geezeh to the island of Roda, for the noise of a Ramadán night on the mainland threatened to drive away sleep from our eyes. At Roda the sounds reached us still, but they were softened by distance. Guns were firing, 'tom-toms' playing, people shouting, singing, and talking all night long; and by the noise over our heads we strongly suspect that a large entertainment was given on board the 'Cairo' herself during the early morning hours. How lovely was this last evening in our boat-home at Roda! Long did we sit and watch the exquisite moon and star-lit sky, never, perhaps, till this moment, when we were about to lose it, fully appreciating the unlimited range over which our eyes had wandered for the last four months. How should we bear the change? The glorious curtain of night could henceforth be only partially peeped at through the limits of a window-frame.

Saturday, March 16th.—To conclude our cruise, we sailed round the pretty island of Roda, and took our last look at the Nilometer. The green trees, the flowering gardens, the comfortable palaces of this favoured spot, were clothed with new interest and beauty after all the barren sands upon which we had looked for so long a time. After our four months of comparative solitude, with silent temples and thinly populated villages, how noisy, busy, and bustling did the shores of 'Old Cairo' and Boulak appear! How populous their streets, how inviting the baskets full of green vegetables, brought down by the women to the water's edge to be well washed, freshened up, and carried away to the markets for sale; and, to crown all, how fair the complexions of the populous city compared to what we had judged them on our departure. Had they been bleaching whilst we had been burning on the river? Be that as it may, a large number of them now bore a very fair comparison with the ladies of our party, while 'Cousin Phil' himself did not hesitate to say that the Cairenes had even the advantage over him in this respect.

The harbour of Boulak was full of dahabëéhs, despoiled of their banners and deserted by the various parties, grave and gay, who had found in them their homes some few weeks back. The gaily-painted vessels would now lie idle till the next season on the Nile should begin, with the exception of a few that were

The first evening on shore was spent in reviewing our life on the Nile. More and more dreamlike it seemed, and as we heard the reports of other travellers, the questions suggested themselves: How was it that, instead of enjoying it, we had not rather died of *ennui?* Was Selina the better or the worse for her journey? Would either of us willingly go up the Nile again? Many other travellers, before six weeks were over, had returned with all speed, finding the monotony of the trip unbearable. Perhaps they had not stocked their cabins so well with books and drawing-paper as we had, and perhaps their dragomen were not so amusing as ours was, let alone the engrossing interest of 'Cousin Phil' and his wonderful chair. Selina certainly returned far stronger than she went, but she had suffered much from the inequalities of temperature, the cold nights, and high winds. She says the risk is too great, though the pleasure was also great, and many objects of interest are still left to be seen. 'Cousin Phil' says he would rather not start again to-morrow, but some future day the brave old gentleman would see no reason against enjoying another similar cruise. Thomas, who on this one subject alone had never said anything before, says nothing now. Sarah turns aside and whispers audibly, "Catch me there again if you can." And I say, "Let well alone;" we have made the most of our trip, we have enjoyed it thoroughly, and have brought home a fund of interest and amusement, which will last by many a winter fireside, and we are very glad to get back again to enjoy the recollections of our cruise.

No trip could be more full of interest, or better calculated for diverting the thoughts of invalids from their ailments; and the bracing, invigorating properties of the desert air cannot be denied for those who, in the earlier stage of disease, are still strong enough to stand the inequalities of the temperature of Egypt; but in cases where consumption is far advanced, it would seem that a more equable climate must be preferable. In such cases it appeared to us that the Nile trip was full of risk. Five of the invalids whom we met this year died before the excursion was over; two returned no better; one only, who was in comparatively good health at starting, and who was not suffering from a chest complaint, unhesitatingly pronounced himself much benefited.

CHAPTER X.

FROM CAIRO TO SUEZ.

CONCLUSION.

ONCE more we met a large concourse of fellow-countrymen and women in the English church at Cairo, and joined in the public worship, from which we had been so long debarred, offering our thankful acknowledgment for the safety in which our long journey had been accomplished. The room was full, as it always is when Shepherd's Hotel is full, and the singing was sweet and melodious—at least by comparison with that of our Arab crew.

In the afternoon a mail arrived from Southampton, and a number of omnibuses and carriages of various descriptions disgorged their living loads at the door of the hotel, where we sat to receive them. The passengers tumble out pell-mell, and, knowing full well that the hotel will not hold them all, they rush wildly along the passages, and up and down the stairs, forgetful of all Christian charity on the occasion, and solely impressed with the propriety of the maxim, "First come first served." In the *mêlée* we discover no less than three parties of our acquaintances, one of them in a state of utter destitution, the luggage of papa, mamma, and baby having been sent on to Suez by mistake, when they had purposed remaining at Cairo until the last necessary moment of departure.

Monday, March 18th.—There was no alternative for our friends but to follow their luggage on to Suez. We saw them off, and then commenced a second week of 'sight-seeing' at Cairo. The Turkish and Syrian bazaars engaged our attention for two successive days. It is necessary to take your time when you wish to bargain with a merchant in these bazaars—he certainly will take his, and that is not less than three-quarters of an hour's parleying for each article to be purchased. Very beautiful handkerchiefs and scarfs, from Damascus and Constantinople, were displayed before us.

We discovered, towards the end of the visit, that the merchant in the Syrian bazaar understood English perfectly, but he feigned entire ignorance of the language in order not to hamper our intercourse with the dragoman on the subject of his wares. Mohamed also was perfectly aware of this fact, but he did not let it out, and continued to bargain for us, prefacing each fresh proposal with a washing of his hands, whereby he declared himself incapable of taking any of the extra prices for himself, as he loudly asserted that "all other dragomen" did. We had good reason to believe that both merchant and dragoman were well up to their own interests on this occasion; yet, from future considerations, and comparisons with other travellers and their bargains, we found that these fatiguing hours in the bazaar had not been ill spent. The articles Mohamed el Adlëëh procured for us were of the best materials, and not too highly priced, as times go; indeed, we should not hesitate to apply to him for future bargains.

The next object of interest was the museum of Egyptian antiquities, collected by the Viceroy, and opened at Boulak since we left in November last. This museum is well worth seeing, and contains some very handsome specimens. In the first room the chief object of interest is the mummy-case of one of the ancient princesses. It is very elaborately painted, and the colours remain in perfect preservation. The treasures which were found in it are arranged under a glass case in the middle of the room. They consist of handsome chains, brooches, bracelets, and ear-rings, in various devices, all of gold, a handsome collar necklace, in the same metal, besides many other articles of curious and unintelligible shapes, and two very pretty silver boats, with their crews sitting at the oars. Round the room stand other mummy-cases, and the contents of many more. In a second apartment are many specimens of the ancient blue and green ware of Egypt; some small alabaster figures, exquisitely sculptured; images of heathen gods innumerable; mummied birds and crocodiles, wrapped in rags of two colours—yellow and brown—in such a manner as to retain their true forms. These are very beautifully done, and are still in perfect preservation. A number of statues in granite and alabaster are placed along the centre and round this room. One of the figures squatted, in the same attitude as that in which the Egyptians of the present day still squat, and two others, sitting cross-legged, reading a roll of papyrus, are particularly interesting.

The Turk who was in charge could not speak one word of any European language, so that a catalogue was sadly needed, and one short visit is not enough to impress on the mind half the objects in this excellent, though comparatively small collection, which is well worth several visits.

Five days of the atmosphere of Cairo was sufficient to excite a desire for a little fresher air; accordingly, on Thursday, March 21st, we set out for a drive to the 'Petrified Forest.' Four horses were required for this excursion; and after a drive, rush or jolt, across the Desert for one hour and a half, over sand, rock, and hill, we arrived at the outskirts of the forest.

We had been jolted and shaken in the most unmerciful manner, the unfortunate horses beaten and urged on more mercilessly still by the indefatigable running 'saïs.'

The Arabs, convinced that there is no other way of inducing the horses to get over the uneven surface, and that, if they once suffer them to rest, they will never move again, treat them so cruelly that the poor beasts are at length obliged to stop, and require some little time to recover, before they can proceed any further. After several pauses for this purpose, we arrived in sight of the curious natural phenomenon called the 'Petrified Forest.'

We stood on the outskirts only of a forest of palm-trees, which once stretched many miles away on the now barren, sandy plain. Fragments of petrified wood lie in all directions on the sand. The pieces have so entirely lost their original nature, that on striking them against one another, they emit a clear, metallic sound; but the veining and knots of the wood remain so distinct as to leave no doubt as to its normal condition. The largest piece we saw was, perhaps, between three feet and four feet in length. The greater number of those which were scattered about the plain resembled blocks cut for firewood. Several of these blocks lie collected together in small, circular spaces, carpeted with petrified shavings and splinters of all sizes (some as sharp and fine as needles), as though a carpenter or hewer of wood had sat there at his work, and, being called suddenly away, had left the sweepings of his shop behind him. Some miles further on, whole trunks of petrified trees are to be seen; and there are many other places in Egypt where such are found. Between Cairo and Suez, mention is made of a palm-tree, petrified in the sandstone rock, measuring from twenty-five feet to thirty feet in length.

The pure desert air was thorough enjoyment

after the few last days' confinement to the streets and bazaars of Cairo, to which we returned when we had gathered up reminiscences of the forest, almost sufficient, Mohamed said, to build ourselves a house.

The two remaining days of our intended stay were devoted to the mosques, which we had not yet visited. These buildings form the principal features of this great city—the 'mother of the world;' and at every turn in its streets, a mosque or minaret, new or old, meets the eye. That of 'Ahmed Ebn e' Tooloon' is the most ancient, and many unlikely and impossible traditions are connected with its site. It bears date A.D. 879, about ninety years previous to the foundation of any other part of the city.

It consists of a large open court, surrounded by colonnades, with many rows of columns supporting pointed arches, which prove the existence of the pointed arch about three hundred years before it was in use in England, where it was not general till A.D. 1200. An outer wall surrounds the court, at each corner of which formerly rose a minaret. One of these has a spiral staircase on the outside, still remaining. It is said that its founder being one day observed by his 'Wizeer' in an absent moment, rolling up a piece of parchment in a spiral form, the minister reproved him for having no better employment for his royal dignity. "On the contrary," said the Prince; "I am thinking that a minaret, erected on this principle would have many advantages; I could even ride up it on horseback."

The staircase of the new mosque was accordingly built after thát manner. Whether the monarch ever did ride up it is not related; but in March 1861, we walked up its broken and dilapidated steps, and, not without some difficulty, I reached the summit. The dragoman accompanied me; and gloried in the splendid view of the city which is obtained from thence. The citadel with the whole of Cairo, the Uzbekëéh, the Shoobra Gardens, and the distant Pyramids, are plainly seen. It was in vain that I endeavoured to draw from the Arab head the situation of one single street or bazaar in the city. He had not the most remote idea where this or that was situated. From such a position he declared it was impossible. How could he tell? He could not see streets; when we came down again, and passed by the various objects, then he would tell me where they stood. Cairo was three times the size of London, and he was quite sure no one could describe London from the top of St. Paul's. Such was our dragoman's idea of the greatest city in the world and the intelligence of its inhabitants, and he spoke from personal observation, for he had been twice in London with an English gentleman, in whose service he had remained for three years.

We next visited the mosque of Sultan Kalaoon. It is near the Turkish bazaar, and is attached to the madhouse (Morostán) founded by the Sultan

A.D. 1287. The tomb of the Sultan within this mosque, is very handsome, and the light tracery, and inlaid work of mother of pearl and mosaic very pretty and curious. In this mosque, Mohamed pointed out a small niche, which was, he said, always kept miraculously filled with water, of which all those partook who entered the mosque for prayer. There was a jar of water standing near at the time to account for the miracle; but Mohamed's faith was in no way shaken hereby, neither apparently was that of the Moslem, whose business it was to replenish the holy vessel whenever it was emptied.

The lunatics have since been removed to another hospital, where they are tended by Europeans. The court of the mosque has now the appearance of a number of almshouses, filled with poor families. Mohamed said that it was a kind of 'poor-house,' in which a certain number of persons were clothed and fed, at the expense of the Sultan.

During the nights of Ramadán the mosque of the citadel is illuminated, and the people resort thither in large numbers at the hours of prayer. It is usual to allow strangers to enter and witness the illumination; but there was at this time some difficulty in gaining admittance to this as well as to some of the other mosques, in consequence of the ill behaviour of a few travellers, who, for the sake of the good name of their nation, if not for their own, should have been more careful in their proceedings. We resolved, however, to try.

Selina's throat would not allow her to go out in the evening air, and 'Cousin Phil' and I went alone to the citadel. The minarets were very prettily encircled with lights; but when we arrived at the entrance of the mosque, far from being admitted ourselves, crowds of natives were being driven away by the guards stationed within. All the eloquence of Mohamed, upon 'Cousin Phil's' importance, and his enfeebled state, were for a long time unavailing. The Pasha was praying. If we chose to wait for half-an-hour or more, when his prayers would be over, we might see him, and ask permission for ourselves; but now, go we must. 'Cousin Phil' could not stand for so long a time, and we were going off, when the guard relented sufficiently to say, that if we chose to go round to the side-door we might peep in. This we did, and saw very nearly all.

The illumination consisted of large coronas of small oil lamps, which had a brilliant, and very pretty effect, though not coming up to the reports which we had heard of the illumination. A crowd of persons were assembled, prostrated on the beautiful marble pavement, engaged in prayer. A sound as of chanting came from the extremity of the mosque, where all the derweesh were assembled, invisible to us, and the people rose, and prostrated themselves again several times. But here, we were not allowed to remain, and we left them, to return again through the lighted busy streets, where buying and selling, feasting and story-telling, intermingled with the readings of the Korán, and prayers in the mosque, were carried on till two o'clock in the morning.

The temporary cessation of smoking, which is general, if not universal, during Ramadán, causes considerable improvement in the atmosphere of the streets and bazaars; and tended much, no doubt, to the extra enjoyment of our last Cairo excursion— a donkey-ride through the oldest and narrowest parts of the city.

The first time that we mounted on donkey-back in Egypt, the bewildering novelty of the scenes around us completely silenced our tongues, and left eyes and brains alone in full and earnest play. Now we were novices no longer, and off we started, ambling along; the amble of the Cairo donkeys being a very comfortable pace, though their trotting is not quite so agreeable. We could chat and laugh now, as we rode on almost as unconcernedly as the Arabs themselves; Mohamed cleared the way for us, in a state of great excitement about the old city, which he declared it would take us one whole year to explore. Some of the oldest streets are so narrow that the pretty projecting 'mushrabëéh,' literally touch each other from the opposite houses; and throughout the whole of this quarter of the town, the narrowest aperture only is left between them to admit the light or heat of the burning sun. Some of the fret-work of these 'mushrabëéh' is very elaborate. Numberless objects of interest are seen in the crowded shops of the old narrow streets, as well as in the bazaars, which are a very little more spacious. Amongst them all, the very primitive door-bolts or locks, still in use in Egyptian houses, claimed our attention. They are made of wood; three, four, or six tiny pins, or bolts suspended from the top, drop into corresponding holes in the wooden latch, and thus secure it. The key, which is also of wood, is armed with similar pins, fixed firmly upon it; when this is slid into the groove of the latch, the pins enter the holes, raise the suspended bolts, and the latch may be drawn out. As soon as it is pushed back again, and the key withdrawn, the bolts fall, and secure it once more. Similar wooden locks were used by the Greeks and Romans, and in the Highlands wooden locks still exist, so artfully contrived, by notches made at unequal distances, on the inside, that they can only be opened by the wooden key which belongs to them. But this is also the case with at least the greater number of the wooden locks in Egypt. We purchased three of them from the manufacturer, and neither of these three can be opened by the keys belonging to the other two. The Shoe Bazaar also claimed some time, for admiration of the brilliant red and yellow leather in its well-stocked shops, and the busy workmen, who seem to have constant occupation for every day, notwithstanding that so large a proportion of the population wear no shoes at all.

The ride itself was the greatest fun imaginable, the populace, who were almost exclusively of the male sex, crowded round us, and were perpetually sent flying away by the shouts of our attendants; and on our return, Selina congratulated herself that her donkey had not knocked over more than three men and one child in the course of the journey. The narrow streets exclude all wheeled conveyances of any description, but heavily laden donkeys, and even camels, pass through in long files, so that when any of these meet there is but little room left for pedestrians, who consequently learn all kinds of ingenious and agile contrivances for keeping their ten toes in safety. To Europeans the lack of women in these streets and bazaars is very striking; they sit in the market-places offering things for sale, but are elsewhere seen only in very small proportions to the other sex.

Sunday, March 24th.—We were occupied with the morning public worship—a broiling walk in the afternoon; and after dinner a turn in the Uzbekëéh, to see the house of the Sardinian Consul, which was very prettily illuminated with small oil-lamps, branching up in festoons on either side the doorway as well as round all the window-frames, in honour of Garibaldi's late victory over the Neapolitan troops.

Monday, March 25th.—We set out for Suez, still keeping Mohamed as dragoman. The heat in Cairo was becoming oppressive. The thermometer was at 70° in our well-sheltered bed-rooms, and walking or driving about before four P.M., was beginning to be even beyond the enduring powers of my non-combustible companions.

In the space of five hours and a half, the railway carriages conveyed us to Suez, across the same sandy plains over which the Israelites of old had journeyed when, under the immediate protection of Heaven, they fled from the pursuing hosts of Pharaoh, laden with the spoils of their task-masters. Laborious, indeed, must their journey have been through the dry, burning sand, and requiring a lively faith even in those to whom the difficulties of the desert may not have been quite so great as they would appear to Europeans. As we passed by a few toiling pedestrians and heavily laden dromedaries, and saw how deeply they sank at each step in the sand, and how slowly they proceeded, we pictured to ourselves the travelling hosts and the hardships they must have had to endure in their long and weary wanderings; and inexcusable though they were, we wondered less than we had formerly done, at the murmurings of the faithless people. Had we moderns been placed in the same circumstances, would many of us have been found with those whose faith shone so brightly through all their long trial ?

Passing by a long vista of years, imagination next called up visions of uncles, brothers, and cousins innumerable, jolting, in the service of their Queen and country, over the same road, in the crazy caravan in momentary expectation of tumbling through and lying on the sand, till a more crazy concern should pass by and pick them up; or, after a succession of unexpectedly affectionate embraces with their opposite neighbours, arriving at their journey's end with a fractured skull from a series of salutary reminders overhead, that the 'caravan,' if crazy at bottom, was at least sound and solid at the top.

The third picture was that of modern 1861 rushing to and fro, because one ingenious contrivance after another has so arranged it, that people may leave their homes at a moment's notice, with the least possible regret; the level road, the luxurious railway-carriage, the puffing steam-engine, carrying invalided 'seventy-five,' with his younger companions, quickly and quite at their ease to Suez, because, forsooth, brave 'seventy-five' has seen the Pyramids of Egypt, and he naturally wishes to cross the Red Sea also.

Thus we were set down at Suez, in an hotel which would have done credit to London itself. The present proprietor is assisted by the Peninsular and Oriental Company, and the hotel, formerly so indifferent, now ranks as a first-rate establishment. The change from Shepherd's was striking and most welcome. In the first place, the bed-rooms were clean; then there were no fleas, and comparatively few mosquitoes or flies, in any part of the house. The servants were cleanly, active, intelligent Bengalese, and waited at table extremely well; the cooking was excellent (the cook an Indian), the table was served like a gentleman's table ; and to complete our luxury, there was a pleasant-looking, carpeted parlour, with window-curtains, couches, and a supply of newspapers and books on the table, open to every one.

Either we were particularly good-tempered on this occasion, or peculiarly fortunate in our visit, or the generality of our countrymen are great grumblers (a British privilege, it is true), or the whole agreeable result may have been due solely to contrast with Cairo and with Shepherd's; but we enjoyed our stay at Suez extremely. The hotel was excellent, the sea-breeze delightfully refreshing, the Red Sea a lovelier blue than any sea we had yet seen,—a clear, transparent turquoise blue; the Arabian hills on the opposite coast, with the 'Wells of Moses' in the distance, the recollections of the miraculous passage of the Israelites under Moses, supposed according to some authorities to have taken place just above the town; all was full of such deep interest, that the notions of dreariness and loneliness, which might otherwise be connected with the very name of Suez, retreated immediately into the back-ground.

Tuesday, March 26th.—We embarked soon after breakfast in a small sailing vessel, manned by five rather Indian-looking sailors, and set sail for the 'Wells of Moses.' Mohamed had provided a new chair for 'Cousin Phil;' luncheon and all necessaries for the day's excursion. The sea looked beautiful, and the hills on both sides were tipped with lovely purple hues.

One hour and a half conveyed our little vessel across, within three miles of the interesting Wells. 'Cousin Phil' was carried by the crew in his new chair, which was a simple arm-chair supported on two poles, by no means as safe as the former contrivance, but there was no way of getting anything else. Selina and I rode on donkeys, which had been sent across for us previously. We were out of Africa now, and for the first time set foot on the Asiatic continent.

Situated on the border of the wide-spreading, barren desert of Arabia, are three gardens, lately planted near the Wells, which have always been known to the natives of these parts by the name of the 'Wells of Moses,' and at which we again pictured the children of Israel refreshing themselves on their weary march.

The gardens are the property of persons residing in Suez, and there are gardeners appointed to look after them. Their produce did not appear to be great, but anything green here was extremely refreshing to the eye. There are seven springs, or wells as they are called. One bubbles up through the sand on the surface of the desert, others are sunk and walled in with masonry. Three of them are situated outside the gardens, the others are within; and the waters of the principal well run through them in a beautifully clear, sparkling stream. We put our hands in to taste a draught of the inviting beverage, but a simultaneous expression of horror was the result. The water was inviting indeed to the eye, and the plants drank of it thankfully and greedily, but it was bitter and horrid to the taste. "The waters of Marah," we exclaimed, "could not have been worse;" and here again another picture rose up before us, of Israel murmuring because of the bitter waters, and we tried to believe that this was the actual spot where that event took place, in spite of the fact, that the best authorities place it at least three days' journey further on.

The heat was intense, and we were glad to take our luncheon under the shelter of a small summer-house, erected in one of the gardens. A low mud-seat ran all round the mud walls, and upon this we sat and refreshed ourselves, with our own provisions and some new milk which the gardener sent to us.

Once in Asia, it was but natural that our thoughts should turn with increased longings towards the Holy Land. Mount Sinai at least seemed within our grasp; and Mohamed eagerly detailed how comfortably the expedition might be accomplished with invalid chairs, dromedaries, and tents. The difficulties and imprudence of the undertaking, for such a party as ours, began to vanish before our excited imaginations; but a kind Providence interfered to stay the wild project. An accident befell us, on this our last excursion, which brought us back to our senses, and put an end to the scheme. On all former occasions, notwithstanding Mohamed's constant exclamations of 'Trust to me! trust to me!' we had been careful that extra hands should always be in readiness, to balance the wonderful chair, as the bearers raised it from the ground. Mohamed looked upon this precaution of ours as a personal insult; but now, at the last moment, we all became aware how necessary the precaution had been. Our heads, no doubt still running upon Mount Sinai, we obeyed the dragoman's excited shout, "Trust to me! Get up if you please." We mounted our donkeys, turned round to look for 'Cousin Phil,' and saw him fall forward upon the sand. The bearers, at a signal from Mohamed, had raised the chair before he was aware of their intention; he had not had time to lay hold of the arms, before the sudden jerk had thrown him out of it, and he was taken up bleeding and stunned. Happily he soon came to himself, and we were satisfied that this would not prove a serious accident, though we were much frightened, and our stay at Suez was prolonged until 'Cousin Phil' should recover from the effects of his fall.

Our return was tedious. The sea had receded so much, that we had a long way to go over wet sand and through the water before reaching the boat. Our donkeys carried us as far as their nerves would allow them to face the treacherous element. Neither coaxing nor beating could get them beyond a certain point, nor could the shouting of our attendants awake the sleepers in our vessel, which seemed to lie hopelessly out of reach. Most travellers make a long circuit, and return from the Wells to Suez by land, on account of the receding of the tide, but this would have been too fatiguing for our party at any time, and now next to impossible.

Mohamed and one sailor carried 'Cousin Phil' through the water to the boat, with some difficulty succeeding in keeping his feet from the surface, for, as they neared the vessel, the water reached up to the men's waists. Selina's light weight was easily carried by the remaining sailor, as she was seated on his shoulder, and rested her hands on his turban. I waited patiently till Mohamed and another sailor returned, they put their shoulders together, and, seated upon them, with my hands resting on a turbaned head on either side, they carried me safely to the vessel. We congratulated ourselves on being re-embarked without a wetting; though dry we did not long remain.

The wind was blowing fresh and contrary, so that we were obliged to tack in order to make any way. The sea became rougher, the vessel danced merrily up and down, and the waves dashed over her with increased force till we were all wet through. But 'Cousin Phil' was recovering fast, our spirits rose again, and we remembered that sea-water could do no harm, except to the cloaks and shawls. We sat close together to keep out the cold; but at every fresh 'tack,' the cold was let in, as it was necessary to divide our party in order to balance the vessel more evenly.

The sun set while we were still on the water; the Ramadán gun fired, and the hungry Arabs attacked their bread and raw onions with eagerness, for they had tasted nothing the whole day; the moon and stars shone out brilliantly; we had at least gained a lovely moonlight scene on the Red Sea. We watched the steamer from Mauritius arriving, bearing an acquaintance, who, could he have recognised us at that moment in our little bark, would have been even more astonished, than when he did so a few days later at Shepherd's Hotel in Cairo.

The band on board a man-of-war steamer played pleasantly as we passed by—strains which were to us a comforting assurance, that music such as we had been taught to appreciate was not lost to us for ever. The friendly sounds died away, and at length the human voice from the shore greeted our longing ears. After five weary hours and a half, at half-past nine P.M., we disembarked at Suez, and re-entered the hotel, to the no small relief of those who were on the look-out for us. At this late hour dinner was served for us, hot and comfortable, with exactly the same variety of dishes, and the same attention as at the regular dinner-hour. Seldom had dinner or bed been more welcome than this evening to each one of our party, not excluding Mohamed, who, still white, and trembling for the results of the accident, for which he was in great measure responsible, came up to us with a low 'salaam,' saying pathetically, "My two legs shaked together when I see him fall."

Wednesday, March 27th.—The fall had produced considerable stiffness, and 'Cousin Phil' was quite helpless this morning, but under Mohamed's directions he submitted to a course of lentil poultices, which proved very efficacious. We saw the passengers from the Mauritius steamer land, and set off again in the train for Cairo; walked through the very dirty bazaar and the uninteresting-looking town, and took a stroll on the beach to pick up a few shells. Very beautiful shells are found under the hills lower down, but they were beyond our reach. The many different kinds of vessels in the harbour, and the Indian costumes of their crews, were interesting and amusing, while a little further excitement was caused towards evening by the arrival of the 'Shereef,' a great man, from Mecca, who, having escorted the Viceroy back to Cairo, after his late pilgrimage to the holy city of the Mahometans, was now returning homewards.

Thursday, March 28th.—We were amusing ourselves with our sketch-books. In the train of the 'Shereef' there was a man so remarkably fat, we could not resist trying, in a sly way, to take his portrait. He immediately placed himself in front of the artists; we were half afraid, but he pretended to be quite unconscious of our intention, and the opportunity was too good to be lost. In a few minutes Selina was alarmed by a request from the dignitary, to send up her sketch for inspection. She was dreadfully afraid of losing an ear or a nose for her impertinence; but up went the book, and she was relieved by the decided approval of the fat man, who very nearly expressed a command that the portrait should be finished, coloured, and so forth.

My book was next called for, and imagine the state of my nerves when it met with such high approbation, that the dignitaries begged leave to carry it upstairs to the 'great man,' the 'Shereef' himself. I dared not refuse, but expected never to see my treasure again. He looked it all through, however, and then sent it down, appearing himself on the balcony to have a look at the artist, to honour her with his *vivâ voce* approval, which was expressed in the single word "buono" (good). It was a relief to have the books safe again in our own hands, and we had now no lack of subjects, for the whole concourse of 'Governors' in attendance on the 'Shereef' henceforth seated themselves near us, in their most becoming attitudes, and smoked immovably, in the fond hope, no doubt, that their portraits would some day be exhibited in one of the London galleries. We had recovered from our fright, and having nothing better to do, continued drawing, to the admiration of the assembled crowd of all nations that was gathered on the quay. Even the two miserable derweesh, who surpassed all those we had yet seen in their wild and wretched appearance, exciting mingled feelings of repugnance and pity, ventured to draw near to take a peep.

We had good reason to wish that our friends at home would take pattern from the cleverness of this motley crowd, for they showed a very just appreciation of our art, and invariably recognised striking likenesses in all the portraits, even when the likeness was not so apparent to the artists themselves.

Good Friday, March 29th.—The only outward sign of this solemn day at Suez consisted in our being obliged to partake, soon after breakfast, of two separate batches of 'hot-cross buns.' The first were presented by the Captain of one of the Peninsular and Oriental vessels then at Suez, much to the discomfiture of the attentive landlord of the hotel, who hastened forward with an apology, that his buns, through some mistake, were "still in the oven." In less than an hour they also appeared, piping hot, and both batches were pronounced excellent.

The lentil poultices had succeeded admirably; 'Cousin Phil' was quite himself again, and Mohamed's peace of mind was restored. He evidently fancied that it would be at the risk of his head, or something very near it, were he to bring "Pap-pa" back to Mr. B—— in the least degree "damaged," as he expressed it, and he watched the result of his medical proceedings with the greatest anxiety. All was well now, however, and we left Suez on Easter Eve, carrying away with us, as tokens of our excursion thither, two shells which had been picked off the electric cable in the Red Sea, and which were kindly presented to me by a gentleman in the hotel. The shells had stuck to the cable, had grown upon it, and were deeply indented by it. We had also a few which we gathered ourselves, and some bought at one of the little French shops in the town, besides two small splinters of petrified wood which we picked up in the sand on the Arabian side, and which we see no reason against labelling in our collection as a portion of Pharaoh's chariot-wheels.

At half-past seven P.M. Cairo, with all the noise, bustle, and hum of a Ramadán evening, received us again. Shepherd's Hotel seemed worse than before, by comparison with Suez. Its landlord did not consider that late comers deserved a better dinner than those who were ready for it at the appointed hour. These in general get their dinner cold and tough ; ours was colder and tougher, in just and due proportion. Our famished appetites in consequence fed chiefly upon the letters which we found awaiting us, and we made a speedy retreat to bed.

Easter-Day had its own peculiar joy and blessing even in Cairo, and we felt this strongly as we knelt with the little company of our fellow-Christians to commemorate the death and resurrection of our blessed Lord. The truths of Christianity seemed to have double power, and to take stronger hold of the mind, when we felt, as we did here, that our little band was confessing a faith which was openly denied by the population of the country. The bulk of the people are Mahometans, but there are a large number of Coptic Christians in Cairo, having their own missionaries and places for public worship.

After service we looked at a large Coptic church, which is being built at no great distance from the house in which the English service is held; but it was not sufficiently advanced to enable us to understand the plan.

Towards evening Colonel C——, whom we had recognised on our return from Suez, kindly showed us a number of sketches of Mauritius, giving many little reminiscences of its Bishop, a friend of both parties, and who was daily expected in Cairo, on his return from England to his episcopal duties.

Easter Monday, April 1st.—The thermometer was at 72° in the coolest part of the hotel, which heat we all found so unbearable, we were not sorry to think that our stay in Cairo was drawing to a close. This was our last day, and Heliopolis was destined to receive the parting visit.

A ride of two hours led us through a garden of orange and lemon trees and a long shady avenue of acacias to the village of Matarëëh, near which stood the ancient city of Heliopolis, supposed by some authorities to have been the abode of the Pharaohs before the rise of Memphis. Here stood the famed Temple of the Sun, of which Potipherah, the father-in-law of Joseph, was priest; the Scripture names of the city being 'On' and 'Bethshemesh.' Here the father and brothers of Joseph first arrived in Egypt, and the neighbouring land of Goshen was given to them for their dwelling.

Heliopolis was the seat of learning and the arts till the time of the Ptolemies. It was looked upon as the University of Egypt, and to its College of Priests the learned of other countries resorted for instruction. Herodotus the historian, Eudoxus the astronomer, and Plato the philosopher, visited Heliopolis, that they might become acquainted with the sciences and mysteries of Egypt. The two latter are said to have resided thirteen years under the tuition of the priests of Heliopolis, and their houses were pointed out to Strabo when he visited the city about thirty years before the Christian era. Priests and philosophers had at that time deserted the abode of learning; but the 'Temple of the Sun' was still standing, and apparently employed as a place of worship.

Almost the only remains of the celebrated city is the Obelisk of Osirtasen the First, B.C. 2020. The name of this monarch is inscribed on its four faces, attesting its antiquity. It is composed of a block of rose-coloured granite, in perfect preservation, measuring sixty-eight feet in height from its base. It stands on a pavement sunk nearly six feet below the present level of the ground, whereas the whole city is described as having originally stood on a raised mound, before which were some lakes which received the waters of the inundation, and conveyed them into the neighbouring canals: a fact which, with many others of a similar nature, proves the great change which has taken place in the level of the soil of Egypt and the bed of its mighty river. A garden is planted round the obelisk, which is very prettily shadowed on one side by a pepper and a cyprus tree. At the entrance of the garden is a fountain, invested by tradition with many a tale in connexion with the flight of the Holy Family into Egypt. This fountain is said to have been miraculously produced and rendered sweet to quench the thirst of the holy fugitives. It is said that here the Virgin, with her own hands, washed the clothes of the infant Saviour; and a tree at a short distance, in another garden, is hallowed, even in the eyes of the natives, and called the 'Virgin's tree,' as having afforded shelter to the 'Family from Judea.' The tree is an Egyptian sycamore; and, whatever truth may rest in the story, it bears every appearance of the greatest antiquity. The trunk is very remarkable, being extremely broad, and flattened on two sides like a wall. A portion of it overhangs on one side from the top, thus affording a shelter, under which at this moment (as though to give truth to the tradition) a party of Damascene women and children were seated, in their brilliantly-coloured costumes. From the withered and blasted-looking trunk (said to flourish miraculously to this day) spring young spreading branches, which, when in full foliage, must afford an agreeable shelter. They were just now coming into leaf.

It was pleasant to sit there and to think that these things might have been. If this were the part of Egypt to which the Holy Family resorted, what more natural than that they should have reposed in this spot, or refreshed themselves at that fountain, without any superstition with regard to the recorded miracles? The possibility of these two simple facts is sufficient to invest the place with peculiar interest to the Christian traveller; and we could have sat there much longer, in imagination filling up the landscape with the Holy Family and with the patriarchs and saints of old; but the heat was too intense: it was mid-day, and we were exposed to its full power. Moreover, the days of our romance were drawing to a close; and we knew that in the hotel at Cairo 'Cousin Phil' sat, impatiently awaiting our return, his whole soul bent upon 'packing up.'

Back, then, we trotted, as briskly as possible, for there was no shade at this hour, and our donkeys seemed well aware that this was the only way of passing over the grilling road in safety, till the narrow streets of Cairo again sheltered our heads.

At two P.M. we reached the hotel. The last scene here was certainly not without its amusement. Mohamed el Adlëëh — on the principle, no doubt, that if he did not speak for himself nobody would speak for him—gave out that he was the first packer in the universe; no one could stow away things as he could; he would ensure the safety of every article, and, as usual, pay for anything that should be found damaged. This last assertion he considered indisputably convincing; and so, with tucked-up sleeves, the dragoman proceeded to the work, very much as though he were at a washtub or a kneading-trough. We had our notions of packing as well as he; and as we watched the violent proceedings, 'Cousin Phil' trembled for his wine, we for our crocodiles and treasures of Egyptian ware, &c. In they all went, and out 'Cousin Phil' ordered them all again several times, till the Arab became so excited that we were fairly forced to give in, and let him fill the boxes his own fashion, leaving the consequences to fate. The result was that the wine arrived in safety, but everything else that was breakable suffered more or less.

Easter Tuesday, April 2nd.—We took an early breakfast, and at eight A.M. the carriage was at the door, ready to convey us from Cairo to the terminus. We speeded along, and at the end of our journey Alexandria claimed us as old acquaintances.

We looked at one another in astonishment. On our arrival from Europe, Alexandria had appeared to us the essence of Orientalism; now that we came from Cairo and Nubia, it boasted European houses, streets, and squares, together with costumes and features, if not English, at least French and Italian. Had we passed through the city blindfold before, or what had come over it since our departure?

In the Hôtel d'Europe, sitting once again in a comfortable parlour, carpeted, curtained, and well furnished with sofas and easy chairs, looking out upon the 'Place' below, in which Paris fashions promenaded before us, it was difficult to remember that we were in Egypt still, and not rather at Marseilles or Brussels — nay, even Paris itself. It is true that the carriages which stood in the sun, waiting to be hired, were still driven by Arab coachmen of all shades of brown, in their white or blue dresses and turbaned heads, with their bare legs hanging carelessly over the coach-boxes. The money-changers were still at all the corners of the streets, rattling their coins to attract attention. Donkeys trotted by, and donkey-boys grunted and shouted still, whilst amongst the European fashionables strange-looking groups of shrouded nurses and gaily-dressed Levantine ladies and children promenaded as before. Yet this was the 'Frank Quarter,' and our enlarged minds were *now* capable of acknowledging the justice of the term, and the Oriental features of the scene required to be sought for ere they struck our eye.

We found the sea-breeze fresh and invigorating after the dust and heat of Cairo ; and although there may have been some charm in the thought of the fertile land to which it was soon to lead us, still the thermometer did point three or four degrees lower. The flies and mosquitoes, which had devoured 'Cousin Phil' so voraciously, and had nearly driven me and my companion crazy on our arrival, had not yet revived from their winter's sleep. The hotel was far better than Shepherd's, and far less infested with fleas; and we were enabled to receive, with becoming composure, the intelligence which was soon brought us, that there was no further accommodation in the first steamer for Malta, and that we must wait until the arrival of the 'Pera,' on the 10th or thereabouts. Two ladies could easily find a little shopping for every intervening day, and a number of neglected odds-and-ends for which this extra week was indispensable. Mr. B—— took tea with us more than once; Mrs. S—— crowned our good fortune by a visit to the Pasha's Haréem; the church and the church-service was a decided improvement upon that at Cairo; and upon the Sunday, which we should have spent upon the 'high seas,' Col. C—— arrived, with his portfolio replenished in Cairo, to be our companion in the miseries of the coming sea-voyage. We made a new and very pleasant acquaintance of our own sex; and the second impression which Alexandria left on our minds considerably modified the first.

On Tuesday, April 9th, Mrs. S——, with another lady, who was to act as interpreter, introduced us into the Haréem. It is not seen to advantage during the season of Ramadán; but it was better to see it then than not at all. The Princess and her ladies were residing, at the time, in a small palace on the banks of the canal. She was dressed in a plain cotton dress, and wore one diamond ornament only in her black hair. She sat on a divan on one side of the room, in a listless attitude, with one leg tucked under her, which she exchanged every now and then for the other. Her handsome, sad face raised much sympathy towards her in our minds. She looks as though born to something better than the listless, idle life to which these unfortunate women are all condemned. We were told that she had enjoyed a superior education, and often pined for the greater happiness of English ladies. Having no child of her own, she has adopted a pretty little girl, whom she was caressing. The Princess rose to receive us as we entered the room. According to instructions, we offered to take her hand and to kiss it; but she withdrew it immediately, not allowing the compliment.

We were next introduced to the Pasha's sister, who was on a visit at the Haréem. She was very fat, which is esteemed a great beauty in this country, was rather untidily dressed, and had so little dignity of manner that, when she required some instructions concerning the slippers she was working, she merely rolled herself over on the divan on which she was sitting '*à la Turque*,' spoke to her neighbour, and rolled herself back again. She allowed us to raise her hand close to our lips, and then, with a sudden jerk, she set it free.

Next came the Pasha's second wife. A true and faithful Mussulman is legally allowed by the Korán to have four wives at the same time, provided he has the means of supporting them in conformity with his rank and social position. The Pasha's second wife is the mother of his son and heir. She was dressed in scarlet, but equally simply, and is a very pleasing-looking person, though quite a different style of beauty to the Princess. She understands a few words of English, so that, while she was present, no remarks could be made nor questions put in that language. But few words were spoken during the hour and a half through which our visit lasted; but we had plenty to look at and to think about.

The ladies examined us closely: we dressed as handsomely as we could, for the dress of visitors to the Harêem is much thought of. Several of the Princess's attendants were seated on low divans round the room; they were all attired in simple cotton dresses, and, like the Princess, were working slippers on canvas, with German wool, all of one and the same pattern. This is a new accomplishment in the Harêem, and its only pastime, save that of playing at childish games.

Two very pretty Circassian slaves, with painted eyebrows, stood with folded arms, statue-like, on either side the doorway, in which a curtain was hung. They wore large loose trousers and flowing drapery, mostly white, red, or yellow, with small fez-caps upon their heads. These are now replaced, in the harêems, by small muslin handkerchiefs. The slaves stood at their posts for a certain time, till others came to relieve them. Along the marble pavement of the hall beyond we could see a great many, constantly passing and repassing, with no other apparent object than to show that they were in attendance, unless, perhaps, they wanted to take a peep at us. A eunuch came in, knelt, and kissed the hand of the Princess, and then spoke to her, apparently on some matter of business. A strange, little, ugly, witch-like woman, dressed in bright yellow, also entered, and kissed the Princess's hand: she seemed to be on most intimate terms with her, and rattled away with chat and joke — a strange contrast, both in this point and in her personal appearance, to the silent beauties around her.

Pipes are not always presented during Ramadán, but we were honoured not only with one such presentation, but with two. Four very pretty slaves advanced, bearing a long, handsome pipe in one hand and a small silver dish in the other. They placed the dish on the floor, at a certain distance from each guest, rested the bowl of the pipe in it, and then presented the handles. The pipes must have been five feet in length; they were covered with gold twist, had large amber mouth-pieces, and were encircled with diamonds. It is considered rude not to accept of any such compliment in the East; so, of course, we all did our best to smoke nicely: Selina coughed at the first puff, and she was let off; I tried honestly to smoke, but could not manage it at all: the tiny whiff which reached my mouth at one attempt was so particularly disagreeable, that it may have paralyzed my further efforts, and it certainly confirmed my former aversion to this luxury. Our kind escort smoked delightfully for the whole party, so that we hoped the Princess would feel sufficiently honoured. Coffee was offered us in cups of filagree-gold, set with diamonds and emeralds. These, I fear, we actually coveted, though we should have been but too glad to have had our dragoman at hand to make away with their black contents.

In due course of time it was supposed that we had emptied our pipes, and the slaves took them away to replenish them, presenting them again as before. To crown all her attentions, the Princess expressed a hope that we would attend the Haréem on the coming festival of 'Biram,' which succeeds 'Ramadán:' then she and her ladies would be seen in the State Palace, dressed in gorgeous Eastern costume, covered with jewels and precious stones; and numbers of slaves in attendance, splendidly attired, would dance before the Princess and her guests.

We could almost willingly have lost the 'Pera' for this sight, but not quite, and we lost the sight instead. On the very morning of the opening 'Biram' we left the shores of Egypt, taking away with us a very sufficient idea of the Pasha's Haréem to convince us of its wealth, beauty, and the unfortunate destiny of its inmates, and to make us prize doubly the liberty and domestic happiness of our English homes.

Wednesday, April 10th.—At four P.M. a loud cannonading announced the termination of the Mahometan fast. The whole population of Alexandria started to their feet as though an electric shock had passed through the city. The poor, famished-looking people rushed to whatever food was nearest at hand; pipes and tobacco appeared again, and on the morrow the whole place wore a changed aspect.

The Arabs looked positively clean. Gaily dressed groups of all classes were to be seen passing by or chatting merrily in the streets. The very poorest had found means to provide some new, bright-coloured article of clothing; and notwithstanding the alleged enjoyment of the nightly meals, all seemed as happy as possible at the restoration of day and night to their natural order and use.

Our dragoman had received his dismissal soon after we returned to Alexandria, there being literally no occupation for him now in our service. We made him a parting present, whereupon he looked at us sentimentally and with one finger in the corner of each eye, whined out, "I don't like to leave you at all, Mrs. L——, indeed—I can't help it, Mrs. C." What the good man thought he could not help, did not quite appear, but Selina and I were under the impression that he wanted to cry, so we immediately hardened our hearts in order to avoid a scene. We wished him many more journeys up the Nile, promised to recommend him to our friends, and after an unintentional disclosure of our having been "taken in" after all by the clever Arabs, inasmuch as the good ship 'Cairo' turned out to have been all the time 'The Fairy Queen,' famous for herds of rats, bearing her true name all the while on her bow, though most cleverly hidden from our sight, and thus accounting for a difficulty we had had in ascertaining her character at the first—Mohamed left us with an '*au revoir;*' for he was to keep us informed of the arrival of the 'Pera,' and to see us safely on board.

Dress makes the man, even here in Egypt. When Mohamed el Adlééh appeared again, we scarcely recognised him. The ludicrous change which had taken place in the appearance of our high-minded servitor was so great, that we could not refrain from asking what he had done to himself. His dragoman dress was laid aside till the next season, he looked like a pilgrim ready to start for Mecca, in a long loose black garment, bare feet, and sandals, with green and brown straps across the foot, such as we had seen in the bazaar at Suez, and which are manufactured in Medina. "Of course," was the only explanation we could get out of him.

Thursday, April 11th. The hotel was filled with the arrivals from Suez; bag, baggage, and children, crowded the passages, our beautiful drawing-room had served as bed-room to four of the new-comers; it was time for us to be off; Mohamed was in readiness, and at half-past eight A.M. we again drove to the harbour of Alexandria. How composedly we now looked upon all its confusion and bustle. The first impression it had made upon our minds endeavoured to revive; we compared the two scenes, they were in every respect alike, but the glare and charm of entire novelty had passed away for us. The scene was still interesting and enjoyable, but it was not the same.

The hour of starting approached, Mohamed made a last affectionate dive into 'Cousin Phil's' pockets, for boat, luggage, carriage, sound limbs, &c., &c.; the last shaking of hands took place between the white and the brown, and the efficient though benighted dragoman returned to his native shore; "to pray," (he says,) till the next Nile season comes.

The same little steamer, which had taken our fellow-passengers away, on our arrival in the 'Vectis,' came puffing along to the 'Pera,' with her living load now bound for home, and with three only of whom we were acquainted.

We are off;—and thought turns with pleasurable anticipations homeward. One last look at Alexandria and its windmills, over the high sides of the 'Pera,' which do their best to place the scene of our wanderings immediately both out of sight and out of mind.

The former it will be without doubt to our trio for ever; but the memories of the past five months and a half can hardly fade from the minds of any one of our party. Rather will they serve to kindle a warm, cheerful glow, by many a winter fireside, while public readings of Thomas' carefully kept Journal will no doubt shortly be announced in some of the country towns of Scotland, infusing into that national mind, also, a kindred sympathy with his adventures.

FINIS.

London:—STRANGEWAYS & WALDEN, 28 Castle Street, Leicester Square.

Milton Keynes UK
Ingram Content Group UK Ltd.
UKHW020955090124
435730UK00007B/307